SEW YOUR OWN WARDROBE

SEW YOUR OWN WARDROBE

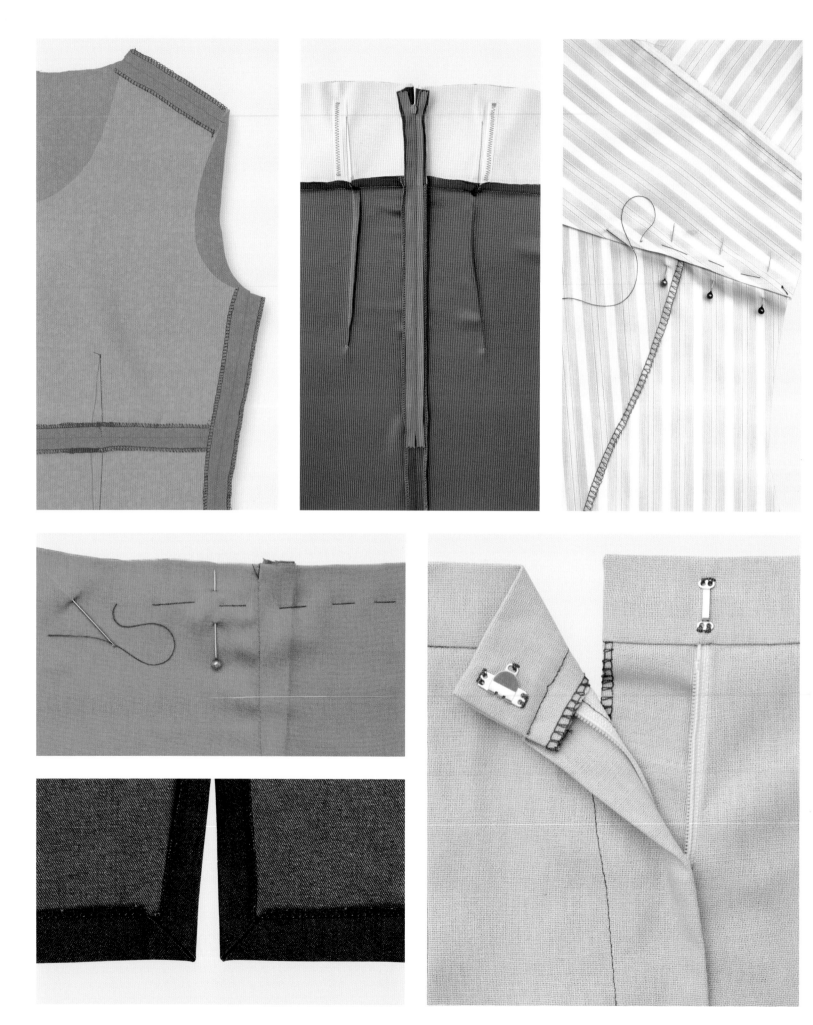

CONTENTS

INTRODUCTION

My passion is sewing. I'm never happier than when I'm in front of my sewing machine creating a new garment, so I wanted to share that enjoyment with everyone who loves clothes and would like to sew their own. This book offers you thirteen basic patterns ranging from skirts and dresses through pants and tops to jackets, which you can download via a dedicated website.

The bonus is that these basic patterns can then be adapted to make a total of thirty-one fabulous garments. If you make them all, you will have a complete wardrobe, whatever your age and lifestyle.

Beginners can start with the basic patterns and quickly progress to the more complex ones. For the

more experienced sewer, there are plenty of new ideas and techniques to try, or you may feel like making the same pattern several times in different fabrics for a variety of looks. I've also included detailed instructions for the techniques needed to make every garment in the book. This section will also help you to work with any commercial pattern. And, finally, there are sections dedicated to mending and customizing, enabling you to prolong the useful life of your clothes.

Happy sewing!

Alison Smith

HOW TO USE THIS BOOK

This book contains all the information you need to make your own clothes.
There are patterns and step-by-step instructions for twelve classic garments, and variations of each. Additional guidance, if needed, is to be found in sections on key dressmaking techniques, tools, fabrics, and pattern alterations. Finally, sections on mending and customizing show how to prolong the life of your garments, both old and new.

GARMENT SECTION

▶ GARMENT OVERVIEWS

An overview of each type of garment showcases the classic garments and all the possible variations you can make with the patterns provided. Use these to see the full range of options available as you plan your next project.

▶ CLASSIC GARMENT OPENERS

Each classic garment is profiled in an introduction spread that tells you what you need to begin your project, followed by clear step-by-step instructions with close-up photography.

▶ VARIATION PAGES

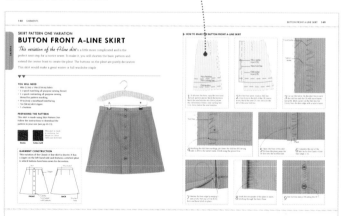

At least one possible variation is suggested for each classic pattern, along with alternative fabric choices. Variations begin with pattern alterations. Detailed step-by-step instructions then guide you through sewing the garment.

OTHER USEFUL SECTIONS

▶ ESSENTIAL TOOLS

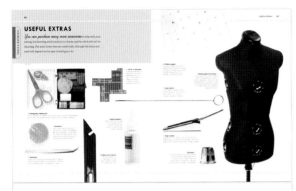

All the essential tools and materials you may need are contained in a gallery at the beginning of the book. Full-color photographs and clear text explain the uses of each.

▶ FABRICS

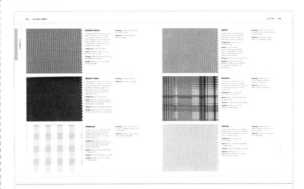

This gallery showcases more than 30 dressmaking fabrics and explains the uses of each. Use it to find more information on the suggested fabrics for your garment or to find inspiration for future projects.

▶ GENERAL TECHNIQUES

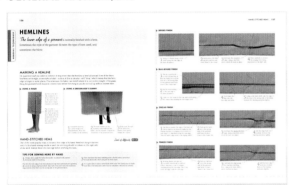

All key dressmaking techniques are shown and explained, step-by-step, in a self-contained section. Turn to this section for extra guidance when completing a project, or use it as a general reference for dressmaking questions.

▶ PATTERN ALTERATION

A chapter on pattern alterations teaches you to customize patterns to fit your body shape—for example, shortening arms or lengthening a top. These techniques can be used with the patterns in this book or with commercial patterns.

▶ MENDING AND REPAIRS

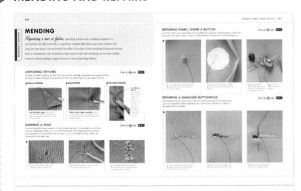

This section contains all the skills you need to repair worn items. Here you will learn the essentials, such as how to mend tears, darn holes, and replace lost buttons.

▶ CUSTOMIZING

Get inspiration on how to update and personalize your existing pieces in a section on customizing. Six complete projects teach you how to breathe new life into old garments.

USING THE PATTERN SECTION

To create any of the garments in this book, you will first need to download and prepare the corresponding pattern. Head to our website, dk.com/sew-your-own-wardrobe, to choose from a selection of thirteen classic patterns, each in a range of sizes that can be adapted to suit your own unique body size and shape.

FIND YOUR SIZE

Find your size by taking your bust, waist, and hip measurements and finding the closest set of measurements in the table below. If you are between sizes, choose the larger of the two.

Size	2–4	4–6	6–8	8–10	10–12	12–14	14–16	16–18	18–20
BUST	32¼in (82cm)	33¼in (84.5cm)	34¼in (87cm)	36¼in (92cm)	38in (97cm)	40in 102cm)	42in (107cm)	44in (112cm)	46in (117cm)
WAIST	24½in (62cm)	25¼in (64.5cm)	26¼in (67cm)	28¼in (72cm)	30¼in (77cm)	32¼in (82cm)	34¼in (87cm)	36¼in (92cm)	38 in (97cm)
HIP	34¼in (87cm)	35¼in (89.5cm)	36¼in (92cm)	38in (97cm)	40in (102cm)	42in (107cm)	44in (112cm)	46in (117cm)	48in (122cm)

▶ VARIED SIZES

You may have noticed that your size in the table differs from what you would buy in a store. In general, dressmaking sizes tend to be smaller than sizes in stores. It is always a good idea to make a garment in a toile first (see **pp.74–75**) to make sure that the size is right and the garment fits.

SEAM ALLOWANCE

▶ Seam allowance is the amount of fabric that is taken up by the seam. It is usually given as the distance between the cutting line and the stitching line.

The patterns in this section include ⅝in (1.5cm) seam allowance. This means that to make a garment that is the correct size and shape, you will need to cut along the line on the pattern, and stitch ⅝in (1.5cm) inside the cutting line. An easy way to remember to do this is to mark a stitching line onto the pattern pieces before you begin.

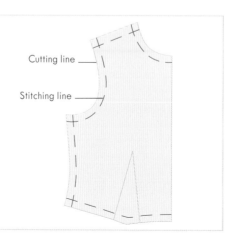

Cutting line

Stitching line

PATTERN MARKINGS

The following markings are used on the patterns in this section.

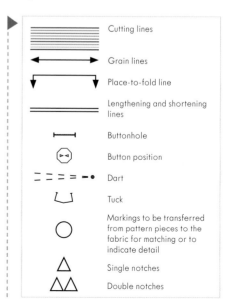

Cutting lines

Grain lines

Place-to-fold line

Lengthening and shortening lines

Buttonhole

Button position

Dart

Tuck

Markings to be transferred from pattern pieces to the fabric for matching or to indicate detail

Single notches

Double notches

THE DRESSMAKING BOOK WEBSITE

All the garment projects featured in this book can be made using patterns downloaded from **dk.com/sew-your-own-wardrobe**.

▶ CLASSIC AND VARIATION PATTERNS

The website features 13 patterns that correspond to the "classic" projects in this book. These patterns are:

Classic A-line skirt (see pp.144–147)
Classic tailored skirt (see pp.150–154)
Classic flared skirt (see pp.158–162)
Classic shift dress (see pp.168–172)
Classic waisted dress (see pp.180–184)
Classic empire line dress (see pp.196–200)
Classic shirtdress (see pp.208–213)
Classic cigarette pants (see pp.220–223)
Classic palazzo pants (see pp.226–231)
Classic shell top (see pp.238–241)
Classic princess-line blouse (see pp.246–250)
Classic boxy jacket (see pp.256–259)
Classic blazer (see pp.264–270)

Each of these patterns can then be adapted to create at least one "variation" project, with a few key changes that transform the garment into something entirely new (see right). To make these garments, download the corresponding classic garment pattern, then follow the steps shown in each individual project.

Sleeveless

Skirt darts

As its name suggests, this variation does not feature the sleeves of the classic pattern. The dress is also lined, and features skirt darts rather than tucks.

VARIATION
Sleeveless empire line dress

CLASSIC
Empire line dress

Strapless

This fully strapless dress adapts an everyday dress pattern to a formal garment. The bodice is boned, interfaced, and interlined, while the skirt is widened, fully lengthened, and features a "puddle" train.

Floor-length skirt

VARIATION
Long empire line dress

DOWNLOAD OR COPY YOUR PATTERN

▶

1 Start by checking which pattern is needed to make the garment or variation. This is listed on the first page of the instructions. Then go to **dk.com/sew-your-own-wardrobe**.

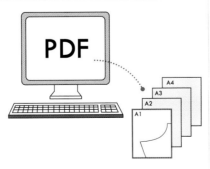

2 Find the correct PDF for your garment and your size. Download the PDF to your computer, and print it out. The pages will be labeled in the order that they fit together.

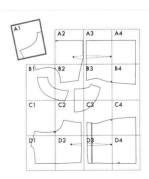

3 Trim the white margins from the printed pages, and tape the pages together, using the letters and gridlines as a guide. Cut out the pattern pieces.

TOOLS & MATERIALS

BASIC SEWING KIT

A well-equipped sewing kit will include all of the items shown below and many more, depending on the type of sewing that you regularly do. It is important to use a suitable container to keep your tools together, so that they will be easy to access and to keep them neat and tidy.

▲ Tape measure
Essential, not only to take body measurements, but also to help measure fabric, seams, etc. Choose one with both metric and standard units. A tape measure made of plastic is best, since it won't stretch.
(See p.20)

Needles ▶
A good selection of different types of needle for sewing by hand. They will enable you to tackle any hand-sewing project.
(See p.16)

Sewing gauge ▶
A handy gadget for small measurements. The slide can be set to measure hem depths, buttonhole diameters, and much more.
(See p.20)

Buttonhole chisel ▶
An exceedingly sharp mini-chisel that gives a clean cut through machine buttonholes. Place a cutting board underneath when using this tool or you might damage the blade.
(See p.23)

▲ Safety pins
Keep a variety of sizes. They are useful for emergency repairs and for threading elastics.
(See p.17)

Cutting shears ▶
Required for cutting fabric. When buying, select a pair that feels comfortable in your hand and that is not too heavy.
(See p.22)

▲ Pincushion
To keep your needles and pins safe and clean. Choose one that has a fabric cover and is firm.
(See p.17)

◄ Zippers
It is always a good idea to keep a couple of zippers in your sewing kit. Black, cream, and navy are the most useful colors. (See pp.129–132)

▲ Notions
All the odds and ends a sewer needs, including everything from buttons and snaps to trimmings and elastic. A selection of buttons and snaps in your basic kit is useful for a quick repair. (See pp.24–25)

◄ Seam ripper
Also called a stitch ripper, to remove any stitches that have been sewn in the wrong place. Various sizes of seam rippers are available. Keep the cover on when not in use to protect the sharp point. (See p.23)

◄ Thimble
This is useful to protect the end of your finger when hand sewing. Thimbles are available in various shapes and sizes. (See p.27)

▼ Pins
Needed by every sewer to hold the fabric together prior to sewing it permanently. There are different types of pin for different types of work. (See p.17)

▲ Embroidery scissors
Small pair of scissors with very sharp points, to clip threads close to the fabric. (See p.22)

◄ Threads
A selection of threads for hand sewing and machine/serge sewing in a variety of colors. Some threads are made of polyester, while others are cotton or rayon. (See pp.18–19)

BUILD UP YOUR SEWING KIT

CUTTING TOOLS (see pp.22–23)
Bent-handled shears
Paper scissors
Pinking shears
Snips
Trimming scissors
Seam ripper
Buttonhole chisel
Cutting shears
Embroidery scissors

MEASURING TOOLS (see p.20)
Flexible ruler
Other tape measures

MARKING AIDS (see p.21)
Chalk pencil
Drafting ruler
Mechanical pencil
Tailor's chalk
Tracing wheel and carbon paper
Water/air-soluble pen

USEFUL EXTRAS (see pp.26–27)
14-in-1 measure
Beeswax
Collar point turner
Dressmaker's dummy
Liquid sealant
Emergency sewing kit
Loop turner
Pattern paper
Tape maker
Tweezers

NEEDLE THREADERS (see p.16)
Wire needle threader
Automatic needle threader

PRESSING AIDS (see pp.34–35)
Clapper
Iron
Ironing board
Pressing cloth
Pressing mitten
Seam roll
Tailor's ham
Velvet mat

NEEDLES AND PINS

Using the correct pin or needle for your work is extremely important, since the wrong choice can damage fabric or leave small holes. Needles are made from steel, and pins from steel or occasionally brass. Look after them by keeping pins in a pincushion and needles in a needle case—if kept together in a small container they can become scratched and blunt.

NEEDLES AND THREADERS

Needles are available for all types of fabrics and projects. Keep a good selection of needles on hand at all times, whether for emergency mending of tears, sewing on buttons, or adding trimmings to special-occasion wear. With a special needle threader, inserting the thread through the eye of the needle is simplicity itself.

Sharps An all-purpose hand-sewing needle, with a small, round eye. Available in sizes 1 to 12. For most hand sewing use a size 6 to 9.

Crewel Also known as an embroidery needle, a long needle with a long, oval eye that is designed to take multiple strands of embroidery thread.

Milliner's or straw A very long, thin needle with a small, round eye. Good for hand sewing and basting, since it doesn't damage fabric. A size 8 or 9 is most popular.

Betweens or quilting Similar to a milliner's needle but very short, with a small, round eye. Perfect for fine hand stitches and favored by quilters.

Beading Long and extremely fine, to sew beads and sequins to fabric. Since it is prone to bending, keep it wrapped in tissue paper when not in use.

Darner's A long, thick needle that is designed to be used with wool or thick yarns and to sew through multiple layers.

Tapestry A medium-length, thick needle with a blunt end and a long eye. For use with wool yarn in tapestry. Also for darning in serger threads.

Chenille This looks like a tapestry needle but it has a sharp point. Use with thick yarns or wool yarns for darning or heavy embroidery.

Bodkin A strange-looking needle with a blunt end and a large, fat eye. Use to thread elastic or cord. There are larger eyes for thicker yarns.

Self-threading needle A needle that has a double eye. The thread is placed in the upper eye through the gap, then pulled into the eye below for sewing.

Wire needle threader
A handy gadget, especially useful for needles with small eyes. Also helpful in threading sewing-machine needles.

Automatic needle threader
This threader is operated with a small lever. The needle, eye down, is inserted and the thread is wrapped around.

PINS

There is a wide variety of pins available, in differing lengths and thicknesses and ranging from plain household pins to those with colored balls or flower shapes on their ends.

Household
All-purpose pins of a medium length and thickness. Can be used for all types of sewing.

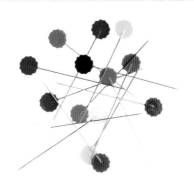

Flowerhead
A long pin of medium thickness with a flat, flower-shaped head. It is made to be ironed over, since the head lies flat on the fabric.

Pearl-headed
Longer than household pins, with a colored pearl head. They are easy to pick up and use.

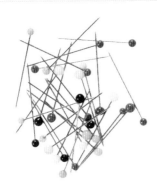

Glass-headed
Similar to pearl-headed pins but shorter. They have the advantage that they can be ironed over without melting.

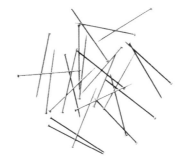

Dressmaker's
Similar to a household pin in shape and thickness, but slightly longer. These are the pins for beginners to choose.

Extra fine
Extra long and extra fine, this pin is favored by many professional dressmakers because it is easy to use and doesn't damage finer fabrics.

Safety pins
Available in a huge variety of sizes and made either of brass or stainless steel. Used for holding two or more layers together.

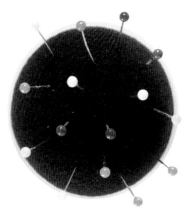

Pincushion
To keep pins clean and sharp. Choose a fabric cover: a foam cushion may blunt pins.

THREADS

There are so many threads available that knowing which ones to choose can be confusing. There are specialty threads designed for special tasks, such as machine embroidery or decorative stitching. Threads also vary in fiber content, from pure cotton to rayon to polyester. Some threads are very fine, while others are thick and coarse. Failure to choose the correct thread can spoil your project and lead to problems with the stitch quality of the sewing machine or serger.

Cotton thread
A 100 percent cotton thread. Smooth and firm, this is designed to be used with cotton fabrics.

Polyester all-purpose thread
A good-quality polyester thread that has a very slight "give," making it suitable for sewing all types of fabrics and garments. It is the most popular type of thread.

Silk thread
A sewing thread made from 100 percent silk. Used for machining delicate silk garments because it can be removed without leaving an imprint, it is also used for basting or temporary stitching in areas that are to be pressed, such as jacket collars.

Elastic thread
A thin, round elastic thread normally used on the bobbin of the sewing machine for stretch effects such as shirring.

Embroidery thread

Machine embroidery thread is a finer embroidery thread that is usually made from rayon or cotton. Also available on larger spools for economy.

VARIEGATED MACHINE EMBROIDERY THREAD

LARGE SPOOL OF RAYON EMBROIDERY THREAD

COTTON MACHINE EMBROIDERY THREAD

RAYON MACHINE EMBROIDERY THREAD

Topstitching thread

A thicker polyester thread used for decorative topstitching and buttonholes. Also for hand sewing buttons on thicker fabrics.

Serger thread

A dull yarn on a larger spool designed to be used on the serger. This type of yarn is normally not strong enough to use on the sewing machine.

MEASURING AND MARKING TOOLS

A huge range of tools enables a sewer to measure accurately. Choosing the correct tool for the task at hand is important, so that your measurements are precise. After measuring, the next step is to mark your work using the appropriate marking technique or tool.

MEASURING TOOLS

There are many tools available to help you measure everything from the width of a seam or hem to body dimensions. One of the most basic yet invaluable measuring tools is the tape measure. Be sure to keep yours in good condition—once it stretches or gets snipped on the edges, it will no longer be accurate and should be replaced.

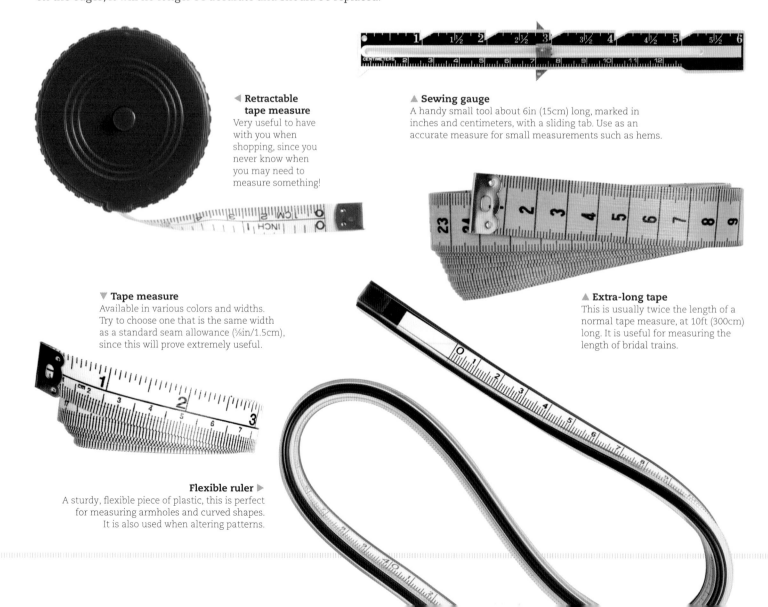

◀ **Retractable tape measure**
Very useful to have with you when shopping, since you never know when you may need to measure something!

▲ **Sewing gauge**
A handy small tool about 6in (15cm) long, marked in inches and centimeters, with a sliding tab. Use as an accurate measure for small measurements such as hems.

▼ **Tape measure**
Available in various colors and widths. Try to choose one that is the same width as a standard seam allowance (⅝in/1.5cm), since this will prove extremely useful.

▲ **Extra-long tape**
This is usually twice the length of a normal tape measure, at 10ft (300cm) long. It is useful for measuring the length of bridal trains.

Flexible ruler ▶
A sturdy, flexible piece of plastic, this is perfect for measuring armholes and curved shapes. It is also used when altering patterns.

MARKING AIDS

Marking certain parts of your work is essential, to make sure that elements such as pockets and darts are placed correctly and seam lines are straight as drawn on the pattern. With some marking tools, such as pens and a tracing wheel and carbon paper, it is always a good idea to test on a scrap of fabric first to make sure that the mark made will not be permanent.

◀ Chalk mechanical pencil
Chalk leads of different colors can be inserted into a mechanical pencil, making it a very versatile marking tool. The leads can be sharpened.

Chalk pencil ▶
Available in blue, pink, and white. It can be sharpened like a normal pencil, so will draw accurate lines on fabric.

◀ Tailor's chalk
Also known as French chalk, this solid piece of chalk in either a square or triangular shape is available in a wide variety of colors. The chalk easily brushes off fabric.

Drafting ruler ▼
A plastic curved tool, also called a pattern-marking ruler, used primarily when drafting or altering patterns.

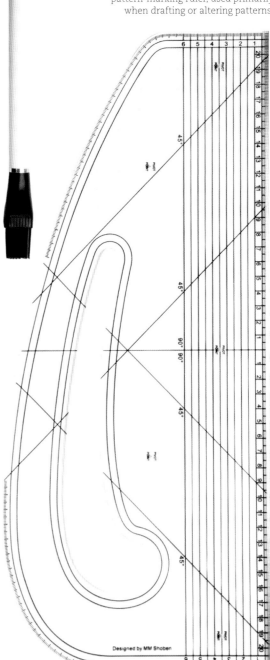

▼ Tracing wheel and carbon paper
These two items are used together to transfer markings from a paper pattern or a design onto fabric. Not suitable for all types of fabric though, since marks may not be easily removable.

Water/air-soluble pen ▶
This resembles a felt-tip pen. Marks made can be removed from the fabric with either a spray of water or by leaving to air-dry. Be careful—if you iron over the marks, they may become permanent.

CUTTING TOOLS

There are many types of cutting tools, but one rule applies to all: buy good-quality products that can be resharpened. When choosing cutting shears, make sure that they fit the span of your hand so that you can comfortably open the entire blade with one action. This is very important to allow clean and accurate cutting lines. Shears and scissors of various types are not the only cutting tools required; everyone will at some time need a seam ripper to remove misplaced stitches or to unpick seams for mending.

Cutting shears ▷
The most popular type of shear, used for cutting large pieces of fabric. The length of the blade can vary from 8 to 12in (20 to 30cm) in length.

Trimming scissors ▷
These scissors have a 4in (10cm) blade and are used to trim away surplus fabric and neaten ends of machining.

▲ **Snips**
A very useful, small, spring-loaded tool that easily cuts the ends of thread. Not suitable for fabrics.

▲ **Embroidery scissors**
A small and very sharp scissor used to get into corners and clip threads close to the fabric.

◀ Seam ripper
A sharp, pointed hook to slide under a stitch, with a small cutting blade at the base to cut the thread. Various sizes are available, to cut through light to heavyweight fabric seams.

◀ Buttonhole chisel
A smaller version of a carpenter's chisel, to cut cleanly and accurately through buttonholes. Since this is very sharp, use a cutting board underneath.

Pinking shears ▶
Similar in size to cutting shears but with a blade that cuts with a zigzag pattern. Used for neatening seams and decorative edges.

Paper scissors ▶
Use these to cut around pattern pieces—cutting paper will dull the blades of fabric scissors and shears.

▼ Bent-handled shears
This type of blade has an angle between the blade and the handle that enables the shears to sit flat on the table when cutting out. Popular for cutting long, straight edges.

NOTIONS

The term notions covers all of the odds and ends that a sewer needs, for example, fasteners such as buttons, snaps, hooks and eyes, and Velcro™. But notions also includes elastics, ribbons, trimmings of all types, and boning.

BUTTONS

Buttons can be made from almost anything—shell, bone, coconut, nylon, plastic, brass, silver. They can be any shape, from geometric to abstract to animal shapes. A button may have a shank or have holes on the surface so that it can be attached to fabric.

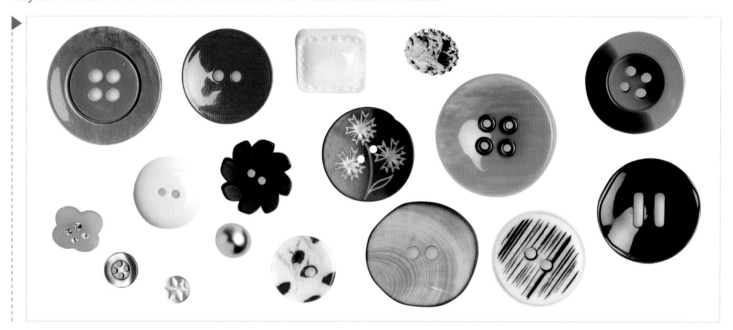

OTHER FASTENERS

Hooks and eyes, snaps, and Velcro™ all come in a wide variety of forms, differing in size, shape, and color. Some hooks and eyes are designed to be seen, while snaps and Velcro™ are intended to be hidden fasteners.

HOOKS AND EYES

VELCRO™

SNAPS

TRIMMINGS, DECORATIONS, FRINGES, AND BRAIDS

Decorative finishing touches—fringes, strips of sequins, rickrack braids, feathers, pearls, bows, flowers, and beads—can embellish or personalize a garment. Some are designed to be inserted into seams while others are surface-mounted.

RICKRACK TRIM

RIBBON TRIM

BEADED FRINGE

RIBBONS

From the narrowest strips to wide swathes, ribbons are made from a variety of yarns, such as nylon, polyester, and cotton. They can be printed or plain and may feature metallic threads or wired edges.

ELASTIC

Elastic is available in many forms, from very narrow, round cord elastic to wide strips. The elastic may have buttonhole slots in it or even a decorative edge.

WIDE ELASTIC

NARROW ELASTIC

BUTTONHOLE ELASTIC

BONING

Boning comes in various types and in different widths. You can sew through polyester boning, used in boned bodices, while nylon boning, also used on boned bodices, has to be inserted into a casing. Specialized metal bones, which may be either spiral or straight, are for corsets and bridal wear.

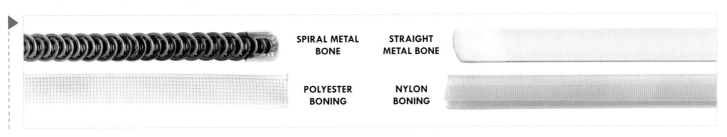

SPIRAL METAL BONE

STRAIGHT METAL BONE

POLYESTER BONING

NYLON BONING

USEFUL EXTRAS

You can purchase many more accessories to help with your sewing, but knowing which products to choose and for which job can be daunting. The tools shown here are useful aids, although the items you need will depend on the type of sewing you do.

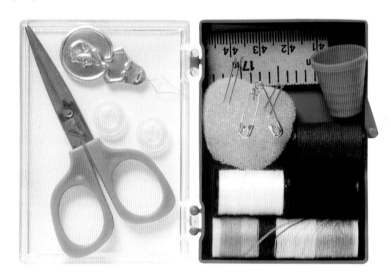

◄ 14-in-1 measure
A strange-looking tool that has 14 different measurements on it. Use to turn hems or edges accurately. Available in both standard and metric.

▲ Emergency sewing kit
All the absolute essentials to fix loose buttons or dropped hems while away from your sewing machine. Take it with you when traveling.

◄ Beeswax
When hand sewing, this will prevent the thread from tangling, and will strengthen it. First draw the thread through the wax, then press the wax into the thread by running your fingers along it.

Liquid sealant ▶
Used to seal the cut edge of ribbons and trims to prevent fraying. Also useful to seal the ends of serger stitching.

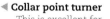

▲ Tweezers
These can be used for removing stubborn basting stitches that are caught in the machine stitching. Also an essential aid to threading the serger.

◄ Collar point turner
This is excellent for pushing out those hard-to-reach corners in collars and cuffs.

▲ Pattern paper
This can be plain or printed with dots and crosses at regular intervals. The paper can be used for drafting patterns or for altering or tracing patterns.

Dressmaker's dummy ▶
An adjustable form that is useful when fitting garments, since it can be adjusted to personal body measurements. Excellent to help in turning up hemlines. Available in female, male, and children's shapes and sizes.

▼ Loop turner
A thin metal rod with a latch at the end. Use to turn narrow fabric tubes or to thread ribbons through slotted lace.

▲ Tape maker
Available in ½, ¾, and 1in (12, 18, and 25mm) widths, this tool evenly folds the edges of a fabric strip, which can then be pressed to make binding.

Thimble ▶
An essential item for many sewers, to protect the middle finger from the end of the needle. There are many types of thimbles, so choose one that fits your finger comfortably.

SEWING MACHINE

A sewing machine will quickly speed up any job, whether it's a quick repair or making a dress for a special occasion. Most sewing machines today are aided by computer technology, which enhances stitch quality and ease of use. Always spend time trying out a sewing machine before you buy, to really get a feel for it.

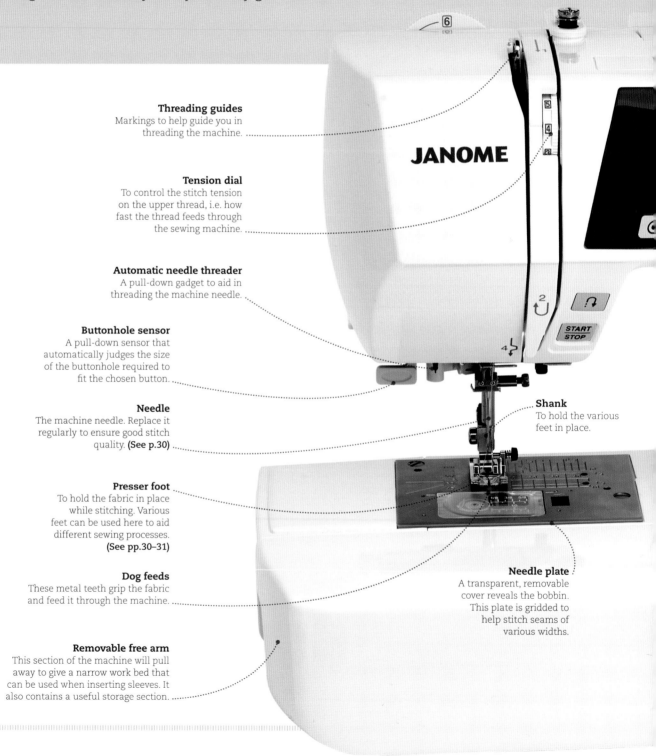

Threading guides
Markings to help guide you in threading the machine.

Tension dial
To control the stitch tension on the upper thread, i.e. how fast the thread feeds through the sewing machine.

Automatic needle threader
A pull-down gadget to aid in threading the machine needle.

Buttonhole sensor
A pull-down sensor that automatically judges the size of the buttonhole required to fit the chosen button.

Needle
The machine needle. Replace it regularly to ensure good stitch quality. **(See p.30)**

Presser foot
To hold the fabric in place while stitching. Various feet can be used here to aid different sewing processes. **(See pp.30–31)**

Dog feeds
These metal teeth grip the fabric and feed it through the machine.

Removable free arm
This section of the machine will pull away to give a narrow work bed that can be used when inserting sleeves. It also contains a useful storage section.

Shank
To hold the various feet in place.

Needle plate
A transparent, removable cover reveals the bobbin. This plate is gridded to help stitch seams of various widths.

JANOME

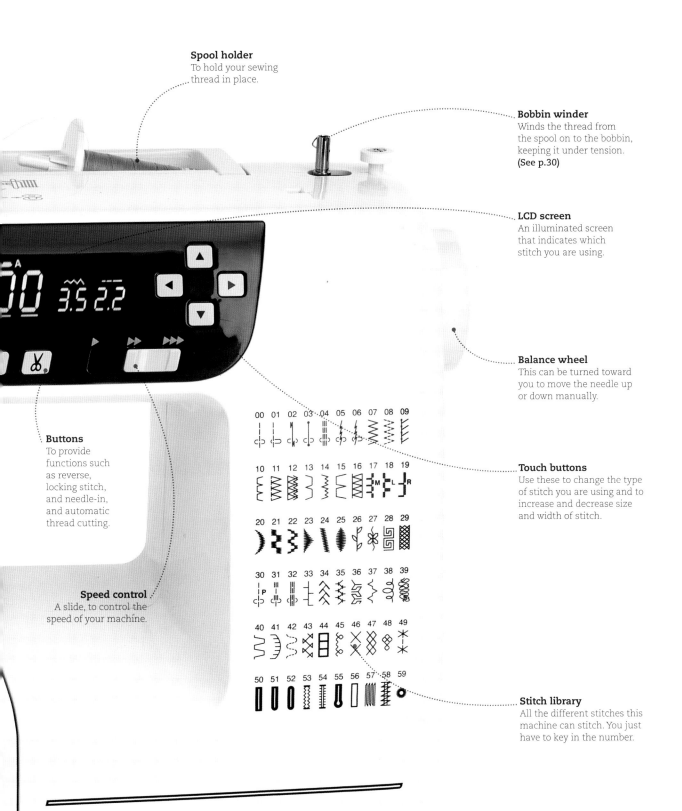

Spool holder
To hold your sewing
thread in place.

Bobbin winder
Winds the thread from
the spool on to the bobbin,
keeping it under tension.
(See p.30)

LCD screen
An illuminated screen
that indicates which
stitch you are using.

Balance wheel
This can be turned toward
you to move the needle up
or down manually.

Buttons
To provide
functions such
as reverse,
locking stitch,
and needle-in,
and automatic
thread cutting.

Touch buttons
Use these to change the type
of stitch you are using and to
increase and decrease size
and width of stitch.

Speed control
A slide, to control the
speed of your machine.

Stitch library
All the different stitches this
machine can stitch. You just
have to key in the number.

SEWING-MACHINE ACCESSORIES

You can purchase a variety of accessories for your sewing machine to make certain sewing processes much easier. There are different machine needles not only for different fabrics but also for different types of thread. There is also a huge number of sewing-machine feet, and new feet are constantly coming on to the market. Those shown here are some of the most popular.

Plastic bobbin
The bobbin is for the lower thread. Some machines take plastic bobbins, others metal. Always check which kind of bobbin your machine uses, since the incorrect choice can cause stitch problems.

Metal bobbin
Also known as a universal bobbin, this is used with many types of sewing machines. Be sure to check that your machine requires a metal bobbin before you buy.

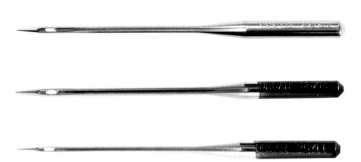

Machine needles
There are different types of sewing machine needle to handle different fabrics. Machine needles are sized from 60 to 100, a 60 being a very fine needle. There are special needles for machine embroidery and also for metallic threads.

Overedge foot
A foot that runs along the raw edge of the fabric and holds it stable while an overedge stitch is worked.

Embroidery foot
A clear plastic foot with a groove underneath that allows linear machine embroidery stitches to pass under.

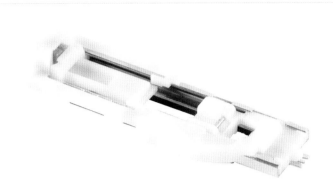

Buttonhole foot
This extends so the button can be placed in the back of the foot. The machine will stitch a buttonhole to fit thanks to the buttonhole sensor.

Blind hem foot
Use this foot in conjunction with the blind hem stitch to create a neat hemming stitch.

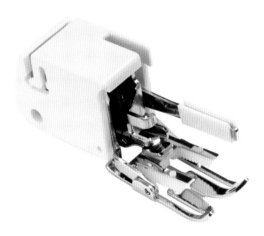

Walking foot
This strange-looking foot "walks" across the fabric, so that the upper layer of fabric does not push forward. Great for matching checks and stripes and also for stitching difficult fabrics.

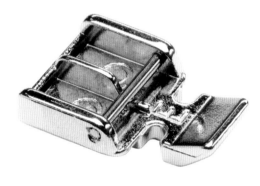

Zipper foot
This foot fits to either the right- or left-hand side of the needle to enable you to stitch close to a zipper.

Invisible zipper foot
A foot that is used to insert an invisible zipper—the foot holds the coils of the zipper open, enabling you to stitch behind them.

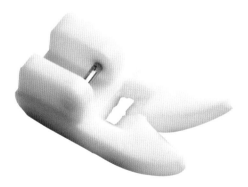

Ultra-glide foot
A foot made from Teflon™ that glides over the fabric. Useful for synthetic leathers.

SERGER

This machine is often used in conjunction with the sewing machine, since it gives a very professional finish to your work. The serger has two upper threads and two lower threads (the loopers), along with two knives that remove the edge of the fabric. Used extensively for neatening the edges of fabric, the serger can also be used for construction of stretch knits.

SERGER ACCESSORIES

You can purchase additional feet for the serger. Some will speed up your sewing by performing tasks such as gathering.

Serger needles
The serger uses a ballpoint needle, which creates a large loop in the thread for the loopers to catch and produce a stitch. If a normal sewing machine needle is used it can damage the serger.

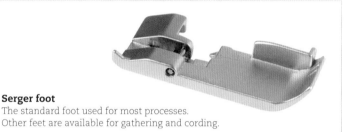

Serger foot
The standard foot used for most processes. Other feet are available for gathering and cording.

SERGER STITCHES

As the serger works, the threads wrap around the edge to give a professional finish. The 3-thread stitch is used primarily for neatening. A 4-thread stitch can also be used for neatening, but its fourth thread makes it ideal for constructing a seam on stretch knits.

▶ 3-THREAD SERGER STITCH

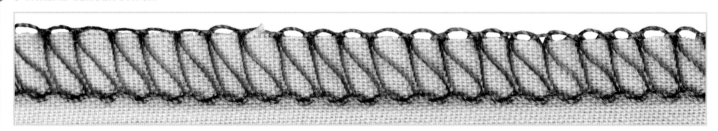

▶ 4-THREAD SERGER STITCH

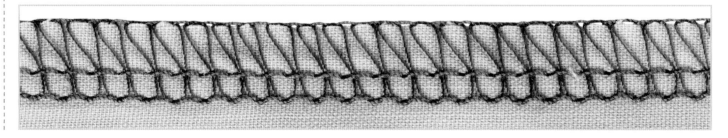

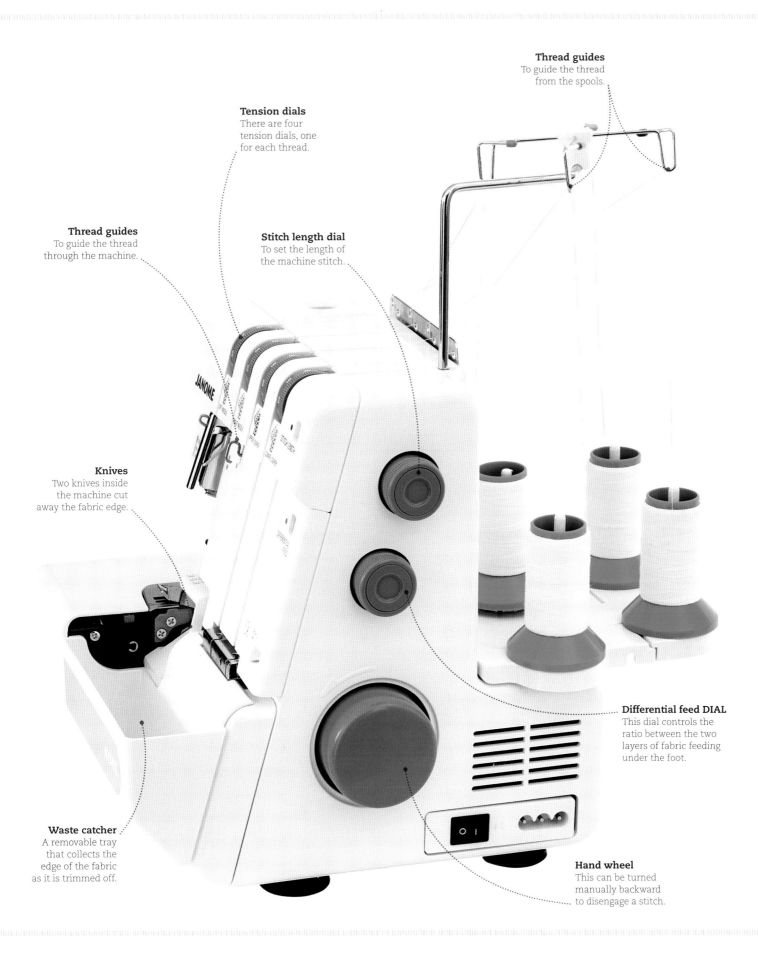

Thread guides
To guide the thread
from the spools.

Tension dials
There are four
tension dials, one
for each thread.

Thread guides
To guide the thread
through the machine.

Stitch length dial
To set the length of
the machine stitch.

Knives
Two knives inside
the machine cut
away the fabric edge.

Differential feed DIAL
This dial controls the
ratio between the two
layers of fabric feeding
under the foot.

Waste catcher
A removable tray
that collects the
edge of the fabric
as it is trimmed off.

Hand wheel
This can be turned
manually backward
to disengage a stitch.

PRESSING AIDS

Successful sewing relies on successful pressing. Without the correct pressing equipment, sewing can look too "homemade," whereas if correctly pressed any sewn item will have a neat, professional finish.

Clapper ▶
A wooden aid that pounds creases into a heavy fabric after steaming. The top section is used to help press collar seams and points.

◀ **Seam roll**
This tubular pressing aid is used to press seams open on fabrics that mark, since the iron only touches the seam on top of the roll. Also used for sleeve and pant seams.

Pressing cloth ▶
Choose a cloth made from silk organza or muslin, since you can see through it. The cloth stops the iron from marking fabric and protects delicate fabrics.

◀ Pressing mitten
Slips on to your hand to give more control over where you are pressing.

▲ Velvet mat
A pressing mat with a tufted side to aid the pressing of pile fabrics, such as velvet.

Iron ▶
A good-quality steam iron is a wonderful asset. Choose a reasonably heavy iron that has steam and a shot of steam facility.

▲ Ironing board
Essential to iron on. Make sure the board is height-adjustable.

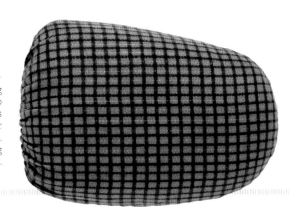

Tailor's ham ▶
A ham-shaped pressing pillow that is used to press darts and press the shape into collar and shoulder curves. Also used in making tailored garments.

FABRICS

WOOL

A natural fiber, wool comes primarily from sheep—Australian merino sheep's wool is considered to be the best. However, we also get wool fibers from goats (mohair and cashmere), rabbits (angora), camels (camel hair), and llamas (alpaca). A wool fiber is either short and fluffy, when it is known as a woolen yarn, or it is long, strong, and smooth, when it is called worsted. The term virgin (or new) wool denotes wool fibers that are being used for the first time. Wool may be reprocessed or reused and is then often mixed with other fibers.

PROPERTIES OF WOOL

▸ **Comfortable to wear** in all climates since it is available in many weights and weaves

▸ **Warm in the winter** and cool in the summer, because it will breathe with your body

▸ **Absorbs moisture** better than other natural fibers—will absorb up to 30 percent of its weight before it feels wet

▸ **Flame-resistant**

▸ **Relatively crease-resistant**

▸ **Ideal to tailor** since it can be easily shaped with steam

▸ **Often blended** with other fibers to reduce the cost of a fabric

▸ **Felts** if exposed to excessive heat, moisture, and pressure

▸ **Will be bleached** by sunlight with prolonged exposure

▸ **Can be damaged** by moths

BOILED WOOL

Made from heat-treated wool or a wool blend, this does not fray or lose its shape. Known for its warmth and durability. It is also known for shrinking (if not bought preshrunk), so always test first by placing in a dryer set on a low temperature with a damp towel.

Cutting out: A nap layout is not required

Seams: Walking foot; plain and neatened edges should not be required but some layering to reduce bulk may be required

Thread: Silk for pure wool; polycotton all-purpose thread for wool blends

Needle: Machine size 14/16 ballpoint needle depending on thickness of the fabric; sharps for hand sewing

Pressing: Wool setting with a pressing cloth; steam-press by holding the iron 1in (2.5cm) above the fabric for approximately 5 seconds

Use for: Coats, jackets, capes, and smaller items such as berets

CASHMERE

Wool from the Kashmir goat, and the most luxurious of all the wools. A soft yet hard-wearing fabric available in different weights.

Cutting out: Since cashmere often has a slight pile, use a nap layout

Seams: Plain, neatened with serger stitch or pinking shears (a zigzag stitch would curl the edge of the seam)

Thread: A silk thread is ideal, or a polyester all-purpose thread

Needle: Machine size 12/14, depending on the thickness of the fabric; sharps for hand sewing

Pressing: Steam iron on a steam setting, with a pressing cloth and seam roll

Used for: Jackets, coats, men's wear; knitted cashmere yarn for sweaters, cardigans, underwear

CREPE

A soft fabric made from a twisted yarn that produces an uneven surface. Crepe will have stretched on the bolt and is prone to shrinkage so it is important to preshrink it by steaming prior to use.

Cutting out: A nap layout is not required

Seams: Plain, neatened with serger stitch (a zigzag stitch may curl the edge of the seam)

Thread: Polyester all-purpose thread

Needle: Machine size 12; sharps or milliner's for hand sewing

Pressing: Steam iron on a wool setting; a pressing cloth is not always required

Used for: All types of clothing

FELTED WOOL

A woven fabric that has been washed and dried at a high temperature. During this process the wool shrinks, becomes thicker, and gains a puffy texture, giving it a soft and fluffy feel.

Cutting out: For plain fabrics a nap layout is not required. Patterns, such as plaids, may need a nap layout

Seams: Plain, neatened edges should not be required but some layering to reduce bulk may be required

Thread: Silk or cotton

Needle: Machine size 14/16 ballpoint needle depending on the thickness of fabric; 14/16 sharps for hand sewing

Pressing: Wool setting with a pressing cloth

Use for: Coats, jackets, vests, and smaller items such as slippers and hats

FLANNEL

A wool with a lightly brushed surface, featuring either a plain or a twill weave. Used in the past for underwear.

Cutting out: Use a nap layout

Seams: Plain, neatened with serger or zigzag stitch or a Hong Kong finish

Thread: Polyester all-purpose thread

Needle: Machine size 14; sharps for hand sewing

Pressing: Steam iron on a wool setting with a pressing cloth; use a seam roll as the fabric is prone to marking

Used for: Coats, jackets, skirts, pants, men's wear

FABRICS

GABARDINE

A hard-wearing suiting fabric with a distinctive weave. Gabardine often has a sheen and is prone to shine. It can be difficult to handle since it is springy and frays badly.

Cutting out: A nap layout is advisable since the fabric has a sheen

Seams: Plain, neatened with serger or zigzag stitch

Thread: Polyester all-purpose thread or 100 percent cotton thread

Needle: Machine size 14; sharps for hand sewing

Pressing: Steam iron on a wool setting; use just the toe of the iron and a silk organza pressing cloth as the fabric will mark and may shine

Used for: Men's wear, jackets, pants

MOHAIR

From the wool of the Angora goat. A long, straight, and very strong fiber that produces a hairy cloth or yarn for knitting.

Cutting out: Use a nap layout, with the fibers brushing down the pattern pieces in the same direction, from neck to hem

Seams: Plain, neatened with serger stitch or pinking shears

Thread: Polyester all-purpose thread

Needle: Machine size 14; sharps for hand sewing

Pressing: Steam iron on a wool setting; "stroke" the iron over the wool, moving in the direction of the nap

Used for: Jackets, coats, men's wear, soft furnishings; knitted mohair yarns for sweaters

PONTE ROMA

A double-knit fabric, less stretchy than other jersey fabrics. No right or wrong side; however, some have a pattern woven into them, which means that each side shows a slightly different version of the pattern that you can mix. It has a tendency to shrink, so wash and dry before cutting out.

Cutting out: A nap layout not required

Seams: Walking or dual feed foot, neatened with a stretch, overlock, or zigzag stitch

Thread: Polyester all-purpose thread

Needle: Machine size 11/14 ballpoint needle; 11/14 sharps for hand sewing

Pressing: Low to medium setting; iron with care

Used for: Skirts, dresses, pants, jackets

TARTAN

An authentic tartan belongs to a Scottish clan, and each has its own unique design that can only be used by that clan. The fabric is made using a twill weave from worsted yarns.

Cutting out: Check the design for even/uneven checks since it may need a nap layout or even a single layer layout

Seams: Plain, matching the pattern and neatened with serger or zigzag stitch

Thread: Polyester all-purpose thread

Needle: Machine size 14; sharps for hand sewing

Pressing: Steam iron on a wool setting; may require a pressing cloth, so test first

Used for: Traditionally kilts, but these days also skirts, pants, jackets, soft furnishings

TWEED

A rough fabric with a distinctive warp and weft, often in different colors. Traditional tweed is associated with the English countryside.

Cutting out: A nap layout is not required unless the fabric features a check

Seams: Plain, neatened with serger or zigzag stitch; can also be neatened with pinking shears

Thread: Polyester all-purpose thread or 100 percent cotton thread

Needle: Machine size 14; sharps for hand sewing

Pressing: Steam iron on a steam setting; a pressing cloth may not be required

Used for: Jackets, coats, skirts, men's wear, soft furnishings

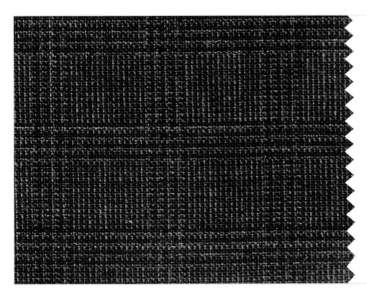

WOOL WORSTED

A light and strong cloth, made from good-quality thin, firm filament fibers. Always steam prior to cutting out since the fabric may shrink slightly after having been stretched around a bolt.

Cutting out: Use a nap layout

Seams: Plain, neatened with serger or zigzag stitch or a Hong Kong finish

Thread: Polyester all-purpose thread

Needle: Machine size 12/14, depending on fabric; milliner's or sharps for hand sewing

Pressing: Steam iron on a wool setting with a pressing cloth; use a seam roll to prevent the seam from showing through

Used for: Skirts, jackets, coats, pants

COTTON

One of the most versatile and popular of all fabrics, cotton is a natural fiber that comes from the seed pods, or bolls, of the cotton plant. It is thought that cotton fibers have been in use since ancient times. Today, the world's biggest producers of cotton include the United States, India, and countries in the Middle East. Cotton fibers can be filament or staple, with the longest and finest used for top-quality bed linen. Cotton clothing is widely worn in warmer climates since the fabric will keep you cool.

PROPERTIES OF COTTON

▶ **Absorbs moisture well** and carries heat away from the body

▶ **Stronger wet** than dry

▶ **Does not build up static electricity**

▶ **Dyes well**

▶ **Prone to shrinkage** unless it has been treated

▶ **Will deteriorate** from mildew and prolonged exposure to sunlight

▶ **Creases easily**

▶ **Soils easily,** but launders well

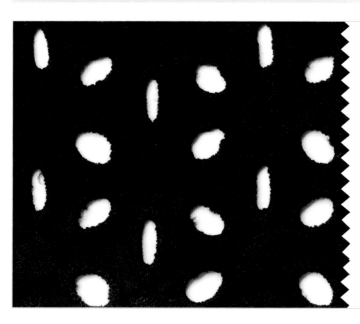

EYELET

A fine, plain-weave cotton that has been embroidered in such a way as to make small holes.

Cutting out: May need layout to place embroidery at hem edge

Seams: Plain, neatened with serger or zigzag stitch; a French seam can also be used

Thread: Polyester all-purpose thread

Needle: Machine size 12/14; sharps for hand sewing

Pressing: Steam iron on a cotton setting; a pressing cloth is not required

Used for: Baby clothes, summer skirts, blouses

MUSLIN

A plain-weave fabric that is usually unbleached and quite firm. Available in many different weights, from very fine to extremely heavy.

Cutting out: A nap layout is not required

Seams: Plain, neatened with serger or zigzag stitch

Thread: Polyester all-purpose thread

Needle: Machine size 11/14, depending on thickness of thread; sharps for hand sewing

Pressing: Steam iron on a steam setting; a pressing cloth is not required

Used for: Toiles (test garments), soft furnishings

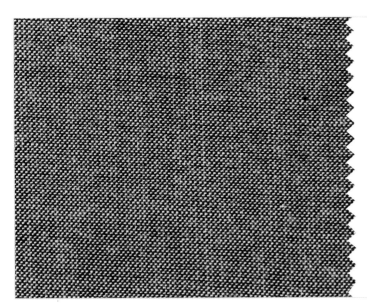

CHAMBRAY

A light cotton that has a colored warp thread and white weft thread. Chambray can also be found as a check or a striped fabric.

Cutting out: A nap layout should not be required

Seams: Plain, neatened with serger or zigzag stitch

Thread: Polyester all-purpose thread

Needle: Machine size 11; sharps for hand sewing

Pressing: Steam iron on a cotton setting; a pressing cloth is not required

Used for: Blouses, men's shirts, children's wear

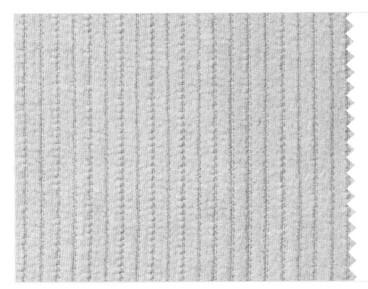

CORDUROY

A soft pile fabric with distinctive stripes (known as wales or ribs) woven into it. The name depends on the size of the ribs: baby or pin cord has extremely fine ribs; needle cord has slightly thicker ribs; corduroy has 10–12 ribs per 1in (2.5cm); and elephant or jumbo cord has thick, heavy ribs.

Cutting out: Use a nap layout with the pile on the corduroy brushing up the pattern pieces from hem to neck, to give depth of color

Seams: Plain, stitched using a walking foot and neatened with serger or zigzag stitch

Thread: Polyester all-purpose thread

Needle: Machine size 12/16; sharps or milliner's for hand sewing

Pressing: Steam iron on a cotton setting; use a seam roll under the seams with a pressing cloth

Used for: Pants, skirts, men's wear

DENIM

Named after Nîmes in France. A hard-wearing, twill-weave fabric with a colored warp and white weft, usually made into jeans. Available in various weights and often mixed with an elastic thread for stretch. Denim is usually blue, but is also available in a variety of other colors.

Cutting out: A nap layout is not required

Seams: Run and fell or topstitched

Thread: Polyester all-purpose thread with topstitching thread for detail topstitching

Needle: Machine size 14/16; sharps for hand sewing

Pressing: Steam iron on a cotton setting; a pressing cloth should not be required

Used for: Jeans, jackets, children's wear

DOUBLE GAUZE

A loosely woven, 100 percent cotton fabric. It is made up of two layers of thin fabric, similar to muslin, and is joined every few inches with small invisible stitches. It is prone to shrinking, so wash using a cold setting before cutting.

Cutting out: Use a nap layout

Seams: Walking or dual feed foot; flat fell or French seam

Thread: Polyester all-purpose thread; 50 weight cotton thread

Needle: Machine size 9/11; sharps for hand sewing

Pressing: Steam press to iron out the crinkle texture

Used for: Loose tops, blouses, dresses, pajamas

FRENCH TERRY

A knitted fabric, often a mix of cotton with elastane or spandex for stretch. It has a brushed, soft surface making the fabric comfortable against the skin. Prewash before cutting out and allow to dry naturally rather than tumble dry.

Cutting out: Use a nap layout

Seams: Stretch, overlock, or zigzag stitch; when sewing multiple layers, a walking foot is advisable

Thread: Polyester all-purpose thread

Needle: Machine size 10/12 ballpoint needle; 10/12 sharps for hand sewing

Pressing: Medium heat only

Used for: All types of clothing

GINGHAM

A fresh, two-color cotton fabric that features a check of various sizes. A plain weave made by having groups of white and colored warp and weft threads.

Cutting out: Usually an even check, so nap layout is not required but recommended; pattern will need to be matched

Seams: Plain, neatened with serger or zigzag stitch

Thread: Polyester all-purpose thread

Needle: Machine size 11/12; sharps for hand sewing

Pressing: Steam iron on a cotton setting; a pressing cloth should not be required

Used for: Children's wear, dresses, shirts, home furnishings

JERSEY

A fine cotton yarn that has been knitted to give stretch, making the fabric very comfortable to wear. Jersey will also drape well.

Cutting out: A nap layout is recommended

Seams: 4-thread serger stitch; or plain seam stitched with a small zigzag stitch and then seam allowances stitched together with a zigzag

Thread: Polyester all-purpose thread

Needle: Machine size 12/14; a ballpoint needle may be required for serger and a milliner's for hand sewing

Pressing: Steam iron on a wool setting since jersey may shrink on a cotton setting

Used for: Underwear, draped dresses, loungewear, bedding

MADRAS

A check fabric made from a fine cotton yarn, usually from India. Often found in bright colors featuring an uneven check. An inexpensive cotton fabric.

Cutting out: Use a nap layout and match the checks

Seams: Plain, neatened with serger or zigzag stitch

Thread: Polyester all-purpose thread

Needle: Machine size 12/14; sharps for hand sewing

Pressing: Steam iron on a cotton setting; a pressing cloth is not required

Used for: Shirts, skirts, shorts, home furnishings

MUSLIN

A plain-weave fabric that is usually unbleached and quite firm. Available in many different weights, from very fine to extremely heavy.

Cutting out: A nap layout is not required

Seams: Plain, neatened with serger or zigzag stitch

Thread: Polyester all-purpose thread

Needle: Machine size 11/14, depending on thickness of thread; sharps for hand sewing

Pressing: Steam iron on a steam setting; a pressing cloth is not required

Used for: Toiles (test garments), soft furnishings

SEERSUCKER

A woven cotton that has a bubbly appearance woven into it, due to stripes of puckers. Do not overpress, or the surface effect will be damaged.

Cutting out: Use a nap layout, due to puckered surface effect

Seams: Plain, neatened with overlock or zigzag stitch

Thread: Polyester all-purpose thread

Needle: Machine size 11/12; milliner's for hand sewing

Pressing: Steam iron on a cotton setting (be careful not to press out the wrinkles)

Used for: Summer clothing, skirts, shirts, children's wear

SHIRTING

A closely woven, fine cotton with colored warp and weft yarns making stripes or checks.

Cutting out: Use a nap layout if fabric has uneven stripes

Seams: Plain, neatened with serger or zigzag stitch; a run and fell seam can also be used

Thread: Polyester all-purpose thread

Needle: Machine size 12; milliner's for hand sewing

Pressing: Steam iron on a cotton setting; a pressing cloth is not required

Used for: Ladies' and men's shirts

VELVET

A pile-weave fabric, made by using an additional yarn that is then cut to produce the pile. Difficult to handle and can be easily damaged if seams have to be unpicked.

Cutting out: Use a nap layout with the pile brushing up from hem to neck, to give depth of color

Seams: Plain, stitched using a walking foot (stitch all seams from hem to neck) and neatened with serger or zigzag stitch

Thread: Polyester all-purpose thread

Needle: Machine size 14; milliner's for hand sewing

Pressing: Only if you have to; use a velvet board, a little steam, the toe of the iron, and a silk organza cloth

Used for: Jackets, coats

SILK

Often referred to as the queen of fabrics, silk is made from the fibers of the silkworm's cocoon. This strong and luxurious fabric dates back thousands of years to its first development in China, and the secret of silk production was well protected by the Chinese until 300 AD. Silk fabrics can be very fine or thick and chunky. They need to be handled with care, since some can be easily damaged.

PROPERTIES OF SILK

▶ **Keeps you warm** in winter and cool in summer
▶ **Absorbs moisture** and dries quickly
▶ **Dyes well**, producing deep, rich colors
▶ **Static electricity can build up** and fabric may cling
▶ **Will fade** in prolonged strong sunlight

▶ **Prone to shrinkage**
▶ **Best dry-cleaned**
▶ **Weaker when wet** than dry
▶ **May watermark**

CHIFFON

A very strong and very fine, transparent silk with a plain weave. Will gather and ruffle well. Difficult to handle.

Cutting out: Place tissue paper under the fabric and pin the fabric to the tissue paper, cutting through all layers if necessary; use extra-fine pins

Seams: French

Thread: Polyester all-purpose thread

Needle: Machine size 9/11; fine milliner's for hand sewing

Pressing: Dry iron on a wool setting

Used for: Special-occasion wear, overblouses

DUCHESSE SATIN

A heavy, expensive satin fabric used almost exclusively for special-occasion wear.

Cutting out: Use a nap layout

Seams: Plain, with pinked edges

Thread: Polyester all-purpose thread

Needle: Machine size 12/14; milliner's for hand sewing

Pressing: Steam iron on a wool setting with a pressing cloth; use a seam roll under the seams to prevent shadowing

Used for: Special-occasion wear

DUPIONI

Woven using a textured yarn that produces irregularities in the weave.

Cutting out: Use a nap layout to prevent shadowing

Seams: Plain, neatened with serger or zigzag stitch

Thread: Polyester all-purpose thread

Needle: Machine size 12; milliner's for hand sewing

Pressing: Steam iron on a wool setting with a pressing cloth, as fabric may watermark

Used for: Dresses, skirts, jackets, special-occasion wear, soft furnishings

HABUTAI

Originally from Japan, a smooth, fine silk that can have a plain or a twill weave. Fabric is often used for silk painting.

Cutting out: A nap layout is not required

Seams: French

Thread: Polyester all-purpose thread

Needle: Machine size 9/11; very fine milliner's or betweens for hand sewing

Pressing: Steam iron on a wool setting

Used for: Lining, shirts, blouses

MATKA

A silk suiting fabric with an uneven-looking yarn. Matka can be mistaken for linen.

Cutting out: Use a nap layout since silk may shadow

Seams: Plain, neatened with serger or zigzag stitch or a Hong Kong finish

Thread: Polyester all-purpose thread

Needle: Machine size 12/14; milliner's for hand sewing

Pressing: Steam iron on a wool setting with a pressing cloth; a seam roll is recommended to prevent the seams from showing through

Used for: Dresses, jackets, pants

ORGANZA

A sheer fabric with a crisp appearance that will crease easily.

Cutting out: A nap layout is not required

Seams: French or use a seam for a difficult fabric

Thread: Polyester all-purpose thread

Needle: Machine size 11; milliner's or betweens for hand sewing

Pressing: Steam iron on a wool setting; a pressing cloth should not be required

Used for: Sheer blouses, shrugs, interlining, interfacing

SATIN

A silk with a satin weave that can be very light to quite heavy in weight.

Cutting out: Use a nap layout in a single layer as fabric is slippery

Seams: French; on thicker satins, use a seam for a difficult fabric

Thread: Polyester all-purpose thread (not silk thread as it becomes weak with wear)

Needle: Machine size 11/12; milliner's or betweens for hand sewing

Pressing: Steam iron on a wool setting with a pressing cloth as fabric may watermark

Used for: Blouses, dresses, special-occasion wear

TAFFETA

A smooth, plain-weave fabric with a crisp appearance. It makes a rustling sound when worn. Can require special handling and does not wear well.

Cutting out: Use a nap layout, with extra-fine pins in seams to minimize marking the fabric

Seams: Plain; fabric may pucker, so sew from the hem upward, keeping the fabric taut under the machine; neaten with serger or pinking shears

Thread: Polyester all-purpose thread

Needle: Machine size 11; milliner's or betweens for hand sewing

Pressing: Cool iron, with a seam roll under the seams

Used for: Special-occasion wear

LINEN

Linen is a natural fiber that is derived from the stem of the flax plant. It is available
in a variety of qualities and weights, from very fine linen to heavy suiting weights.
Coarser than cotton, it is sometimes woven with cotton as well as being mixed with silk.

PROPERTIES OF LINEN

▸ **Cool and comfortable** to wear

▸ **Absorbs moisture well**

▸ **Shrinks** when washed

▸ **Does not ease well**

▸ **Has a tendency to wrinkle**

▸ **Prone to fraying**

▸ **Resists moths** but is damaged by mildew

COTTON AND LINEN MIX

Two fibers may have been mixed
together in the yarn or there may
be mixed warp and weft yarns. It
has lots of texture in the weave.

Cutting out: A nap layout should
not be required

Seams: Plain, neatened with serger
or zigzag stitch

Thread: Polyester all-purpose thread

Needle: Machine size 14; sharps
for hand sewing

Pressing: A steam iron on a
steam setting with a silk organza
pressing cloth

Used for: Summer-weight jackets,
tailored dresses

DRESS-WEIGHT LINEN

A medium-weight linen with
a plain weave. The yarn is often
uneven, which causes slubs
in the weave.

Cutting out: A nap layout is
not required

Seams: Plain, neatened with
serger or zigzag stitch or
a Hong Kong finish

Thread: Polyester all-purpose
thread with a topstitching thread
for topstitching

Needle: Machine size 14; sharps
for hand sewing

Pressing: Steam iron on a cotton
setting (steam is required to
remove creases)

Used for: Dresses, pants, skirts

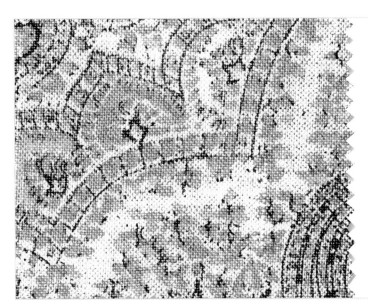

PRINTED LINENS

Many linens today feature prints or even embroidery. The fabric may be light to medium weight, with a smooth yarn that has few slubs.

Cutting out: Use a nap layout

Seams: Plain, neatened with serger or zigzag stitch

Thread: Polyester all-purpose thread

Needle: Machine size 14; sharps for hand sewing

Pressing: Steam iron on a cotton setting (steam is required to remove creases)

Used for: Dresses, skirts

SUITING LINEN

A heavier yarn is used to produce a linen suitable for suits for men and women. Can be a firm, tight weave or a looser weave.

Cutting out: A nap layout is not required

Seams: Plain, neatened with serger or a zigzag stitch

Thread: Polyester all-purpose thread with a topstitch thread for topstitching

Needle: Machine size 14; sharps for hand sewing

Pressing: Steam iron on a cotton setting (steam is required to remove creases)

Used for: Men's and women's suits, pants, coats

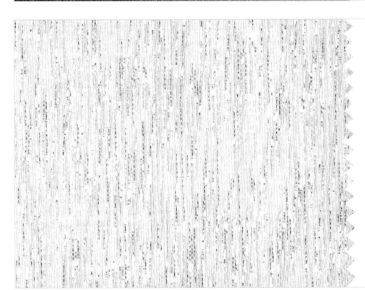

FANCY WEAVE LINEN

A linen woven with additional decorative yarns such as metallic or lurex.

Cutting out: A nap layout is not required

Seams: Plain, neatened with serger or a zigzag stitch

Thread: Polyester all-purpose thread with a topstitch thread for topstitching

Needle: Machine size 14; sharps for hand sewing

Pressing: Press carefully as decorative yarns may melt; use a pressing cloth

Used for: Dresses, jackets

SYNTHETIC FABRICS

The term synthetic applies to any fabric that is not 100 percent natural. Many of these fabrics have been developed over the last hundred years, which means they are new compared to natural fibers. Some synthetic fabrics are made from natural elements mixed with chemicals, while others are made entirely from non-natural substances. The properties of synthetic fabrics vary from fabric to fabric.

PROPERTIES OF SYNTHETIC FABRICS

▶ **Durable** and usually launder well

▶ **Can be prone to static** and "cling" to the body

▶ **Can dye well** and are often digitally printed

▶ **Mix well with natural fibers**

ACETATE

Introduced in 1924, acetate is made from cellulose and chemicals. The fabric has a slight shine and is widely used for linings. Acetate can also be woven into fabrics such as acetate taffeta, acetate satin, and acetate jersey.

Properties of acetate:
• Dyes well
• Can be heat-set into pleats
• Washes well

Cutting out: Use a nap layout due to sheen on fabric

Seams: Plain, neatened with serger or zigzag stitch, or 4-thread serger stitch

Thread: Polyester all-purpose thread

Needle: Machine size 11; sharps for hand sewing

Pressing: Steam iron on a cool setting (fabric can melt)

Used for: Special-occasion wear, linings

ACRYLIC

Introduced in 1950, acrylic fibers are made from ethylene and acrylonitrile. The fabric resembles wool and makes a good substitute for machine-washable wool. Often seen as a knitted fabric, the fibers can be mixed with wool.

Properties of acrylic:
• Little absorbency
• Tends to retain odors
• Not very strong

Cutting out: A nap layout may be required

Seams: 4-thread serger stitch on knitted fabrics; plain seam on woven fabrics

Thread: Polyester all-purpose thread

Needle: Machine size 12/14, but a ballpoint needle may be required on knitted fabrics; sharps for hand sewing

Pressing: Steam iron on a wool setting (fabric can be damaged by heat)

Used for: Knitted yarns for sweaters; wovens for skirts, blouses

FABRICS

POLYESTER

One of the most popular of the man-made fibers, polyester was introduced in 1951 as a man's washable suiting. Polyester fibers are made from petroleum by-products and can take on any form, from a very fine sheer fabric to a thick, heavy suiting.

Properties of polyester:
• Nonabsorbent
• Does not crease
• Can build up static
• May "pill"

Cutting out: A nap layout is only required if the fabric is printed

Seams: French, plain, or 4-thread serger, depending on the weight of the fabric

Thread: Polyester all-purpose thread

Needle: Machine size 11/14; sharps for hand sewing

Pressing: Steam iron on a wool setting

Used for: Office wear, school uniforms

RAYON

Also known as viscose and often referred to as artificial silk, this fiber was developed in 1889. It is made from wood pulp or cotton linters mixed with chemicals. Rayon can be knitted or woven and made into a wide range of fabrics. It is often blended with other fibers.

Properties of rayon:
• Absorbent
• Nonstatic
• Dyes well
• Frays badly

Cutting out: A nap layout is only required if the fabric is printed

Seams: Plain, neatened with serger or zigzag stitch

Thread: Polyester all-purpose thread

Needle: Machine size 12/14; sharps for hand sewing

Pressing: Steam iron on a silk setting

Used for: Dresses, blouses, jackets

SCUBA

A relatively new fabric, scuba is a lofty double-knit of finely spun polyester fibers that creates a super smooth handle, low sheen, and a full-bodied drape. It is often digitally printed to great effect.

Properties of scuba:
• Takes dye well, especially digital prints
• Holds its shape after construction
• Does not absorb moisture well

Cutting out: A nap layout is not required unless the fabric is printed

Seams: Plain seam; no need to neaten but you can pink the edge or overlock

Thread: Polyester all-purpose thread

Needle: Machine size 14; some scubas may require a ballpoint needle

Pressing: Steam iron, with a pressing cloth (fabric can melt)

Used for: Skirts and dresses

ECO-FRIENDLY FABRICS

Traditional fabric production methods may have a negative impact on the environment, with some using harmful chemicals or large amounts of water. Fabric stores now sell a growing number of eco-friendly fabrics. Such fabrics are produced using raw ingredients that do not use pesticides, synthetic fertilizers, or chemicals that damage the environment and wildlife. They may also use fibers from sustainable and renewable sources, such as hemp and bamboo, and can be easier to recycle, too.

WHAT MAKES A FABRIC ECO-FRIENDLY?

▸ **Eco-fabrics are fabrics** that use plant-based, biodegradable raw materials, and are produced using ethical and environmentally sustainable methods. Unlike traditional textile production, eco-fabric production does not utilize chemicals that may harm the environment and wildlife.

▸ **Not all natural fibers** are necessarily eco-friendly—it is all down to the way they are produced. For example, most bamboo viscose is manufactured in a way that is harmful to both workers and the environment. However, bamboo fabrics produced in a closed-loop system reuse chemicals rather than releasing them. Even better are those that use natural enzymes—this process results in a soft yarn used to make bamboo linen.

▸ **Some eco-fabrics** are made solely from recycled textiles, helping to reuse some of the 14 million tons of clothing thrown out each year.

BAMBOO JERSEY

Bamboo is a soft fabric that feels comfortable against the skin and is breathable, making it cool to wear. It is also hypoallergenic, antifungal, light, and strong. Wash prior to use. Bamboo fabrics are manufactured in different ways, so choose fabrics produced in a closed-loop system.

Cutting out: Use a nap layout

Seams: Plain, but use a stretch stitch or narrow zigzag; should not need neatening but can be neatened with a 3-thread overlock or zigzag stitch

Thread: Polyester all-purpose thread

Needle: Machine size 11/12 stretch or jersey needle; sharps for hand sewing

Pressing: Low to medium iron

Used for: T-shirts, skirts, dresses, and smaller items such as scarves

BIO LINEN

A fabric made from the flax plant, which requires less water during the growing process than cotton. This fabric is absorbent and breathable, which means it is cool to wear in the summer but provides an insulating layer during the colder months. It is washed with bio enzymes, rather than chemicals, making it soft.

Cutting out: A nap layout is only required if the fabric is printed

Seams: Plain, neatened with a 3-thread overlock or zigzag stitch; a run and fell seam could also be used

Thread: Polyester all-purpose thread

Needle: Machine size 11/12; sharps for hand sewing

Pressing: Steam iron on a cotton setting; a pressing cloth should not be required

Used for: Skirts, shirts, tunics, pants, shorts, dresses

ECO-VISCOSE

Viscose comes from wood pulp cellulose from fast-growing, regenerative trees. It absorbs moisture well but can shrink during washing, so it is advisable to wash prior to cutting.

Cutting out: A nap layout is only required if the fabric is printed; it has a tendency to move while cutting, so use a rotary cutter rather than scissors to cut out

Seams: Plain, neatened with a 3-thread overlock or zigzag stitch

Thread: Polyester all-purpose thread

Needle: Machine size 10/11; sharps for hand stitching; the use of a walking foot may make sewing easier

Pressing: Medium heat setting; use a pressing cloth

Used for: Blouses, dresses, skirts, coats, jackets

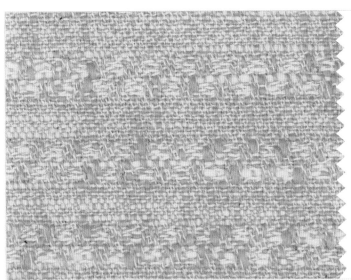

RAMIE

A hard-wearing fabric made from nettle fibers. It is often mixed with other fibers such as cotton, wool, and silk. It is a breathable fabric, similar in appearance to linen, and is cool to wear. Resistant to shrinking but creases easily. It is also bacteria resistant.

Cutting out: Use a nap layout

Seams: Plain, neatened with a 3-thread overlocker or zigzag stitch

Thread: Polyester all-purpose thread

Needle: Machine size 14; sharps for hand sewing

Pressing: Use a high temperature and a pressing cloth

Used for: All types of garments

RECYCLED POLYESTER SATIN

While not made from natural fibers, recycled polyester is an eco-friendly, less wasteful alternative to virgin synthetic fabrics. It is made from recycled plastic bottles, which means less energy is required to make it than virgin polyester. It has a sheen on one side and a matt finish on the other. It is long lasting, soft to touch, and drapes well; however, it can be less durable than virgin polyester.

Cutting out: A nap layout is only required if the fabric is printed

Seams: Plain, with a 3-thread overlocker or zigzag stitch

Thread: Polyester all-purpose thread

Needle: Machine size 14; sharps for hand sewing

Pressing: Cool iron; swatch test advised

Used for: Blouses, dresses, skirts, coats, jackets

PATTERNS &
CUTTING OUT

READING PATTERNS

Most dressmakers buy a commercial paper pattern to make a garment. A pattern has three main components: the envelope, the pattern sheets, and the instructions. The envelope gives an illustration of the garment that can be made from the contents, together with fabric suggestions and other requirements. The pattern sheets are normally printed on tissue paper and contain a wealth of information, while the instructions tell you how to construct the garment.

READING A PATTERN ENVELOPE

The envelope front illustrates the garment that can be made from the contents of the envelope. The illustration may be a line drawing or a photograph. There may be different versions, known as views. On the reverse of the envelope there is usually an illustration of the back view and the standard body measurement chart that has been used for this pattern, plus a chart that will help you purchase the correct amount of fabric for each view. The reverse of the envelope also includes suggestions for suitable fabrics, together with the notion, which are all the odds and ends you need to complete the project.

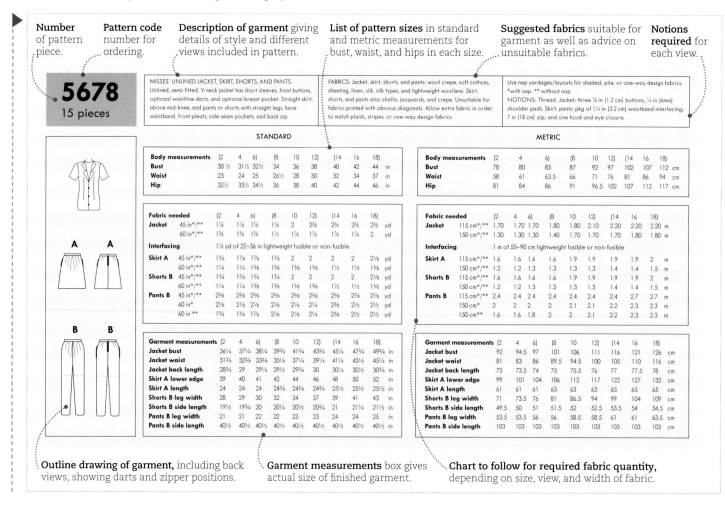

Number of pattern piece.

Pattern code number for ordering.

Description of garment giving details of style and different views included in pattern.

List of pattern sizes in standard and metric measurements for bust, waist, and hips in each size.

Suggested fabrics suitable for garment as well as advice on unsuitable fabrics.

Notions required for each view.

5678
15 pieces

MISSES' UNLINED JACKET, SKIRT, SHORTS, AND PANTS. Unlined, semi-fitted, V-neck jacket has short sleeves, front buttons, optional waistline darts, and optional breast pocket. Straight skirt, above mid-knee, and pants or shorts with straight legs, have waistband, front pleats, side seam pockets, and back zip.

FABRICS: Jacket, skirt, shorts, and pants: wool crepe, soft cottons, sheeting, linen, silk, silk types, and lightweight woollens. Skirt, shorts, and pants also challis, jacquards, and crepe. Unsuitable for fabrics printed with obvious diagonals. Allow extra fabric in order to match plaids, stripes, or one-way design fabrics.

Use nap yardages/layouts for shaded, pile, or one-way design fabrics. *with nap. ** without nap NOTIONS: Thread. Jacket: three ⅞ in (1.2 cm) buttons; ¼ in (6mm) shoulder pads. Skirt, pants: pkg of 1¼ in (3.2 cm) waistband interfacing; 7 in (18 cm) zip; and one hook and eye closure.

STANDARD

Body measurements	(2	4	6)	(8	10	12)	(14	16	18)	
Bust	30 ½	31½	32½	34	36	38	40	42	44	in
Waist	23	24	25	26½	28	30	32	34	37	in
Hip	32½	33½	34½	36	38	40	42	44	46	in

Fabric needed		(2	4	6)	(8	10	12)	(14	16	18)	
Jacket	45 in*/**	1⅞	1⅞	1⅞	1⅞	2	2⅜	2⅜	2⅜	2⅜	yd
	60 in*/**	1⅜	1⅜	1⅜	1½	1⅞	1⅞	1⅞	1⅞	2	yd
Interfacing	1⅛ yd of 22–36 in lightweight fusible or non-fusible									
Skirt A	45 in*/**	1¾	1⅞	1⅞	1⅞	2	2	2	2	2⅛	yd
	60 in*/**	1¼	1¼	1⅜	1⅜	1⅜	1⅜	1½	1½	1⅝	yd
Shorts B	45 in*/**	1¾	1¾	1¾	1¾	2	2	2	2	2⅛	yd
	60 in*/**	1¼	1¼	1⅜	1⅜	1⅜	1⅜	1½	1½	1⅝	yd
Pants B	45 in*/**	2⅝	2⅝	2⅝	2⅝	2⅝	2⅝	2⅝	2⅞	2⅞	yd
	60 in*	2⅛	2⅛	2⅛	2⅛	2¼	2¼	2⅜	2½	2½	yd
	60 in **	1¾	1¾	1⅞	2⅛	2⅛	2¼	2⅜	2½	2½	yd

Garment measurements	(2	4	6)	(8	10	12)	(14	16	18)	
Jacket bust	36¼	37¼	38¼	39¾	41¾	43¾	45¼	47¾	49¾	in
Jacket waist	31¾	32¾	33¾	35¼	37¼	39¼	41¼	43¼	45¼	in
Jacket back length	28¾	29	29¼	29½	29¾	30	30¼	30½	30¾	in
Skirt A lower edge	39	40	41	42	44	46	48	50	52	in
Skirt A length	24	24	24	24¾	24¾	24¾	25½	25½	25½	in
Shorts B leg width	28	29	30	32	34	37	39	41	43	in
Shorts B side length	19½	19¾	20	20¼	20½	20¾	21	21¼	21½	in
Pants B leg width	21	21	22	22	23	23	24	24	25	in
Pants B side length	40½	40½	40½	40½	40½	40½	40½	40½	40½	in

METRIC

Body measurements	(2	4	6)	(8	10	12)	(14	16	18)	
Bust	78	80	83	87	92	97	102	107	112	cm
Waist	58	61	63.5	66	71	76	81	86	94	cm
Hip	81	84	86	91	96.5	102	107	112	117	cm

Fabric needed		(2	4	6)	(8	10	12)	(14	16	18)	
Jacket	115 cm*/**	1.70	1.70	1.70	1.80	1.80	2.10	2.20	2.20	2.20	m
	150 cm*/**	1.30	1.30	1.30	1.40	1.70	1.70	1.70	1.80	1.80	m
Interfacing	1 m of 55–90 cm lightweight fusible or non-fusible									
Skirt A	115 cm*/**	1.6	1.6	1.6	1.6	1.9	1.9	1.9	1.9	2	m
	150 cm*/**	1.2	1.2	1.3	1.3	1.3	1.3	1.4	1.4	1.5	m
Shorts B	115 cm*/**	1.6	1.6	1.6	1.6	1.9	1.9	1.9	1.9	2	m
	150 cm*/**	1.2	1.2	1.3	1.3	1.3	1.3	1.4	1.4	1.5	m
Pants B	115 cm*/**	2.4	2.4	2.4	2.4	2.4	2.4	2.4	2.7	2.7	m
	150 cm*	2	2	2	2	2.1	2.1	2.2	2.3	2.3	m
	150 cm**	1.6	1.6	1.8	2	2	2.1	2.2	2.3	2.3	m

Garment measurements	(2	4	6)	(8	10	12)	(14	16	18)	
Jacket bust	92	94.5	97	101	106	111	116	121	126	cm
Jacket waist	81	83	86	89.5	94.5	100	105	110	116	cm
Jacket back length	73	73.5	74	75	75.5	76	77	77.5	78	cm
Skirt A lower edge	99	101	104	106	112	117	122	127	132	cm
Skirt A length	61	61	61	63	63	63	65	65	65	cm
Shorts B leg width	71	73.5	76	81	86.5	94	99	104	109	cm
Shorts B side length	49.5	50	51	51.5	52	52.5	53.5	54	54.5	cm
Pants B leg width	53.5	53.5	56	56	58.5	58.5	61	61	63.5	cm
Pants B side length	103	103	103	103	103	103	103	103	103	cm

Outline drawing of garment, including back views, showing darts and zipper positions.

Garment measurements box gives actual size of finished garment.

Chart to follow for required fabric quantity, depending on size, view, and width of fabric.

SINGLE-SIZE PATTERNS

Some patterns contain a garment of one size only. If you are using a single-size pattern, cut around the tissue paper on the thick black cutting line before making any alterations.

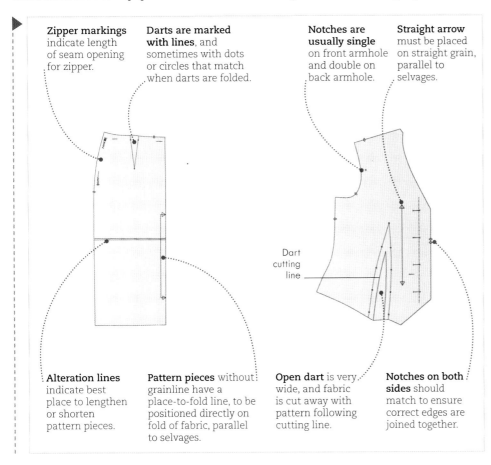

Zipper markings indicate length of seam opening for zipper.

Darts are marked with lines, and sometimes with dots or circles that match when darts are folded.

Notches are usually single on front armhole and double on back armhole.

Straight arrow must be placed on straight grain, parallel to selvages.

Dart cutting line

Alteration lines indicate best place to lengthen or shorten pattern pieces.

Pattern pieces without grainline have a place-to-fold line, to be positioned directly on fold of fabric, parallel to selvages.

Open dart is very wide, and fabric is cut away with pattern following cutting line.

Notches on both sides should match to ensure correct edges are joined together.

MULTISIZE PATTERNS

Many patterns today have more than one size printed on the tissue paper. Each size is clearly labeled and the cutting lines are marked with a different type of line for each size.

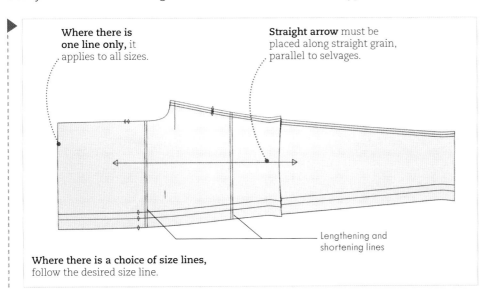

Where there is one line only, it applies to all sizes.

Straight arrow must be placed along straight grain, parallel to selvages.

Lengthening and shortening lines

Where there is a choice of size lines, follow the desired size line.

PATTERN MARKINGS

Each pattern piece will have a series of lines, dots, and other symbols printed on it. These symbols help you to alter the pattern and join the pattern pieces together. The symbols are universal across all major paper patterns.

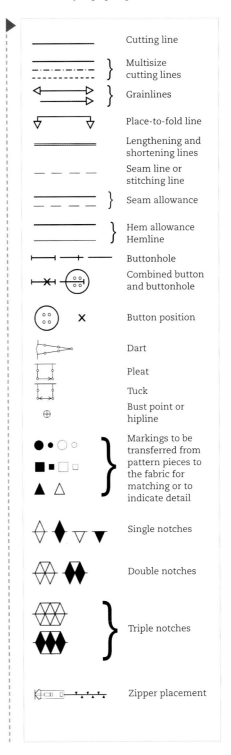

Cutting line

Multisize cutting lines

Grainlines

Place-to-fold line

Lengthening and shortening lines

Seam line or stitching line

Seam allowance

Hem allowance
Hemline

Buttonhole

Combined button and buttonhole

Button position

Dart

Pleat

Tuck

Bust point or hipline

Markings to be transferred from pattern pieces to the fabric for matching or to indicate detail

Single notches

Double notches

Triple notches

Zipper placement

BODY MEASURING

Accurate body measurements are needed to determine the correct pattern size to use and to know if any alterations are required. Pattern sizes are usually chosen by the hip or bust measurement; for tops follow the bust measurement, but for skirts or pants use the hip measurement. If you are choosing a dress pattern, go by whichever of your measurements is the largest.

TAKING BODY MEASUREMENTS

You will need a tape measure and ruler as well as a helper for some of the measuring, and a firm chair or stool.

Wear close-fitting clothes such as a leotard and leggings.

Do not wear shoes.

MEASURING YOUR HEIGHT

Most paper patterns are designed for a woman 5ft 5in to 5ft 6in (165 to 168cm). If you are shorter or taller than this you may need to adjust the pattern prior to cutting out your fabric.

1 Remove your shoes.

2 Stand straight, with your back against the wall.

3 Place a ruler flat on your head, touching the wall, and mark the wall at this point.

4 Step away and measure the distance from the floor to the marked point.

▶ CHEST

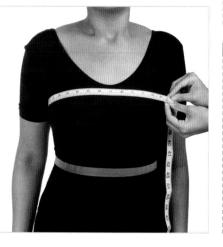

Measure above the bust, high under the arms, keeping the tape measure flat and straight across the back.

▶ FULL BUST

Make sure you are wearing a good-fitting bra and measure over the fullest part of the bust. If your cup size is in excess of a B, you will probably need to do a bust alteration, although some patterns are now cut to accommodate larger cup sizes.

▶ WAIST

This is the measurement around the smallest part of your waist. Wrap the tape around first to find your natural waist, then measure.

▶ HIPS

This measurement must be taken around the fullest part of the hips, between the waist and legs.

▶ HIGH HIPS

Take this just below the **waist** and just above the hip bones to give a measurement across the tummy. Measure around the fullest part of your tummy.

▶ BACK WAIST

Take this measurement **down the center of the back,** from the bony bit at the top of the spine, in line with the shoulders, to the waist.

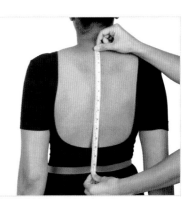

▶ SHOULDER

Hold the end of the tape measure at the base **of your neck** (where a necklace would lie) and measure to the dent at the end of your shoulder bone. To find this dent raise your arm slightly.

▶ OUTSIDE LEG

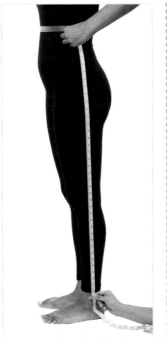

Measure the side of the leg **from the waist,** over the hip, and straight down the leg to the ankle bone.

▶ INSIDE LEG

Stand with your legs apart and measure the inside of one leg from the crotch to the ankle bone.

▶ NECK

Measure around the **neck**—snugly but not too tightly—to determine collar size.

▶ ARM

Bend your elbow and place your hand on your **hip,** then measure from the end of the shoulder over the elbow to the wrist bone.

▶ CROTCH DEPTH

Sit upright on a firm chair or stool and measure from the waist vertically down to the chair.

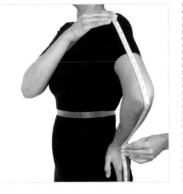

ALTERING PATTERNS

These alterations relate specifically to commercial patterns; the patterns in this book can be altered in a similar way. Your body measurements are unlikely to be exactly the same as those of your chosen pattern, so you will need to alter the pattern. Here is how to lengthen and shorten pattern pieces, and how to make specific alterations at the bust, waist and hips, shoulders and back, and to sleeves and pants.

EQUIPMENT

In addition to scissors and pins or tape, you will need a pencil, an eraser, a ruler that is clearly marked, and possibly a triangle. For many alterations you will also need some paper.

After pinning or taping the pattern to the paper, you can redraw the pattern lines. Trim away the excess paper before pinning the pattern to the fabric for cutting out.

EASY MULTISIZE PATTERN ALTERATIONS

Using a multisize pattern has many advantages, since you can cut it to suit your unique individual shape—for example, to accommodate a hip measurement that may be two sizes different from a waist measurement, if you are not precisely one size or another.

▶ **INDIVIDUAL PATTERN ADJUSTMENT**

To adjust for a wider hip measurement, cut from the smaller pattern size to the larger, curving the line gently to follow the contours of the body.

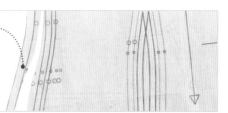

▶ **BETWEEN SIZES**

If your body measurements fall between two pattern sizes, cut carefully between the two cutting lines for the different sizes.

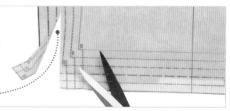

LENGTHENING AND SHORTENING PATTERNS

If you are short or tall, or if your arms or legs are shorter or longer than the pattern allows, you will need to adjust the pattern prior to cutting out. There are lengthening and shortening lines printed on the pattern pieces that will guide you as to the best places. However, you will need to compare your body shape against the pattern. Alter the front and back by the same amount at the same points, and always check finished lengths.

▶ **SLEEVE**

To keep the wrist area intact on the pattern, alter partway down the sleeve, or at the hem.

Wrist

Hem

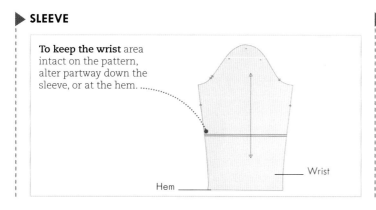

▶ **BODICE**

Alter the back neck to waist length below the bust dart but above the waist. Alter through the waist dart if there is one.

Bust dart

Waist

Waist dart

▶ FITTED DRESS

Mark between the bust and **waist** to alter the back neck to waist length.

Bust dart

Waist

Hipline

Alter below the hipline if not altering at the hem.

Alter below the hem if not altering at the hipline.

▶ SKIRT

Alter below **hipline** or at hem.

Hipline

Hem

▶ PANTS

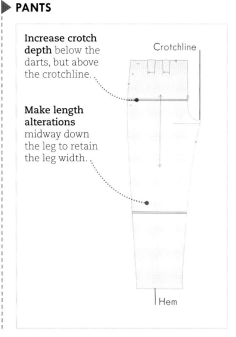

Increase crotch depth below the darts, but above the crotchline.

Crotchline

Make length alterations midway down the leg to retain the leg width.

Hem

▶ LENGTHENING A PATTERN PIECE

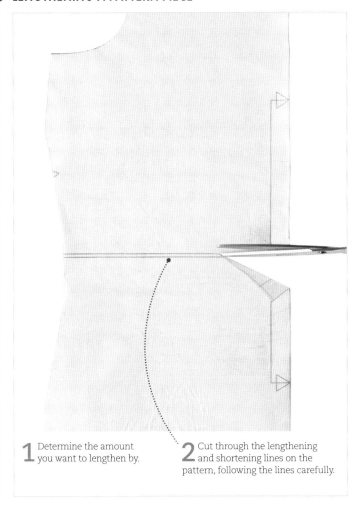

1 Determine the amount you want to lengthen by.

2 Cut through the lengthening and shortening lines on the pattern, following the lines carefully.

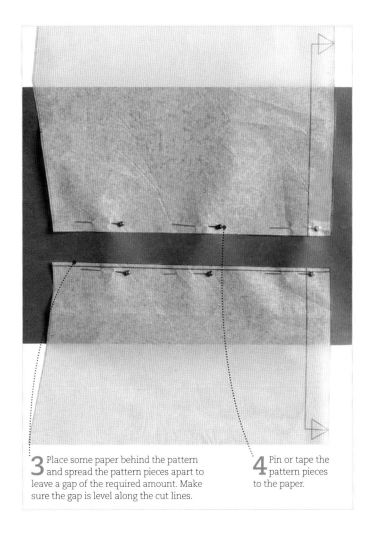

3 Place some paper behind the pattern and spread the pattern pieces apart to leave a gap of the required amount. Make sure the gap is level along the cut lines.

4 Pin or tape the pattern pieces to the paper.

▶ SHORTENING A PATTERN PIECE

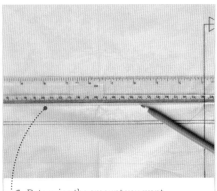

1 Determine the amount you want to shorten by. Mark this amount at intervals above the lengthening and shortening lines, then draw a line through the marks using the ruler as a guide.

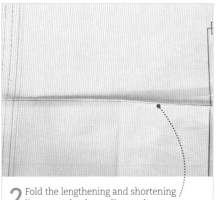

2 Fold the lengthening and shortening line on to the drawn line so the two lines meet neatly.

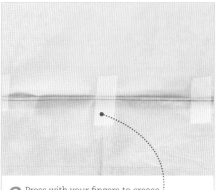

3 Press with your fingers to crease the fold sharply, then secure the fold in the pattern with tape.

▶ LENGTHENING ACROSS DARTS

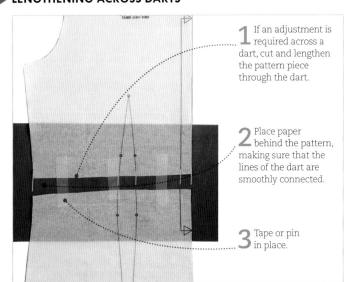

1 If an adjustment is required across a dart, cut and lengthen the pattern piece through the dart.

2 Place paper behind the pattern, making sure that the lines of the dart are smoothly connected.

3 Tape or pin in place.

▶ SHORTENING ACROSS DARTS

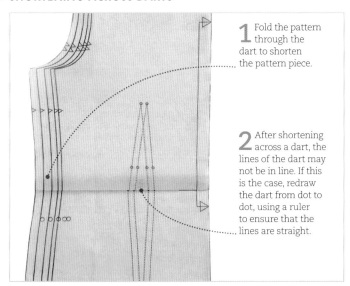

1 Fold the pattern through the dart to shorten the pattern piece.

2 After shortening across a dart, the lines of the dart may not be in line. If this is the case, redraw the dart from dot to dot, using a ruler to ensure that the lines are straight.

▶ LENGTHENING A HEM EDGE

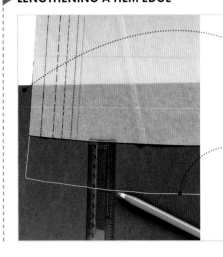

1 Place a sheet of pattern paper under the tissue paper at the hem edge and tape down.

2 Using a ruler as a guide, add on the required amount, marking dots at intervals along the pattern paper first, then connecting them with a line.

▶ SHORTENING A HEM EDGE

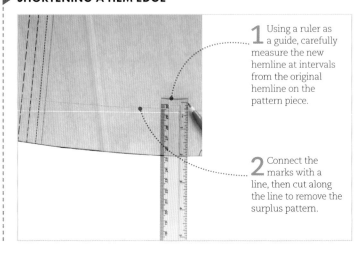

1 Using a ruler as a guide, carefully measure the new hemline at intervals from the original hemline on the pattern piece.

2 Connect the marks with a line, then cut along the line to remove the surplus pattern.

BUST

Some paper patterns today feature various cup sizes, but most are cut to accommodate a B cup, including those in this book. If you are larger than this, you will probably need to adjust your pattern before cutting out. As a general rule, when spreading the pattern pieces apart, try adjusting by ¼in (6mm) per cup size over a B cup.

▶ RAISING A BUST DART

1 If you have a high bust you may need to raise the point of the darts. The bust point is nearly always marked on the pattern. Mark the desired new bust point on the pattern.

2 Redraw the dart, tapering it to the new, higher, point.

▶ RAISING A BUST DART SUBSTANTIALLY

1 Mark the desired new bust point on the pattern.

2 Cut a rectangle out of the bust dart area and move it up to the new position.

3 Tape paper behind and redraw the side seam.

▶ INCREASING A BUST DART FOR A FULL BUST

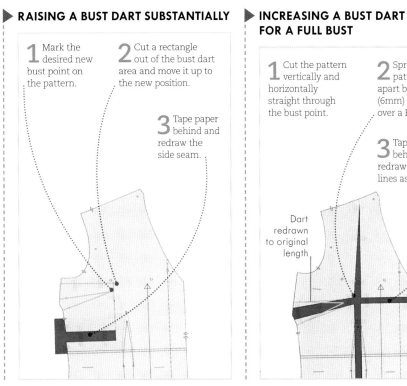

1 Cut the pattern vertically and horizontally straight through the bust point.

2 Spread the cut pattern pieces apart by about ¼in (6mm) per cup size over a B cup.

3 Tape paper behind and redraw the cutting lines as necessary.

Dart redrawn to original length

▶ LOWERING A BUST DART

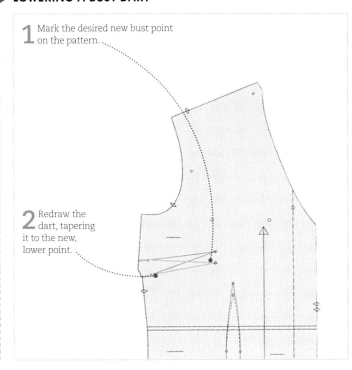

1 Mark the desired new bust point on the pattern.

2 Redraw the dart, tapering it to the new, lower point.

▶ LOWERING A BUST DART SUBSTANTIALLY

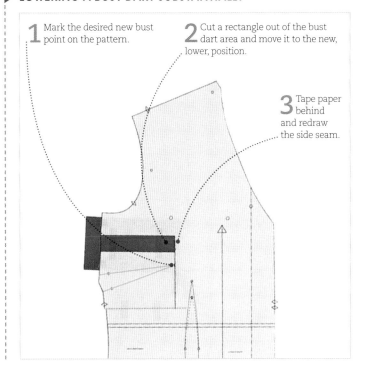

1 Mark the desired new bust point on the pattern.

2 Cut a rectangle out of the bust dart area and move it to the new, lower, position.

3 Tape paper behind and redraw the side seam.

▶ RAISING A CURVED BUST SEAM

1 Fold a pleat in the shoulder area on the center front pattern to raise the bust point by the required amount.

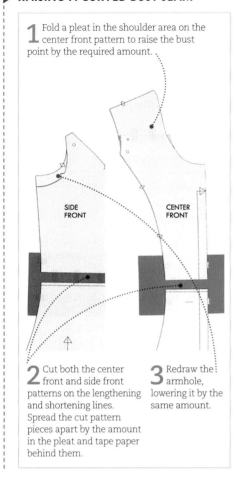

SIDE FRONT

CENTER FRONT

2 Cut both the center front and side front patterns on the lengthening and shortening lines. Spread the cut pattern pieces apart by the amount in the pleat and tape paper behind them.

3 Redraw the armhole, lowering it by the same amount.

▶ LOWERING A CURVED BUST SEAM

1 Cut the center front pattern in the shoulder area and spread the cut pattern pieces apart by the required amount. Tape paper behind the pattern pieces.

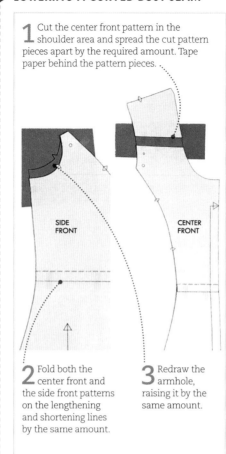

SIDE FRONT

CENTER FRONT

2 Fold both the center front and the side front patterns on the lengthening and shortening lines by the same amount.

3 Redraw the armhole, raising it by the same amount.

▶ ADJUSTING A SEAM FOR A FULL BUST

1 Tape paper under the center front and side front patterns in the bust area.

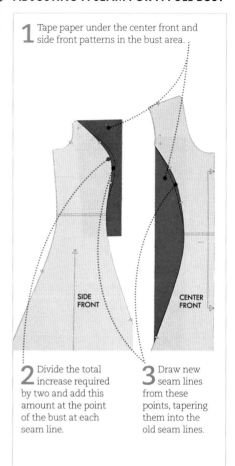

SIDE FRONT

CENTER FRONT

2 Divide the total increase required by two and add this amount at the point of the bust at each seam line.

3 Draw new seam lines from these points, tapering them into the old seam lines.

WAIST AND HIPS

Most people's waists and hips are out of proportion when compared to the measurements of a paper pattern. To alter the pattern to suit your body shape, adjust the pieces for the waist first and then do the hip pieces.

▶ INCREASING THE WAIST ON A FITTED SKIRT

1 Increase the waist at the side seams.

2 Tape paper behind the pattern pieces. Divide the total increase required by four, since there are four seam lines.

3 Add this amount on the paper at the waist edge at each seam line. Draw new seam lines from these points, tapering them into the old seam lines.

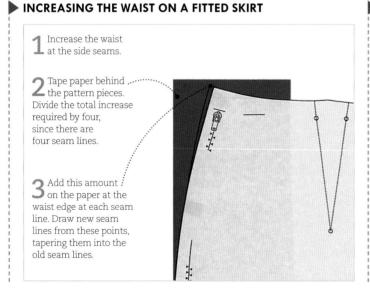

▶ INCREASING THE WAIST ON A GORED SKIRT

1 Tape paper behind the pattern pieces. Since there are many seams, divide the total increase required by the number of seam lines.

2 Add this amount on the paper at the waist edge at each seam line. Draw new seam lines from these points, tapering them into the old seam lines.

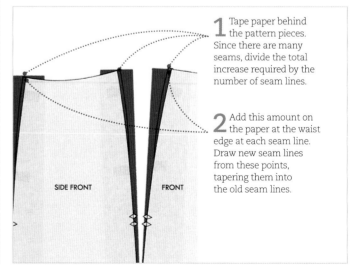

SIDE FRONT

FRONT

▶ INCREASING THE WAIST ON A FULL-CIRCLE SKIRT

1 Carefully check the waist circumference on the pattern against your waist measurement.

2 Draw a new, lower waist stitching line on the pattern. Adjust the finished length of the skirt if necessary.

▶ INCREASING THE WAIST ON A FITTED DRESS

1 Tape paper behind the waist area of the front and back pattern pieces. Divide the total increase required by four, since there are four seam lines.

2 Add this amount on the paper at the waist area of each seam line. Draw new seam lines from these points, tapering them into the old seam lines.

3 If more increase is required, the darts can also be made narrower.

▶ INCREASING THE WAIST ON A PRINCESS-LINE DRESS

1 Tape paper behind the waist area of each pattern piece. Divide the total increase required by the number of seam lines.

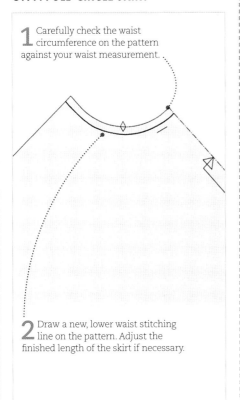

SIDE FRONT CENTER FRONT

2 Add this amount on the paper at the waist area of each seam line. Draw new seam lines from these points, tapering them into the old seam lines.

▶ DECREASING THE WAIST ON A FULL-CIRCLE SKIRT

1 Tape paper behind each pattern piece.

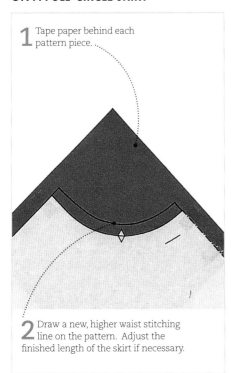

2 Draw a new, higher waist stitching line on the pattern. Adjust the finished length of the skirt if necessary.

▶ DECREASING THE WAIST ON A FITTED SKIRT

1 Decrease the waist at the side seams. Divide the total decrease required by four, since there are four seam lines.

2 Mark this amount on the pattern at the waist edge at each seam line. Draw new seam lines from these points, tapering them into the old seam lines.

▶ DECREASING THE WAIST ON A GORED SKIRT

1 As there are many seams, divide the total decrease required by the number of seam lines.

SIDE FRONT FRONT

2 Mark this amount on the pattern at the waist edge at each seam line. Draw new seam lines from these points, tapering them into the old seam lines.

▶ DECREASING THE WAIST ON A FITTED DRESS

1 Divide the total decrease required by four, since there are four seam lines.

2 Mark this amount on the pattern at the waist on each seam line. Draw new seam lines from these points, tapering them into the old seam lines.

▶ DECREASING THE WAIST ON A PRINCESS-LINE DRESS

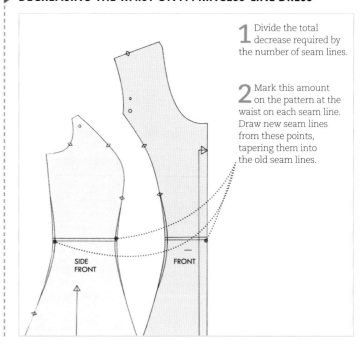

1 Divide the total decrease required by the number of seam lines.

2 Mark this amount on the pattern at the waist on each seam line. Draw new seam lines from these points, tapering them into the old seam lines.

SIDE FRONT

FRONT

▶ INCREASING A FITTED SKIRT AT THE HIPLINE

1 Tape paper behind the pattern pieces. Divide the total increase required by four, since there are four seam lines.

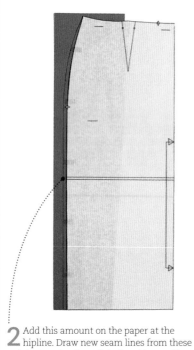

2 Add this amount on the paper at the hipline. Draw new seam lines from these points, tapering them into the old seam lines.

▶ DECREASING A FITTED SKIRT AT THE HIPLINE

1 Divide the total decrease required by four, since there are four seam lines.

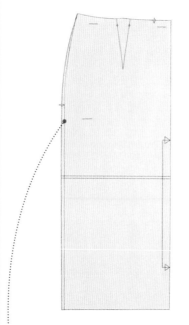

2 Mark this amount on the pattern at the hip on each seam line. Draw new seam lines straight down to the hem from these points, tapering them up into the waist.

▶ ADJUSTING A FITTED SKIRT FOR A LARGE REAR END

1 Cut vertically through the dart to the hem on the skirt back pattern.

2 Cut through the hipline, stopping before you reach the side seam.

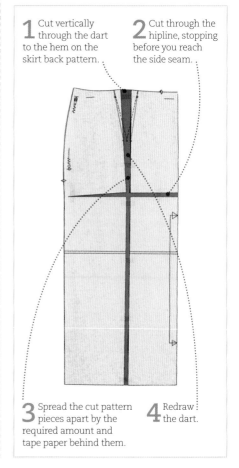

3 Spread the cut pattern pieces apart by the required amount and tape paper behind them.

4 Redraw the dart.

▶ ADJUSTING A FITTED SKIRT FOR EXTRA-LARGE HIPS

1 For an increase over 2in (5cm), cut each pattern piece vertically between the dart and the side seam.

2 Divide the total increase required by four. Spread the cut pattern pieces apart by this amount and tape paper behind them.

3 If the waist is to remain the same, draw in a second dart to remove the increase at the waist.

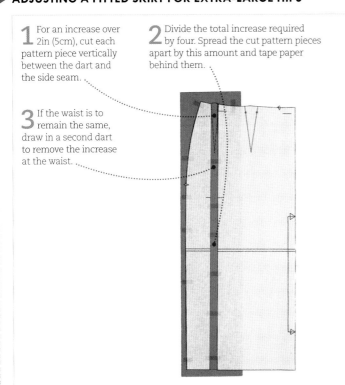

▶ ADJUSTING A GORED SKIRT AT THE HIPLINE

1 Since there are many seams, divide the total decrease or increase required by the number of seam lines.

2 If increasing, tape paper behind the pattern pieces.

3 Mark the reduction at the hipline on the pattern or mark the increase on the paper.

4 Draw new seam lines straight down to the hem from these points, tapering them up into the waist.

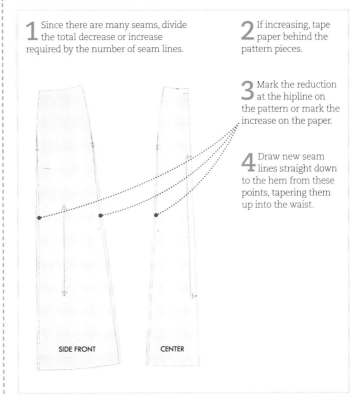

SIDE FRONT   CENTER

▶ MAKING A LARGE INCREASE AT THE HIPLINE ON A FITTED DRESS

1 Divide the total increase required by four.

2 Make a horizontal cut in each pattern piece the length of this amount and just below the waist.

3 Cut vertically from this point to the hem.

4 Spread the cut pattern pieces apart by the required amount and tape paper behind them.

5 Redraw the side seam.

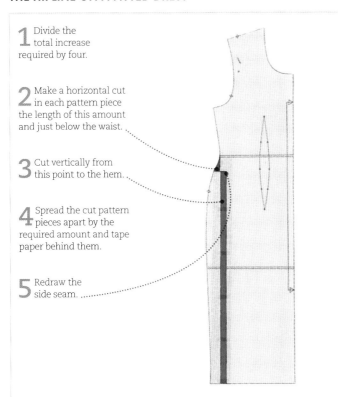

▶ ADJUSTING AT THE HIPLINE TO ALLOW FOR A HOLLOW BACK

1 A hollow back requires a shorter center back seam. Draw a horizontal line on the pattern from the center back across the hipline.

2 Fold along the line to make a pleat at the center back that takes up the required reduction. Taper the pleat to nothing at the side seam. Tape in place.

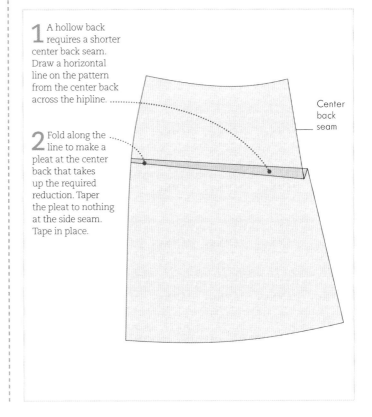

Center back seam

SHOULDERS, BACK, AND SLEEVES

Alterations can be made to accommodate sloping shoulders, square shoulders, and backs that may be wider or narrower than the pattern allowances. It's important to ensure that these alterations have a minimum effect on the armhole. Sleeves need to allow for movement, so should not be too tight; pattern pieces can be enlarged as necessary. Alterations can also be made for thin arms.

▶ ADJUSTING TO FIT SQUARE SHOULDERS

1 Starting at the armhole, slash the pattern about 1¼in (3cm) below and parallel with the shoulder line, stopping before you reach the neck seam line.

2 Spread the cut pattern apart to straighten the shoulder line. Tape paper behind.

3 Redraw the line to close the gap at the armhole.

4 Raise the armhole by the amount added at the shoulder. Mark the new cutting line on the paper.

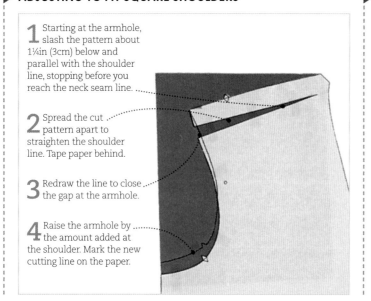

▶ ADJUSTING TO FIT SLOPING SHOULDERS

1 Slash the pattern 1¼in (3cm) below the shoulder line and parallel with it.

2 Overlap the cut pieces by the required amount and tape in place.

3 Lower the armhole by the same amount, marking the new cutting line on the pattern.

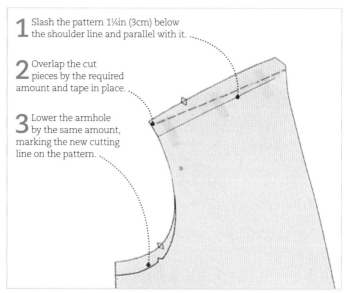

▶ PREPARING THE PATTERN FOR BROAD OR NARROW SHOULDER ALTERATIONS

1 Draw a vertical line 8in (20cm) long on the pattern from the middle of the shoulder.

2 Draw a second, horizontal, line from the end of the first line to the armhole.

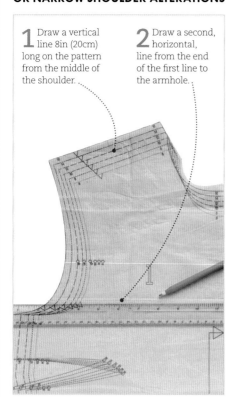

▶ ADJUSTING TO FIT BROAD SHOULDERS

1 Cut along the two drawn lines (see left).

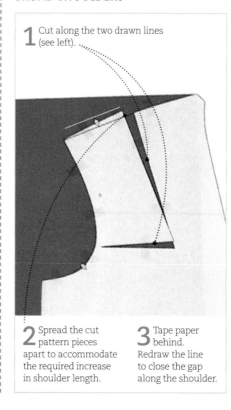

2 Spread the cut pattern pieces apart to accommodate the required increase in shoulder length.

3 Tape paper behind. Redraw the line to close the gap along the shoulder.

▶ ADJUSTING TO FIT NARROW SHOULDERS

1 Cut along the two drawn lines (see far left).

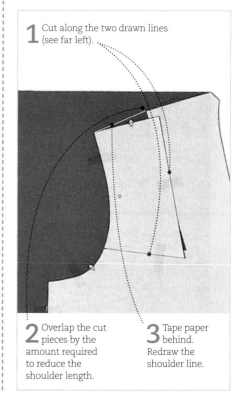

2 Overlap the cut pieces by the amount required to reduce the shoulder length.

3 Tape paper behind. Redraw the shoulder line.

▶ ENLARGING A FITTED SLEEVE

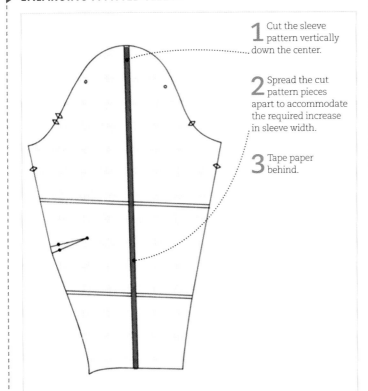

1 Cut the sleeve pattern vertically down the center.

2 Spread the cut pattern pieces apart to accommodate the required increase in sleeve width.

3 Tape paper behind.

▶ ENLARGING THE HEAD OF A FITTED SLEEVE

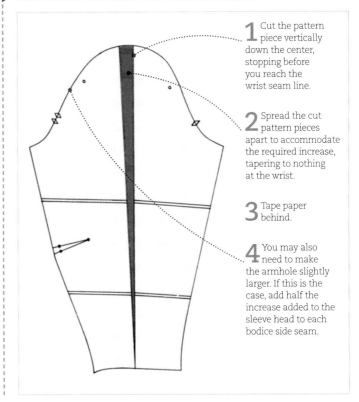

1 Cut the pattern piece vertically down the center, stopping before you reach the wrist seam line.

2 Spread the cut pattern pieces apart to accommodate the required increase, tapering to nothing at the wrist.

3 Tape paper behind.

4 You may also need to make the armhole slightly larger. If this is the case, add half the increase added to the sleeve head to each bodice side seam.

▶ INCREASING A FITTED SLEEVE AT THE UNDERARM

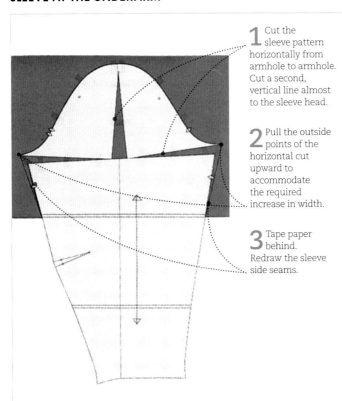

1 Cut the sleeve pattern horizontally from armhole to armhole. Cut a second, vertical line almost to the sleeve head.

2 Pull the outside points of the horizontal cut upward to accommodate the required increase in width.

3 Tape paper behind. Redraw the sleeve side seams.

▶ DECREASING A FITTED SLEEVE TO ACCOMMODATE THIN ARMS

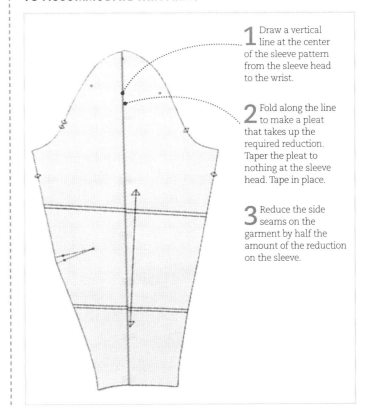

1 Draw a vertical line at the center of the sleeve pattern from the sleeve head to the wrist.

2 Fold along the line to make a pleat that takes up the required reduction. Taper the pleat to nothing at the sleeve head. Tape in place.

3 Reduce the side seams on the garment by half the amount of the reduction on the sleeve.

PANTS

Alterations to pants, to accommodate a large belly, wide hips, or a prominent or flat rear end, can be more complicated than those on other pattern pieces, and need to be done in the correct order. Crotch depth alterations are done first, followed by width alterations, then crotch length alterations, and finally pant leg length. The crotch depth line is only marked on the back pattern pieces.

▶ INCREASING DEPTH AT CROTCH SEAM

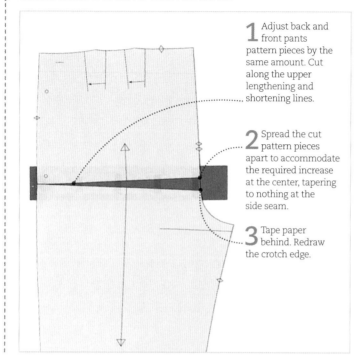

1 Adjust back and front pants pattern pieces by the same amount. Cut along the upper lengthening and shortening lines.

2 Spread the cut pattern pieces apart to accommodate the required increase at the center, tapering to nothing at the side seam.

3 Tape paper behind. Redraw the crotch edge.

▶ DECREASING DEPTH AT THE CROTCH SEAM

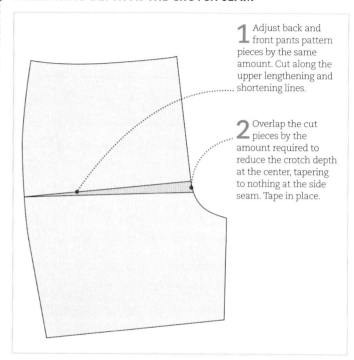

1 Adjust back and front pants pattern pieces by the same amount. Cut along the upper lengthening and shortening lines.

2 Overlap the cut pieces by the amount required to reduce the crotch depth at the center, tapering to nothing at the side seam. Tape in place.

▶ INCREASING THE WAISTLINE

1 Tape paper behind the pattern pieces. Divide the total increase required by eight, since there are eight seam lines.

2 Add this amount on the paper at the waist edge at each seam line. Draw new seam lines from these points, tapering them into the old seam lines.

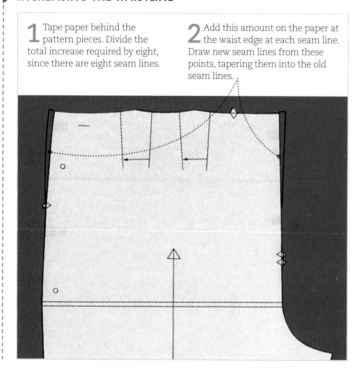

▶ DECREASING THE WAISTLINE

1 Divide the total decrease required by eight, since there are eight seam lines.

2 Mark this amount on the pattern at the waist edge at each seam line. Draw new seam lines from these points, tapering them into the old seam lines.

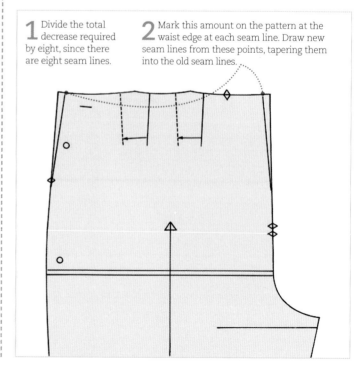

▶ INCREASING AT THE HIPLINE

1 Tape paper behind the pattern pieces. Divide the total increase required by four, since there are four seam lines.

2 Add this amount on the paper at the hipline. Draw new seam lines from these points, tapering them into the old seam lines.

3 For straight pants, draw the new seam lines straight down from the hip to the hem.

▶ DECREASING AT THE HIPLINE

1 Divide the total decrease required by four, since there are four seam lines.

2 Mark this amount on the pattern at the hipline. Draw new seam lines from these points, tapering them into the old seam lines.

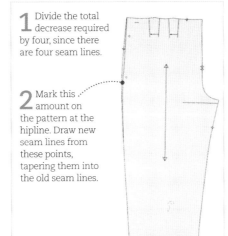

▶ ADJUSTING FOR A LARGE REAR END

1 Cut horizontally through the hipline on the pants back pattern.

2 Spread the cut pattern pieces apart by the required amount and tape paper behind them.

3 Redraw the crotch edge. You may wish to combine this adjustment with a crotch depth adjustment on just the back.

▶ INCREASING LENGTH AT CROTCH POINT

1 If the pants are too tight between the legs, this alteration may be required. The crotch length may need to be increased by a different amount on the front and the back. Tape paper under the crotch seam.

2 Add the required amount to the inside leg seam on the paper. Draw a new seam line from the new crotch point, tapering it into the old seam line.

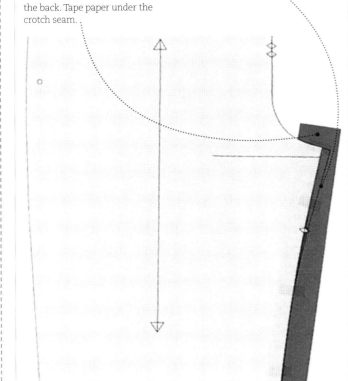

▶ DECREASING LENGTH AT CROTCH POINT

1 If the pants are too loose between the legs, this alteration may be required. Mark the inside leg seam with the position of the new crotch point.

2 Draw a new seam line from the new crotch point, tapering it into the old seam line.

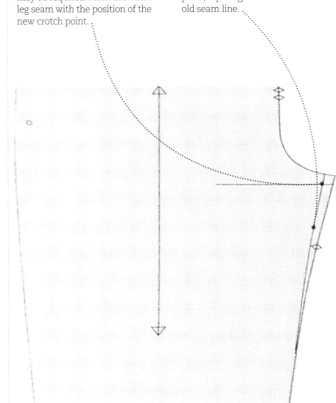

MAKING A TOILE

When using a new pattern for the first time, or if you have made pattern alterations, it is always a good idea to try out the pattern in muslin, making a test garment called a toile. This will tell you if the garment is going to fit you, or whether more alterations are required. It is also a good opportunity to confirm that the style suits your figure type. You will need a helper, or failing that, a dressmaker's dummy.

TOILE TOO BIG

When you try the toile on, if it is too big there will be surplus fabric. Pleat and pin out the surplus fabric, making the pleating equal on both the left- and right-hand sides of the garment. Take off the toile and measure the surplus amount. Alter the pattern pieces to match by pinning out the surplus tissue.

Back adjustment
If the back is too loose, pleat and pin out the surplus fabric parallel to the center back seam. Do this equally on both sides. Make the alteration down the center back seam on the appropriate pattern pieces.

Shoulder adjustment
If the shoulder is too wide it will need a sloping shoulder adjustment (see p.70).

The waist on the bodice and skirt
If the waist is too big, this can easily be adjusted by taking more fabric into the bust dart. If you adjust the bust dart on the bodice, you will need to alter the skirt dart, too, so they join up.

The hip on the skirt
If the hip is too loose, pleat and pin out the surplus fabric on the side seams. Do this equally on both sides. Measure the surplus amount and take in the hipline on the pattern pieces accordingly (see Decreasing a fitted skirt at the hipline, p.68).

TOILE TOO SMALL

If the toile is too small, the fabric will "pull" where it is tight. The garment shown below is too tight over the bust and also over the high hip area. The pattern will need to be adjusted to allow more fabric in these areas. This toile is also snug at the top of the sleeve; this needs to be adjusted, too.

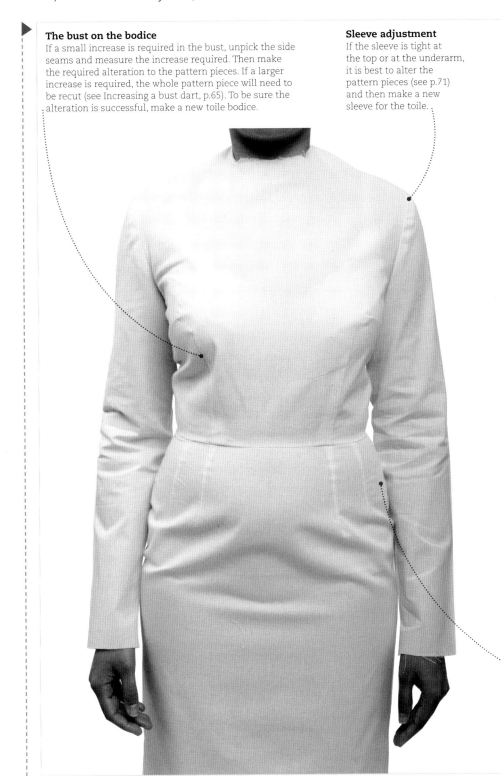

The bust on the bodice
If a small increase is required in the bust, unpick the side seams and measure the increase required. Then make the required alteration to the pattern pieces. If a larger increase is required, the whole pattern piece will need to be recut (see Increasing a bust dart, p.65). To be sure the alteration is successful, make a new toile bodice.

Sleeve adjustment
If the sleeve is tight at the top or at the underarm, it is best to alter the pattern pieces (see p.71) and then make a new sleeve for the toile.

The hip on the skirt
Unpick the side seams and measure the increase required. When you have adjusted the toile with extra muslin and made sure that the fit is right, you can alter the pattern pieces accordingly (see pp.68–69).

ADJUSTING A TOILE THAT IS TOO SMALL

If the toile is too tight, it will require more fabric to cover the contours of the body and you will need to make further alterations to the pattern pieces. For small increases (up to 1½in/4cm), you can adjust the toile as described below and then alter the pattern pieces accordingly, redrawing the seam lines. For more substantial increases, after altering the pattern pieces you will need to make a new toile and try it on.

1 Where the toile is too tight, unpick the side seam on each side, until the garment hangs without pulling.

2 Measure the gap at the fullest point between the stitching lines on the opened-out seam. It should be the same on both sides of the body.

3 Divide this measurement in half—for example, if the gap is 1½in (4cm) at the fullest point, then ¾in (2cm) needs to be added to each side seam seam line.

4 Using a felt-tip pen, mark the top and bottom of the alteration directly on the toile. Also mark the fullest point of the alteration.

5 When the toile has been removed, add muslin to the seam in the given area at the fullest point, tapering back to the original seam at each end.

6 Try the toile on again to be sure your alterations have made it fit properly. Then measure the alterations and make adjustments to the relevant pattern pieces.

CUTTING OUT

Cutting out can make or break your project. But first you need to examine the fabric in the store, looking for any flaws, such as a crooked pattern, and checking to see if the fabric has been cut properly from the roll—that is, at a right angle to the selvage. If it has not been cut properly, you will need to straighten the edge before cutting out. If the fabric is wrinkled, press it; if washable, wash it to prevent shrinkage later. After this preparation, lay the pattern pieces on the fabric, pin in place, and cut out.

FABRIC GRAIN AND NAP

It is important that pattern pieces are cut on the correct grain; this will make the fabric hang correctly. The grain is the direction in which the yarns or threads that make up the fabric lie. The majority of pattern pieces need to be placed with the straight of grain symbol running parallel to the warp yarn. Some fabrics have a nap due to the pile, which means the fabric shadows when it is smoothed in one direction. A fabric with a one-way design or uneven stripes is also described as having a nap. Fabrics with nap are generally cut out with the nap running down, whereas those without nap can be cut out at any angle.

▶ GRAIN ON WOVEN FABRICS

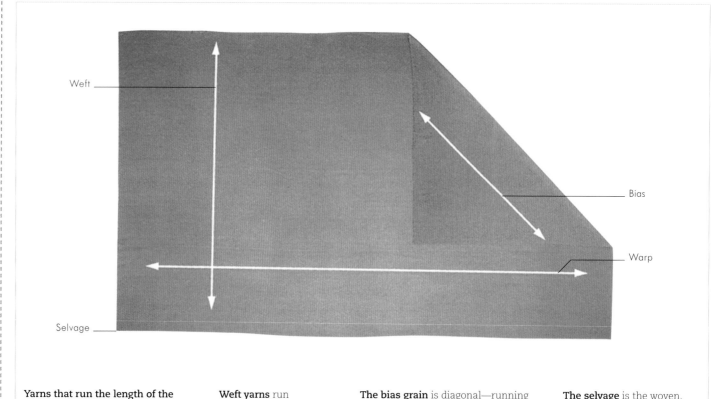

Yarns that run the length of the fabric are called warp yarns. They are stronger than weft yarns and less likely to stretch.

Weft yarns run crosswise, over and under the warp yarns.

The bias grain is diagonal—running at 45 degrees to the warp and weft. A garment cut on the bias will follow the contours of the body.

The selvage is the woven, nonfrayable edge that runs parallel to the warp yarn.

▶ **NAP DUE TO PILE**

Fabrics such as velvet, corduroy, and velour will show a difference in color, depending on whether the nap is running up or down.

▶ **NAP DUE TO ONE-WAY DESIGN**

A one-way pattern—in this case flowers—that runs lenthwise in the fabric will be upside down on one side when the fabric is folded back on itself.

▶ **NAP DUE TO STRIPES**

If the stripes do not match on both sides when the fabric is folded back, they are uneven and the fabric will need a nap layout.

FABRIC PREPARATION

To check if the fabric has been cut properly from the roll, fold it selvage to selvage and see if it lies flat. If the cut ends are uneven and do not match, use one of the following methods to make the edge straight. Then press the fabric.

▶ **PULLING A THREAD TO OBTAIN A STRAIGHT EDGE**

1 On a loose-woven fabric you can pull a weft thread to get a straight edge. First snip the selvage, then find a single thread and tug it gently to pull it out.

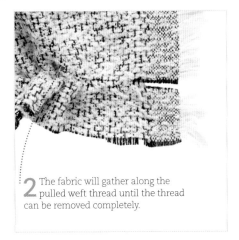

2 The fabric will gather along the pulled weft thread until the thread can be removed completely.

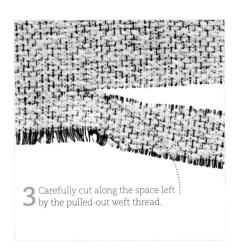

3 Carefully cut along the space left by the pulled-out weft thread.

▶ **CUTTING ON A STRIPE LINE TO OBTAIN A STRAIGHT EDGE**

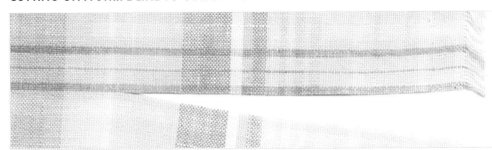

On checks and stripes, cut along the edge of one of the boldest stripes to achieve a straight edge.

PATTERN LAYOUT

For cutting out, fabric is usually folded selvage to selvage. With the fabric folded, the pattern is pinned on top, and both the right- and left-side pieces are cut out at the same time. If pattern pieces have to be cut from single-layer fabric, remember to cut matching pairs. If a fabric has a design, lay the fabric design-side upward so that you can arrange the pattern pieces to show off the design. If you have left- and right-side pattern pieces, they are cut on single fabric with the fabric right-side up and the pattern right-side up.

▶ **PINNING THE PATTERN TO THE FABRIC**

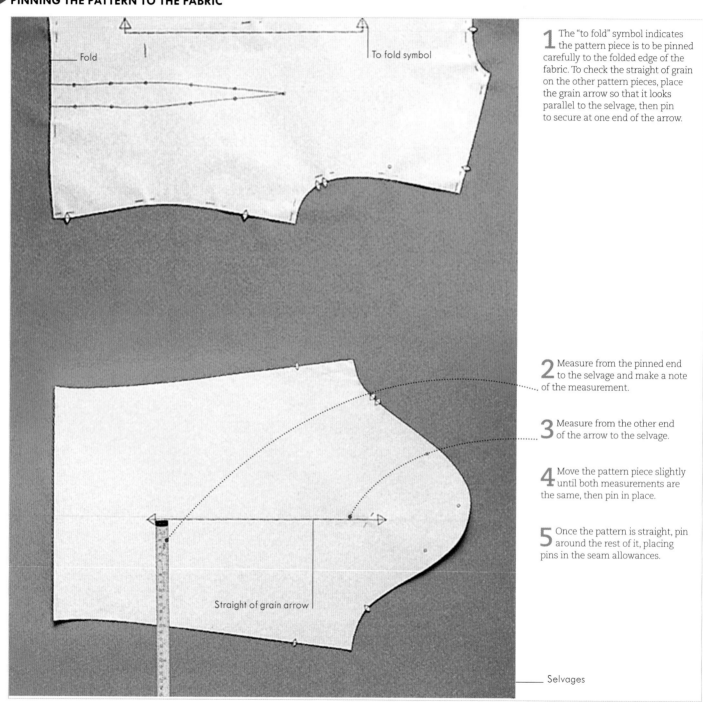

Fold

To fold symbol

1 The "to fold" symbol indicates the pattern piece is to be pinned carefully to the folded edge of the fabric. To check the straight of grain on the other pattern pieces, place the grain arrow so that it looks parallel to the selvage, then pin to secure at one end of the arrow.

2 Measure from the pinned end to the selvage and make a note of the measurement.

3 Measure from the other end of the arrow to the selvage.

4 Move the pattern piece slightly until both measurements are the same, then pin in place.

5 Once the pattern is straight, pin around the rest of it, placing pins in the seam allowances.

Straight of grain arrow

Selvages

▶ GENERAL GUIDE TO LAYOUT

Place the pattern pieces on the fabric with the printed side uppermost. Some pieces will need to be placed on a fold.

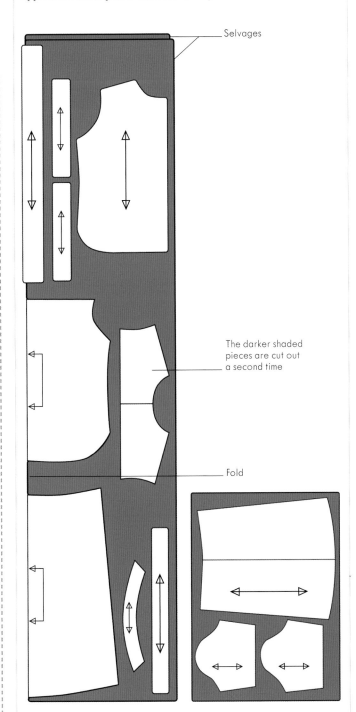

Selvages

The darker shaded pieces are cut out a second time

Fold

If a piece has to be cut twice on a fold, this will need to be done after the other pieces have been cut and the fabric can be refolded.

If using a single layer of fabric, the pieces will need to be cut twice, turning the pattern over for the second piece.

▶ LAYOUT FOR FABRICS WITH A NAP OR A ONE-WAY DESIGN

If your fabric needs to be cut out with a nap, all the pattern pieces need to be placed so the nap will run in the same direction in the completed garment.

"Top" of fabric, from which direction the nap runs

Selvages

Fold

STRIPES AND CHECKS

For fabrics with a stripe or check pattern, a little more care is needed when laying out the pattern pieces. If the checks and stripes are running across or down the length of the fabric when cutting out, they will run the same direction in the finished garment. So it is important to place the pattern pieces to ensure that the checks and stripes match and that they run together at the seams. If possible, try to place the pattern pieces so each has a stripe down the center. With a checked fabric, be aware of the hemline placement on the pattern.

PATTERNS & CUTTING OUT

▶ EVEN AND UNEVEN STRIPES

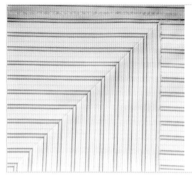

Even stripes When a corner of the fabric is folded back diagonally, the stripes will meet up at the fold.

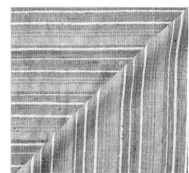

Uneven stripes When a corner of the fabric is folded back diagonally, the stripes will not match at the fold.

▶ EVEN AND UNEVEN CHECKS

Even checks When a corner of the fabric is folded back diagonally, the checks will be symmetrical on both of the fabric areas.

Uneven checks When a corner of the fabric is folded back diagonally, the checks will be uneven lenthwise, widthwise, or both.

▶ MATCHING STRIPES OR CHECKS ON A SKIRT

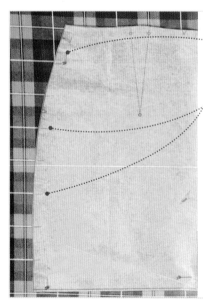

1 Place one of the skirt pattern pieces on the fabric and pin in place.

2 Mark on the pattern the position of the boldest lines of the checks or stripes.

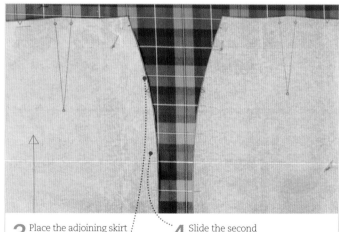

3 Place the adjoining skirt pattern piece alongside, with notches matching and side seams even. Transfer the marks to the second pattern piece.

4 Slide the second pattern piece across, matching up the bold lines. Pin in place.

▶ MATCHING STRIPES OR CHECKS AT THE SHOULDER

1 Mark the boldest lines of the stripes or checks around the armhole on the front bodice pattern.

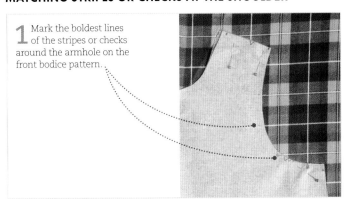

2 Place the sleeve pattern on to the armhole, matching the notches, and copy the marks on to the sleeve pattern.

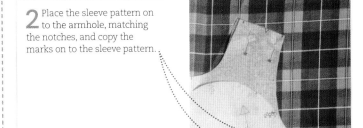

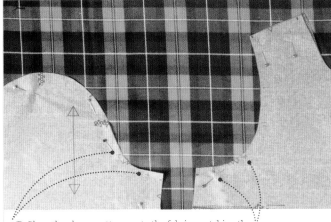

3 Place the sleeve pattern on to the fabric, matching the marks to the corresponding bold lines, and pin in place.

▶ LAYOUT FOR UNEVEN CHECKS OR STRIPES ON UNFOLDED FABRIC

Hem foldline is placed on a prominent stripe

Center back is aligned with a prominent lengthwise stripe

Pattern piece is cut out twice from single layer of fabric

Bars align on both collar pieces

Selvage

▶ LAYOUT FOR EVEN CHECKS ON FOLDED FABRIC

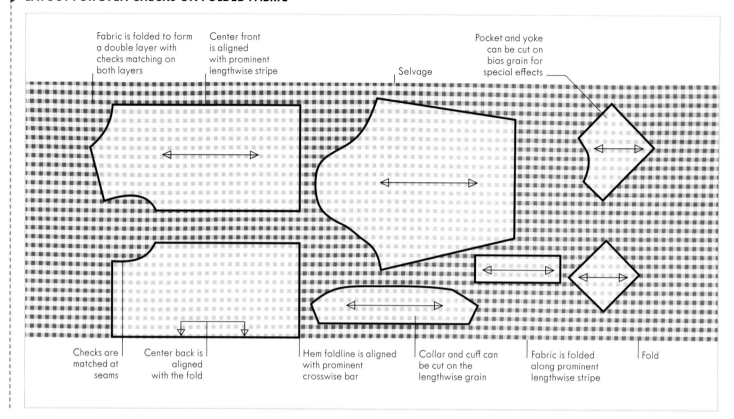

Fabric is folded to form a double layer with checks matching on both layers

Center front is aligned with prominent lengthwise stripe

Selvage

Pocket and yoke can be cut on bias grain for special effects

Checks are matched at seams

Center back is aligned with the fold

Hem foldline is aligned with prominent crosswise bar

Collar and cuff can be cut on the lengthwise grain

Fabric is folded along prominent lengthwise stripe

Fold

▶ LAYOUT FOR EVEN STRIPES ON FOLDED FABRIC

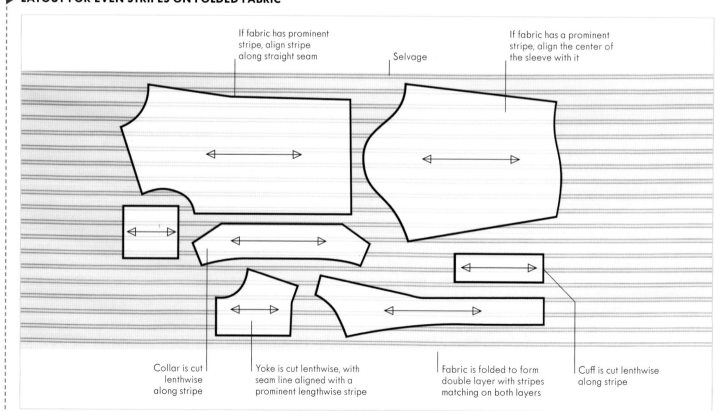

If fabric has prominent stripe, align stripe along straight seam

Selvage

If fabric has a prominent stripe, align the center of the sleeve with it

Collar is cut lenthwise along stripe

Yoke is cut lenthwise, with seam line aligned with a prominent lengthwise stripe

Fabric is folded to form double layer with stripes matching on both layers

Cuff is cut lenthwise along stripe

► LAYOUT FOR PATTERN MATCHING ON UNFOLDED FABRIC

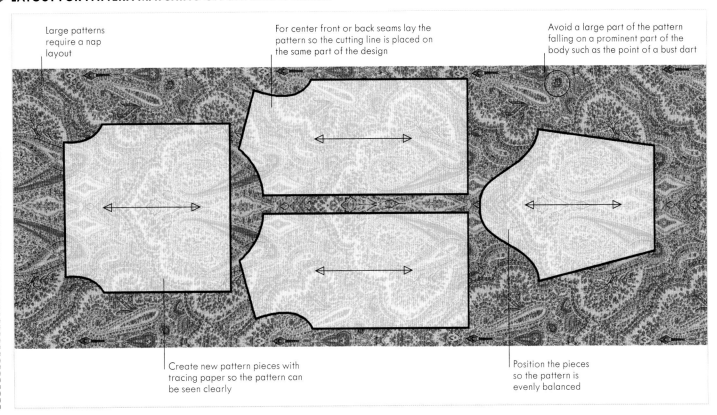

Large patterns require a nap layout

For center front or back seams lay the pattern so the cutting line is placed on the same part of the design

Avoid a large part of the pattern falling on a prominent part of the body such as the point of a bust dart

Create new pattern pieces with tracing paper so the pattern can be seen clearly

Position the pieces so the pattern is evenly balanced

► CUTTING ON THE BIAS

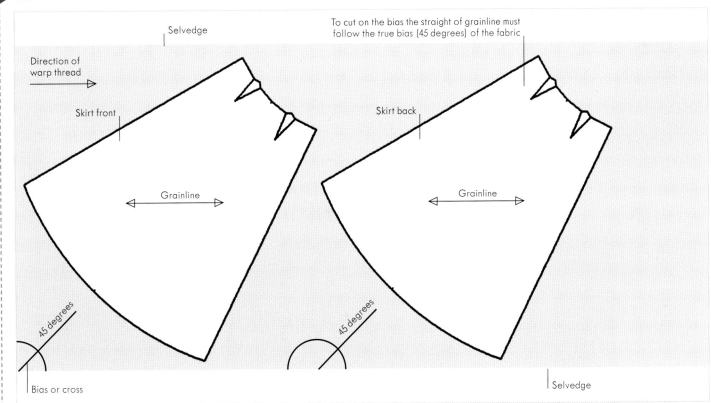

Selvedge

To cut on the bias the straight of grainline must follow the true bias (45 degrees) of the fabric

Direction of warp thread

Skirt front

Skirt back

Grainline

Grainline

45 degrees

45 degrees

Bias or cross

Selvedge

PATTERNS & CUTTING OUT

CUTTING OUT ACCURATELY

Careful, smooth cutting around the pattern pieces will ensure that they join together accurately. Always cut out on a smooth, flat surface such as a table—the floor is not ideal—and be sure your scissors are sharp. Use the full blade of the scissors on long, straight edges, sliding the blades along the fabric; use smaller cuts around curves. Do not nibble or snip at the fabric.

▶ HOW TO CUT

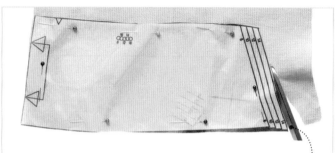

If you are right-handed, place your left hand on the pattern and fabric to hold them in place, and cut cleanly with the scissor blades at a right angle to the fabric.

▶ MARKING NOTCHES

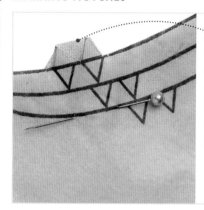

These symbols need to be marked on to the fabric, since they are matching points. One of the easiest ways to do this is to cut out the mirror image of the notches in the fabric. Rather than cutting out double or triple notches separately, cut straight across from point to point.

▶ MARKING DOTS

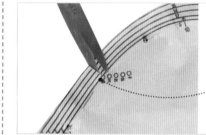

You can cut a small clip into the fabric to mark the dots that indicate the top of the shoulder on a sleeve. Alternatively, these can be marked with tailor's bastes (see opposite).

▶ CLIPPING LINES

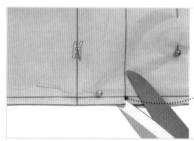

A small clip or snip into the fabric is a useful way to mark some of the lines that appear on a pattern, such as the center front line and foldlines or notches and dart ends.

PATTERN MARKING

Once the pattern pieces have been cut out, but before you remove the pattern, you will need to mark the symbols shown on the pattern through to the fabric. There are various ways to do this. Tailor's bastes are good for circles and dots, or these can be marked with a water- or air-soluble pen. When using a pen, it's a good idea to test it on a piece of scrap fabric first. For lines, you can use trace bastes or a tracing wheel with dressmaker's carbon paper.

▶ TRACE BASTES

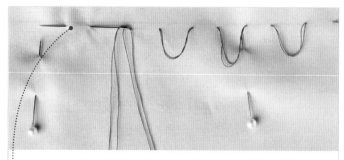

1 This is a really useful technique to mark center front lines, foldlines, and placement lines. With double thread in your needle, stitch a row of loopy stitches, sewing along the line marked on the pattern.

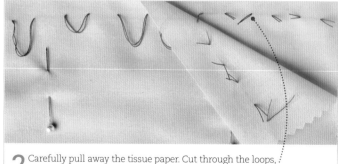

2 Carefully pull away the tissue paper. Cut through the loops, then gently separate the layers of fabric to show the threads. Snip apart to leave thread tails in both of the fabric layers.

▶ TAILOR'S BASTES

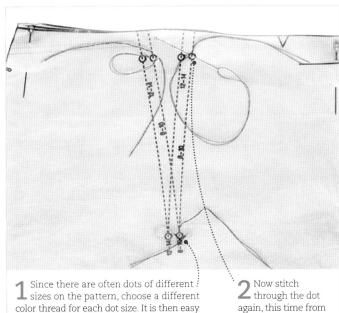

1 Since there are often dots of different sizes on the pattern, choose a different color thread for each dot size. It is then easy to match the colors as well as the dots. Have double thread in your needle, unknotted. Insert the needle through the dot from right to left, leaving a tail of thread. Be sure to go through the pattern and both layers of fabric.

2 Now stitch through the dot again, this time from top to bottom to make a loop. Cut through the loop, then snip off excess thread to leave a tail.

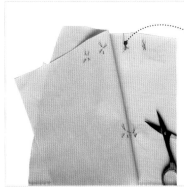

3 Carefully pull the pattern away. On the top side you will have four threads marking each dot. When you turn the fabric over, the dot positions will be marked with an X.

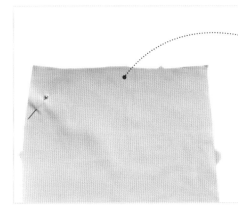

4 Gently turn back the two layers of fabric to separate them, then cut through the threads so that thread tails are left in both pieces of fabric.

▶ TRACING PAPER AND WHEEL

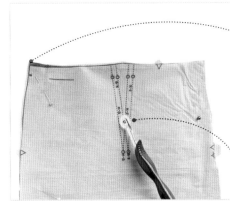

1 This method is not suitable for all fabrics, since the marks may not be easy to remove. Slide dressmaker's carbon paper against the wrong side of the fabric.

2 Run a tracing wheel along the pattern lines (a ruler will help you make straight lines).

3 Remove the carbon paper and carefully pull off the pattern. There will be dotted lines marked on your fabric.

▶ FELT-TIP PENS

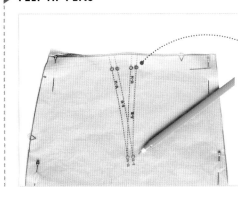

1 This method can only be used with a single layer of fabric. Press the point of the pen into the center of the dot marked on the pattern.

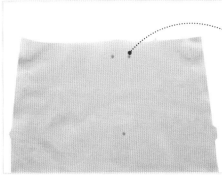

2 Carefully remove the pattern. The pen marks will have gone through the pattern on to the fabric. Be sure not to iron the fabric before the pen marks are removed or they may become permanent.

GENERAL TECHNIQUES

STITCHES FOR HAND SEWING

Although modern sewing machines have eliminated the need for a lot of hand sewing, it is still necessary to use hand stitching to prepare the fabric prior to permanent stitching—these temporary pattern-marking and basting stitches will eventually be removed. Permanent hand stitching is used to finish a garment and to attach fasteners, as well as to help out with a quick repair.

THREADING THE NEEDLE

When sewing by hand, cut your piece of thread to be no longer than the distance from your fingertips to your elbow. If the thread is much longer than this, it will knot as you sew.

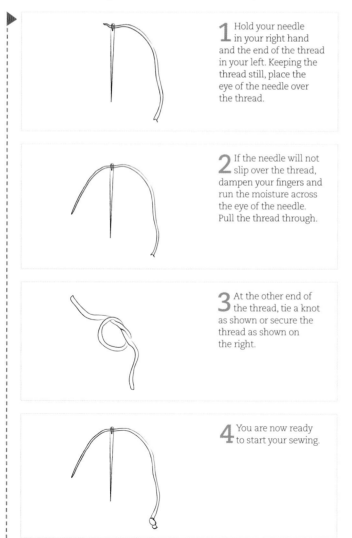

1 Hold your needle in your right hand and the end of the thread in your left. Keeping the thread still, place the eye of the needle over the thread.

2 If the needle will not slip over the thread, dampen your fingers and run the moisture across the eye of the needle. Pull the thread through.

3 At the other end of the thread, tie a knot as shown or secure the thread as shown on the right.

4 You are now ready to start your sewing.

SECURING THE THREAD

The ends of the thread must be secured firmly. A knot (see left) is frequently used and is the preferred choice for temporary stitches. For permanent stitching a double stitch is a better option.

▶ DOUBLE STITCH

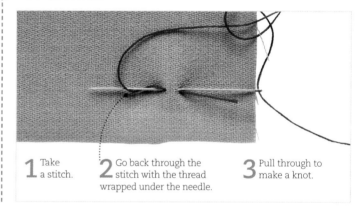

1 Take a stitch.

2 Go back through the stitch with the thread wrapped under the needle.

3 Pull through to make a knot.

▶ BACK STITCH

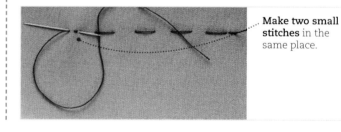

Make two small stitches in the same place.

▶ LOCKING STITCH

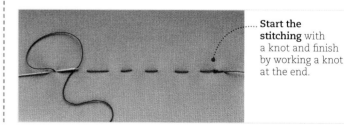

Start the stitching with a knot and finish by working a knot at the end.

HAND STITCHES

There are a number of hand stitches that can be used during the construction of a garment. Some are for decorative purposes, while others are more functional.

▶ RUNNING STITCH

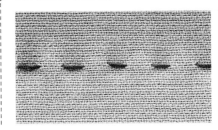

Very similar to basting (see below), but used more for decorative purposes. Work from right to left. Run the needle in and out of the fabric to create even stitches and spaces.

▶ PRICK STITCH

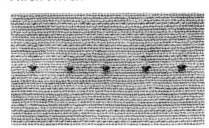

Often used to highlight the edge of a completed garment, such as a collar. Work from right to left. Make small stitches about ¹⁄₁₆in (2mm) long, with spaces between of at least three times that length.

BASTING STITCHES

Each of the many types of basting stitch has its own individual use. Basic bastes hold two or more pieces of fabric together. Long and short bastes are an alternative version of the basic basting stitch, often used when the basting will stay in the work for some time.

▶ BASIC BASTES

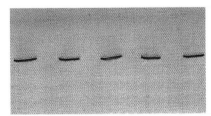

Starting with a knot and using single thread, make straight stitches, evenly spaced.

▶ LONG AND SHORT BASTES

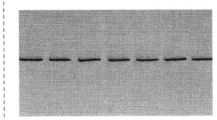

Make long stitches with a short space between each one.

HEM STITCHES

There are various hand stitches that can be used to hold a hem in place. Whichever of these you choose, make sure the stitches do not show on the right side.

▶ FLAT FELL STITCH

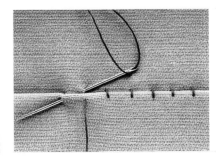

A strong, secure stitch to hold two layers permanently together. In addition to being used for hems, this stitch is often used to secure bias bindings and linings. Work from right to left. Make a short, straight stitch at the edge of the fabric.

▶ BLIND HEM STITCH

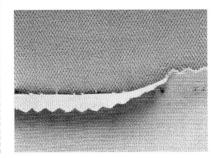

This stitch gives a very discreet finish to a hem. Working from right to left, fold the top edge of the fabric down and use a slip hem stitch (below left).

▶ SLIP HEM STITCH

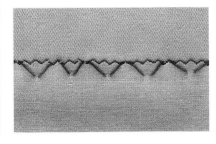

Also called a catch stitch, this is used primarily for securing hems. It looks similar to herringbone (right). Work from right to left. Take a short horizontal stitch into one layer and then the other.

▶ HERRINGBONE STITCH

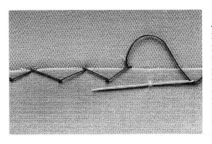

A very useful stitch, since it is secure yet has some movement in it. It is used to secure hems and interlinings. Work from left to right. Take a small horizontal stitch into one layer and then the other, so the thread crosses itself.

MACHINE STITCHES AND SEAMS

When making a garment, fabric is joined together using seams. The most common seam is a plain seam, which is suitable for a wide variety of fabrics and garments. However, there are many other seams to be used as appropriate, depending on the fabric and garment being constructed.

SECURING THE THREAD

Machine stitches need to be secured at the end of a seam to prevent them from coming undone. This can be done by hand, tying the ends of the thread, or using the machine with a reverse stitch or a locking stitch, which stitches three or four stitches in the same place.

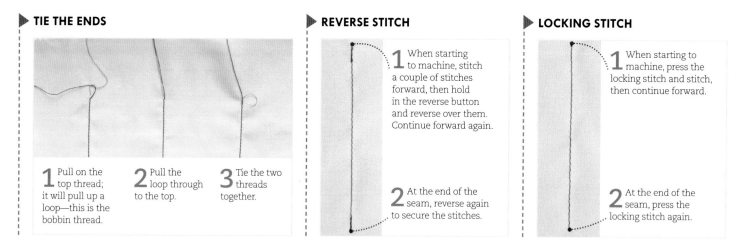

▶ **TIE THE ENDS**

1 Pull on the top thread; it will pull up a loop—this is the bobbin thread.

2 Pull the loop through to the top.

3 Tie the two threads together.

▶ **REVERSE STITCH**

1 When starting to machine, stitch a couple of stitches forward, then hold in the reverse button and reverse over them. Continue forward again.

2 At the end of the seam, reverse again to secure the stitches.

▶ **LOCKING STITCH**

1 When starting to machine, press the locking stitch and stitch, then continue forward.

2 At the end of the seam, press the locking stitch again.

STITCHES MADE WITH A MACHINE

The sewing machine will stitch plain seams and decorative seams as well as buttonholes of various styles. The length and width of buttonholes can be altered to suit the garment.

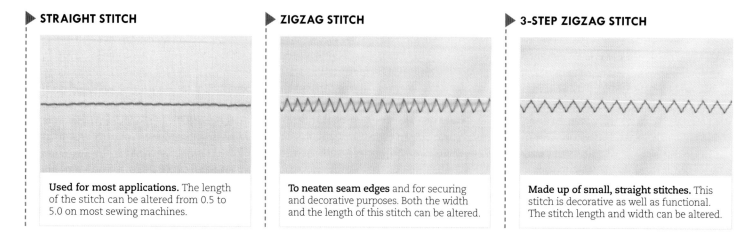

▶ **STRAIGHT STITCH**

Used for most applications. The length of the stitch can be altered from 0.5 to 5.0 on most sewing machines.

▶ **ZIGZAG STITCH**

To neaten seam edges and for securing and decorative purposes. Both the width and the length of this stitch can be altered.

▶ **3-STEP ZIGZAG STITCH**

Made up of small, straight stitches. This stitch is decorative as well as functional. The stitch length and width can be altered.

▶ BLIND HEM STITCH

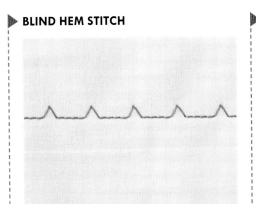

Made in conjunction with the blind hem foot. A combination of straight stitches and a zigzag stitch (see opposite). Used to secure hems.

▶ OVEREDGE STITCH

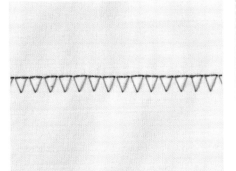

Made in conjunction with the overedge foot. The stitch is used for neatening the edge of fabric. The width and length of the stitch can be altered.

▶ STRETCH STITCH

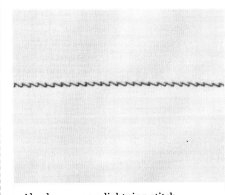

Also known as a lightning stitch. This stitch is recommended for stretch knits but is better used to help control difficult fabrics.

▶ BASIC BUTTONHOLE STITCH

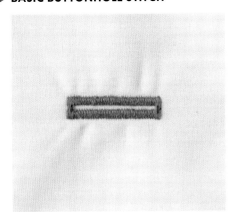

Square on both ends. Used on all styles of garment.

▶ ROUND-END BUTTONHOLE STITCH

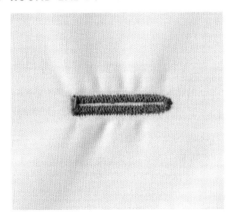

One square end and one round end. Used on jackets.

▶ KEYHOLE BUTTONHOLE STITCH

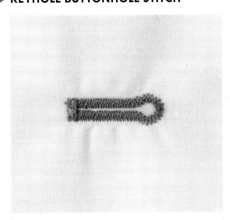

One square end and one end shaped like a loop. Used on jackets.

▶ DECORATIVE STITCHES

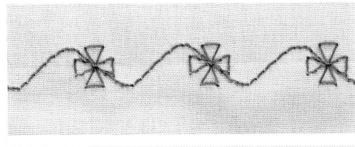

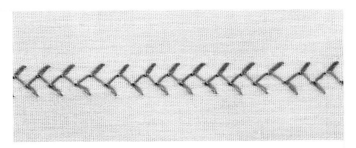

Sewing machines are capable of producing decorative linear stitches. These can be used to enhance a seam or the surface of a garment. Or, when worked as many rows together, they can be used to create a piece of embroidered fabric.

PLAIN SEAM

A plain seam is ⅝in (1.5cm) wide. It is important that the seam is stitched accurately at this measurement, otherwise the garment will end up being the wrong size and shape. There are guides on the plate of the sewing machine to help align the fabric correctly.

Level of difficulty

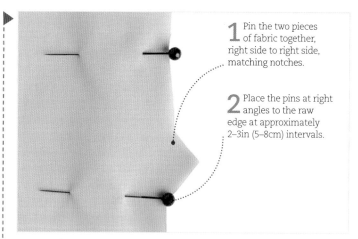

1 Pin the two pieces of fabric together, right side to right side, matching notches.

2 Place the pins at right angles to the raw edge at approximately 2–3in (5–8cm) intervals.

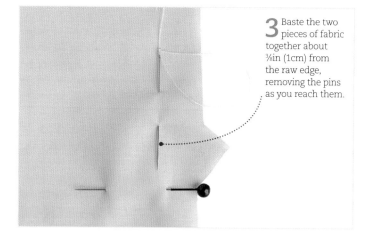

3 Baste the two pieces of fabric together about ⅜in (1cm) from the raw edge, removing the pins as you reach them.

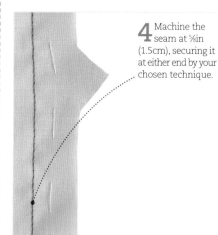

4 Machine the seam at ⅝in (1.5cm), securing it at either end by your chosen technique.

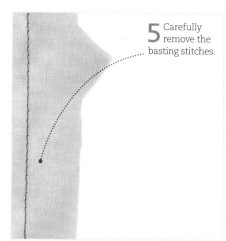

5 Carefully remove the basting stitches.

6 Press the seam open on the wrong side.

SEAM NEATENING

Level of difficulty ✱✱✱

It is important that the raw edges of the seam are neatened or finished—this will make the seam hard-wearing and prevent fraying. The method of neatening will depend on the style of garment that is being made and the fabric you are using.

▶ **PINKED**

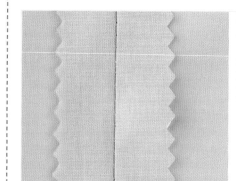

This method of neatening is ideal for fabrics that do not fray badly. Using pinking shears, trim as little as possible off the raw edge.

▶ **ZIGZAGGED**

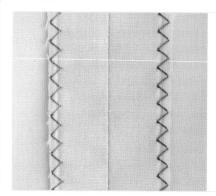

All sewing machines will make a zigzag stitch. It is an ideal stitch to keep the edges from fraying and is suitable for all types of fabric. Stitch in from the raw edge, then trim back to the zigzag stitch. Use a stitch width of 2.0 and a stitch length of 1.5.

▶ **3-THREAD SERGER STITCH**

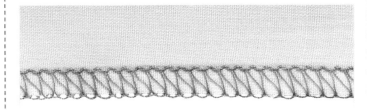

Stitched using three threads on the serger. Used to neaten the edge of fabric to prevent fraying.

▶ **4-THREAD SERGER STITCH**

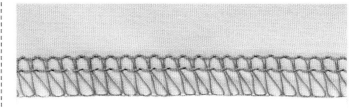

Made using four threads on the serger. Used to neaten edges on difficult fabrics or to construct a seam on stretch knits.

FRENCH SEAM

Level of difficulty ✱✱✱

A French seam is stitched twice, first on the right side of the work and then on the wrong side, enclosing the first seam. It is traditionally used on delicate garments and on sheer and silk fabrics.

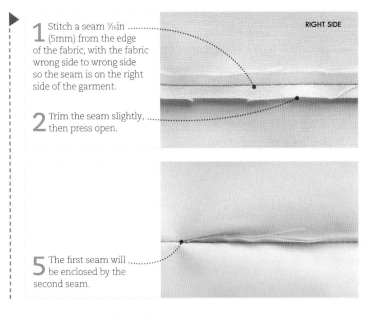

▶ **1** Stitch a seam ³⁄₁₆in (5mm) from the edge of the fabric, with the fabric wrong side to wrong side so the seam is on the right side of the garment.

2 Trim the seam slightly, then press open.

5 The first seam will be enclosed by the second seam.

RIGHT SIDE

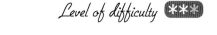

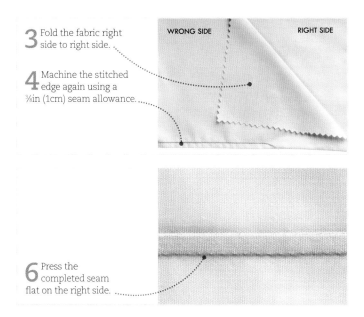

3 Fold the fabric right side to right side.

4 Machine the stitched edge again using a ³⁄₈in (1cm) seam allowance.

WRONG SIDE · RIGHT SIDE

6 Press the completed seam flat on the right side.

RUN AND FELL SEAM

Level of difficulty ✱✱✱

Some garments require a strong seam that will withstand frequent washing and wear and tear. A run and fell seam, also known as a flat fell seam, is very strong. It is made on the right side of a garment and is used on the inside leg seam of jeans and on men's tailored shirts.

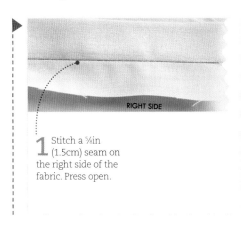

RIGHT SIDE

▶ **1** Stitch a ⁵⁄₈in (1.5cm) seam on the right side of the fabric. Press open.

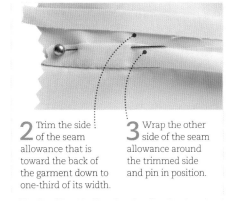

2 Trim the side of the seam allowance that is toward the back of the garment down to one-third of its width.

3 Wrap the other side of the seam allowance around the trimmed side and pin in position.

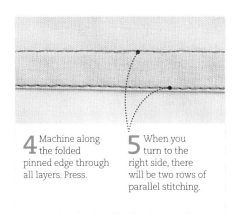

4 Machine along the folded pinned edge through all layers. Press.

5 When you turn to the right side, there will be two rows of parallel stitching.

HONG KONG FINISH

This is a great finish to use to neaten the seams on unlined jackets made from wool or linen. It is made by wrapping the raw edge with bias-cut strips.

1 Cut bias strips of silk organza ¾in (2cm) wide. Good-quality lining fabric or ¾in (2cm) bias binding can also be used.

2 Stitch one raw edge of the bias strip to the raw edge of the seam allowance.

3 Press the other raw edge across the stitching.

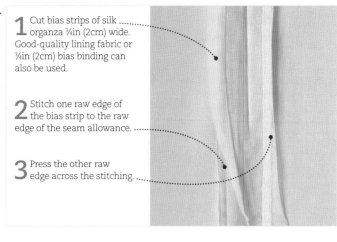

4 Wrap the pressed raw edge over the stitching to the wrong side of the seam allowance.

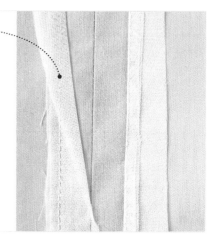

5 Pin the wrapped bias strip to the fabric, then press the folded edge.

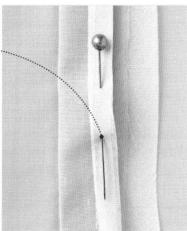

6 Machine the wrapped bias strip to the seam, from the upper side of the seam, stitching alongside the edge of the bias.

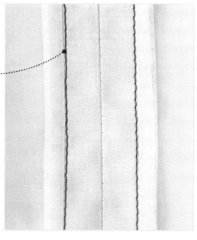

A SEAM FOR SHEER FABRICS

Sheer fabrics require specialized care for seam construction because they are very soft and delicate. The seam shown below is an alternative to a French seam; it is very narrow when finished and presses very flat so is less visible on sheer fabrics.

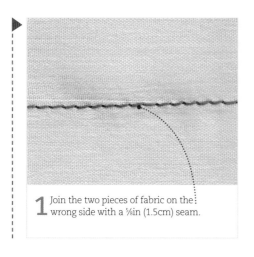

1 Join the two pieces of fabric on the wrong side with a ⅝in (1.5cm) seam.

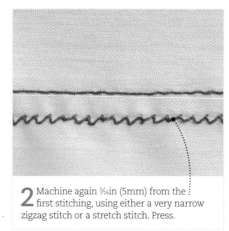

2 Machine again ³⁄₁₆in (5mm) from the first stitching, using either a very narrow zigzag stitch or a stretch stitch. Press.

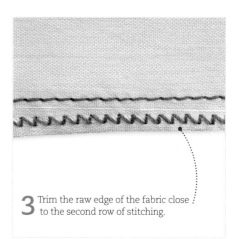

3 Trim the raw edge of the fabric close to the second row of stitching.

STITCHING CORNERS AND CURVES

Not all sewing is straight lines. The work will have curves and corners that require negotiation to produce sharp clean angles and curves on the right side. The technique for stitching a corner shown below applies to corners of all angles. On a thick fabric, the technique is slightly different, with a stitch taken across the corner, and on a fabric that frays badly the corner is reinforced with a second row of stitches.

Level of difficulty ✷✷✷

▶ STITCHING A CORNER

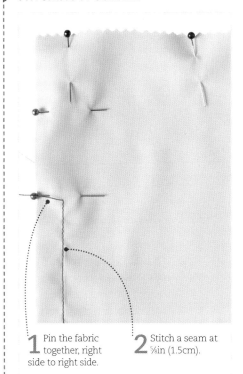

1 Pin the fabric together, right side to right side.

2 Stitch a seam at ⅝in (1.5cm).

3 On reaching the corner, insert the machine needle into the fabric.

4 Raise the presser foot and turn the fabric through 90 degrees to pivot at the corner.

5 Lower the presser foot and continue stitching along the other side.

6 The stitching lines are at right angles to each other, which means the finished corner will have a sharp point when turned through to the right side.

▶ STITCHING A CORNER ON HEAVY FABRIC

1 On a thick fabric it is very difficult to achieve a sharp point, so instead a single stitch is taken across the corner. First, stitch to the corner.

2 At the corner, insert the needle into the fabric, then lift the presser foot. Turn the fabric 45 degrees. Put the foot down again and make one stitch.

3 With the needle in the fabric, lift the foot and turn the fabric 45 degrees again. Lower the foot and continue stitching along the other side.

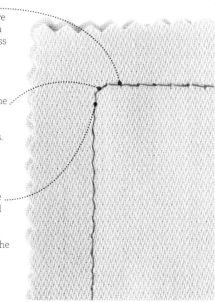

▶ STITCHING A REINFORCED CORNER

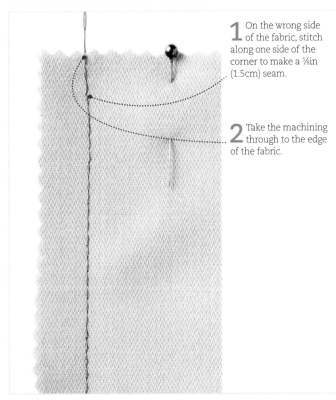

1 On the wrong side of the fabric, stitch along one side of the corner to make a ⅝in (1.5cm) seam.

2 Take the machining through to the edge of the fabric.

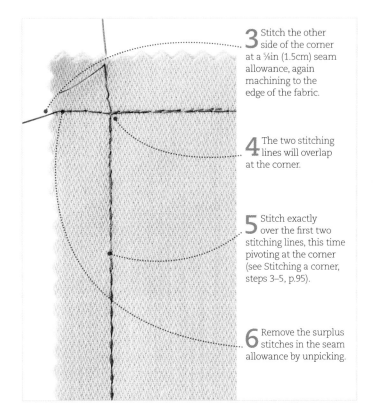

3 Stitch the other side of the corner at a ⅝in (1.5cm) seam allowance, again machining to the edge of the fabric.

4 The two stitching lines will overlap at the corner.

5 Stitch exactly over the first two stitching lines, this time pivoting at the corner (see Stitching a corner, steps 3–5, p.95).

6 Remove the surplus stitches in the seam allowance by unpicking.

▶ STITCHING AN INNER CORNER

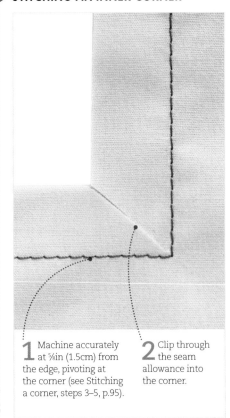

1 Machine accurately at ⅝in (1.5cm) from the edge, pivoting at the corner (see Stitching a corner, steps 3–5, p.95).

2 Clip through the seam allowance into the corner.

▶ STITCHING AN INNER CURVE

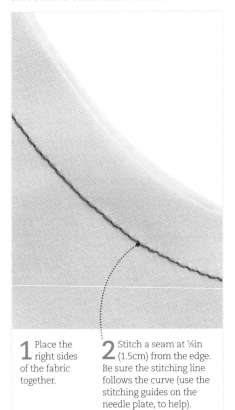

1 Place the right sides of the fabric together.

2 Stitch a seam at ⅝in (1.5cm) from the edge. Be sure the stitching line follows the curve (use the stitching guides on the needle plate, to help).

▶ STITCHING AN OUTER CURVE

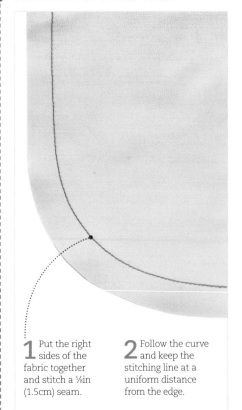

1 Put the right sides of the fabric together and stitch a ⅝in (1.5cm) seam.

2 Follow the curve and keep the stitching line at a uniform distance from the edge.

REDUCING SEAM BULK

It is important that the seams used for construction do not cause bulk on the right side. To make sure this does not happen, the seam allowances need to be reduced in size by a technique known as layering a seam. They may also require V shapes to be removed, which is known as notching, or the seam allowance may be clipped.

LAYERING A SEAM

On the majority of fabrics, if the seam is on the edge of the work, the amount fabric in the seam needs to be reduced. Leave the seam allowance closest to the outside of the garment full width, but reduce the seam allowance that lies closest to the body.

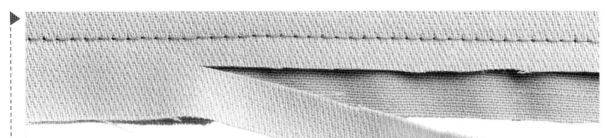

Cut along one side of the seam allowance to reduce the fabric by half to one-third of its original width.

REDUCING SEAM BULK ON AN INNER CURVE

For an inner curve to lie flat, the seam will need to be layered and notched, then understitched to hold it in place (see p.98).

Level of difficulty ✳✳✳

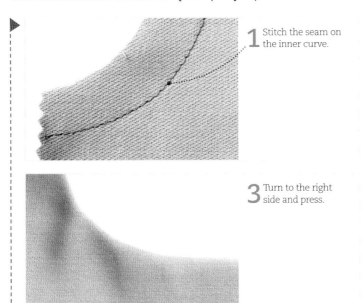

1 Stitch the seam on the inner curve.

2 Layer the seam (see above), then cut out V notches to reduce the bulk.

3 Turn to the right side and press.

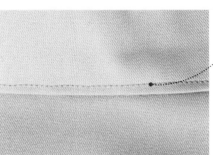

4 Understitch by maching the seam allowances on to the wrong side (see p.98).

REDUCING SEAM BULK ON AN OUTER CURVE

Level of difficulty ✷✷✷

An outer curve also needs layering and notching or clipping to allow the seam to be turned to the right side, after which it is understitched.

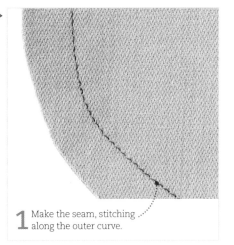

1 Make the seam, stitching along the outer curve.

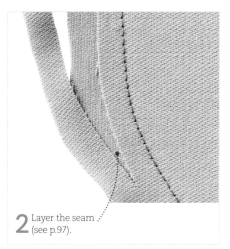

2 Layer the seam (see p.97).

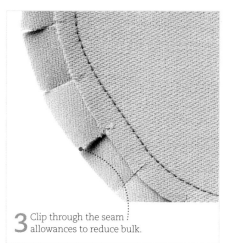

3 Clip through the seam allowances to reduce bulk.

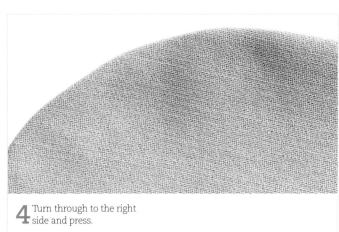

4 Turn through to the right side and press.

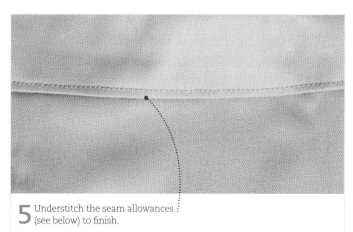

5 Understitch the seam allowances (see below) to finish.

FINISHING EDGES

Level of difficulty ✷✷✷

Topstitching and understitching are two methods to finish edges. Topstitching is meant to be seen on the right side of the work, whereas understitching is not visible from the right side.

▶ TOPSTITCHING

A topstitch is a decorative, sharp finish to an edge. Use a longer stitch length, of 3.0 or 3.5, and machine on the right side of the work, using the edge of the machine foot as a guide.

▶ UNDERSTITCHING

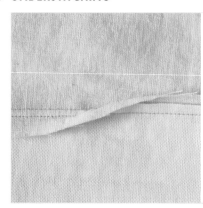

Understitching secures a seam on the fabric's edge. It helps stop the seam from rolling to the right side. First, make the seam, layer (see p.97), turn to the right side, and press. Working from the right side, machine the seam allowance to the facing or the fabric lining. Open the seam; push the allowance over the layered allowance. Machine the seam allowance down.

DARTS

A dart is used to give shape to a piece of fabric so that it can fit around the contours of the body. Some darts are stitched following straight stitching lines and other darts are stitched following a slightly curved line. Always stitch a dart from the point to the wide end since then you will be able to sink the machine needle into the point accurately and securely.

PLAIN DART

Level of difficulty ❋❋❋

This is the most common type of dart and is used to give shaping to the bust in the bodice. It is also found at the waist in skirts and pants to give shape from the waist to the hip.

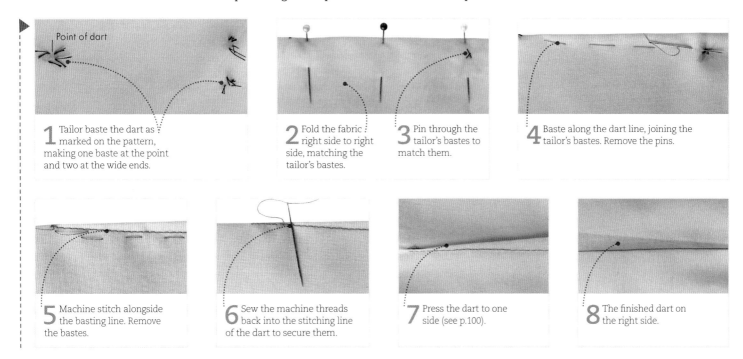

Point of dart

1 Tailor baste the dart as marked on the pattern, making one baste at the point and two at the wide ends.

2 Fold the fabric right side to right side, matching the tailor's bastes.

3 Pin through the tailor's bastes to match them.

4 Baste along the dart line, joining the tailor's bastes. Remove the pins.

5 Machine stitch alongside the basting line. Remove the bastes.

6 Sew the machine threads back into the stitching line of the dart to secure them.

7 Press the dart to one side (see p.100).

8 The finished dart on the right side.

SHAPING DARTS TO FIT

Level of difficulty ❋❋❋

Our bodies have curves, and the straight line of the dart may not sit closely enough to our own personal shape. The dart can be stitched slightly concave or convex so it follows our contours. Do not curve the dart by more than ⅛in (3mm) from the straight line.

▶ **CONVEX DART**

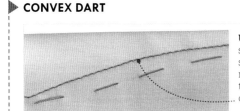

Use this for fuller shapes. Stitch the dart slightly inside the normal stitching line, to make a smooth convex curve.

▶ **CONCAVE DART**

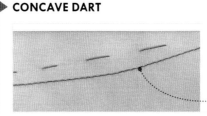

This is for thinner bodies, since it takes up more fabric. Stitch the dart slightly outside the normal stitching line, in a smooth concave curve.

CONTOUR OR DOUBLE-POINTED DART

Level of difficulty ✱✱✱

This type of dart is like two darts joined together at their wide ends. It is used to give shape at the waist of a dress. It will contour the fabric from the bust into the waist and then from the waist out toward the hip.

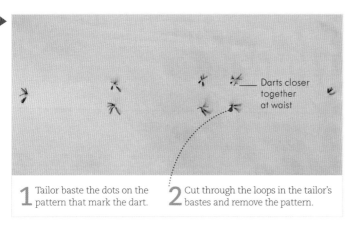

1 Tailor baste the dots on the pattern that mark the dart.

2 Cut through the loops in the tailor's bastes and remove the pattern.

Darts closer together at waist

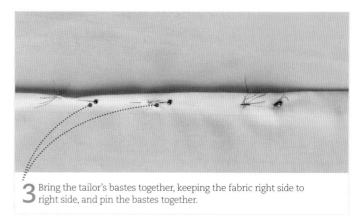

3 Bring the tailor's bastes together, keeping the fabric right side to right side, and pin the bastes together.

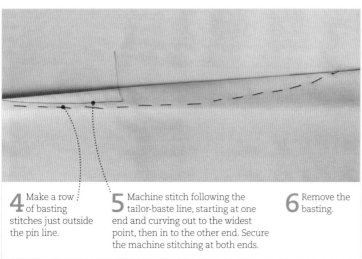

4 Make a row of basting stitches just outside the pin line.

5 Machine stitch following the tailor-baste line, starting at one end and curving out to the widest point, then in to the other end. Secure the machine stitching at both ends.

6 Remove the basting.

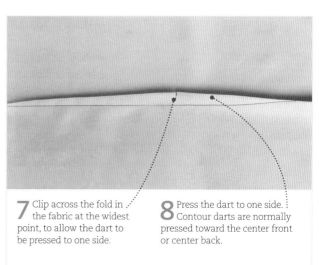

7 Clip across the fold in the fabric at the widest point, to allow the dart to be pressed to one side.

8 Press the dart to one side. Contour darts are normally pressed toward the center front or center back.

PRESSING A DART

If a dart is pressed incorrectly it can spoil the look of a garment. For successful pressing you will need a tailor's ham and a steam iron on a steam setting. A pressing cloth may be required for delicate fabrics such as silk, satin, and chiffon, and for lining fabrics.

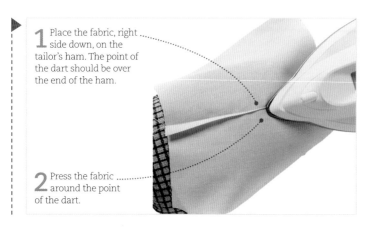

1 Place the fabric, right side down, on the tailor's ham. The point of the dart should be over the end of the ham.

2 Press the fabric around the point of the dart.

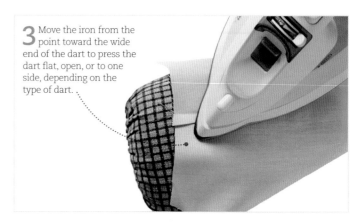

3 Move the iron from the point toward the wide end of the dart to press the dart flat, open, or to one side, depending on the type of dart.

GATHERS

Gathers are an easy way to draw up a piece of larger fabric so that it will fit on to a smaller piece of fabric. They often appear at waistlines or yoke lines. The gather stitch is inserted after the major seams have been constructed. Gathers are best worked on the sewing machine using the longest available stitch length. On the majority of fabrics, two rows of gather stitches are required, but for very heavy fabrics it is advisable to have three rows. Try to stitch the rows so that the stitches line up under one another.

MAKING AND FITTING GATHERS

Level of difficulty ✶✶✶

Once all the main seams have been sewn, stitch the two rows of gathers so that the stitches are inside the seam allowance. This should avoid the need to remove them because doing so after they have been pulled up can damage the fabric. In the example below, we attach a skirt to a bodice.

1 Stitch the first gathers at ⅜in (1cm) and the second at ½in (1.2cm). Leave long tails of thread for gathering. Do not stitch over the seams.

2 Place the skirt against the bodice section, right side to right side.

3 Match the notches and seams, and hold in place with pins.

4 Gently pull on the two long tails of thread on the wrong side of the skirt—the fabric will gather along the threads.

5 Secure the threads at one end to prevent the stitches from pulling out.

6 Even out the gathers and pin.

7 When all the gathers are in place, use a standard machine stitch to stitch a ⅝in (1.5cm) wide seam.

8 Stitch with the gathers uppermost and keep pulling them to the side to stop them from creasing up.

9 Turn the bodice of the garment inside. Press the seam very carefully to avoid creasing the gathers.

10 Neaten the seam by stitching both edges together. Use either a zigzag stitch or a 3-thread serger stitch.

11 Press the seam up toward the bodice.

INTERFACINGS

An interfacing may be non-fusible (sew-in) or fusible (iron-on) and is only attached to certain parts of a garment. Parts that are normally interfaced include the collar and cuffs and the facings.

▶ NON-FUSIBLE INTERFACINGS

Muslin   Silk organza   Non-woven interfacing

All of these interfacings need to be basted to the main fabric around the edges prior to construction of the work or seam neatening.

▶ FUSIBLE INTERFACINGS

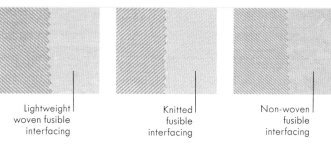

Lightweight woven fusible interfacing   Knitted fusible interfacing   Non-woven fusible interfacing

A fusible interfacing is used in the same areas as a sew-in interfacing. To prevent the fusible interfacing from showing on the right side of the work, use pinking shears on the edge of the interfacing.

▶ HOW TO APPLY A NON-FUSIBLE INTERFACING

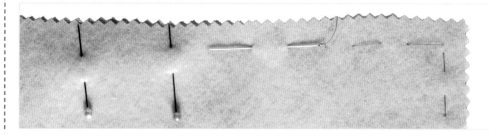

1 Place the interfacing on to the wrong side of the fabric, aligning the cut edges.

2 Pin in place.

3 Using a basic basting stitch, baste the interfacing to the fabric or facing at ⅜in (1cm) within the seam allowance.

▶ HOW TO APPLY A FUSIBLE INTERFACING

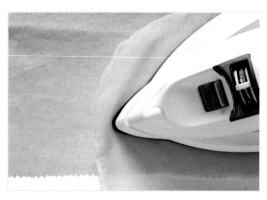

1 Place the fabric on the pressing surface, wrong side up, making sure it is straight and unwrinkled.

2 Place the sticky side (this feels gritty) of the chosen interfacing on the fabric.

3 Cover with a dry pressing cloth and spray the cloth with a fine mist of water.

4 Place a steam iron, on a steam setting, on top of the pressing cloth.

5 Leave the iron in place for at least 10 seconds before moving it to the next area of fabric.

6 Check to see if the interfacing is fused to the fabric by rolling the fabric. If the interfacing is still loose in places, repeat the pressing process.

7 When the fabric has cooled down, the fusing process will be complete. Then pin the pattern back on to the fabric and transfer the pattern markings as required.

FACINGS

The simplest way to finish the neck or armhole of a garment

is to apply a facing. The neckline can be any shape to have a facing applied, from a curve to a square to a V, and many more. Some facings and necklines can add interest to the center back or center front of a garment.

APPLYING INTERFACING TO A FACING

Level of difficulty **✳✳✳**

All facings require interfacing. The interfacing is to give structure to the facing and to hold it in shape. A fusible interfacing is the best choice and should be cut on the same grain as the facing. Choose an interfacing that is lighter in weight than the main fabric.

▶ **INTERFACING FOR HEAVY FABRIC**

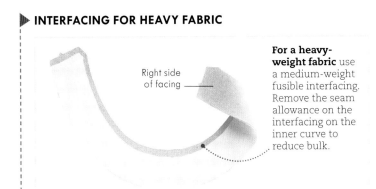

Right side of facing

For a heavy-weight fabric use a medium-weight fusible interfacing. Remove the seam allowance on the interfacing on the inner curve to reduce bulk.

▶ **INTERFACING FOR LIGHT FABRIC**

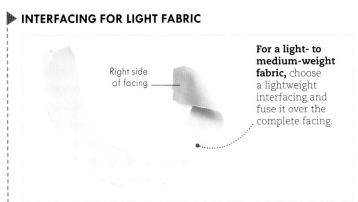

Right side of facing

For a light- to medium-weight fabric, choose a lightweight interfacing and fuse it over the complete facing.

CONSTRUCTION OF A FACING

Level of difficulty **✳✳✳**

The facing may be in two or three pieces in order to fit around a neck or armhole edge. The facing sections need to be joined together prior to being attached. The photographs here show an interfaced neck facing in three pieces.

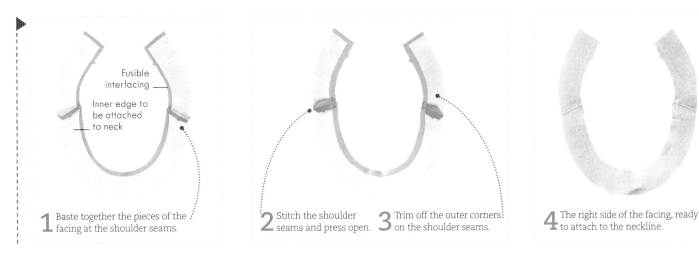

Fusible interfacing

Inner edge to be attached to neck

1 Baste together the pieces of the facing at the shoulder seams.

2 Stitch the shoulder seams and press open.

3 Trim off the outer corners on the shoulder seams.

4 The right side of the facing, ready to attach to the neckline.

NEATENING THE EDGE OF A FACING

Level of difficulty ✱✱✱

The outer edge of a facing will require neatening to prevent it from fraying, and there are several ways to do this. Binding the lower edge of a facing with a bias strip makes the garment a little more luxurious and can add a designer touch inside the garment. Alternatively, the edge can be stitched or pinked (see opposite).

▶ CUTTING BIAS STRIPS

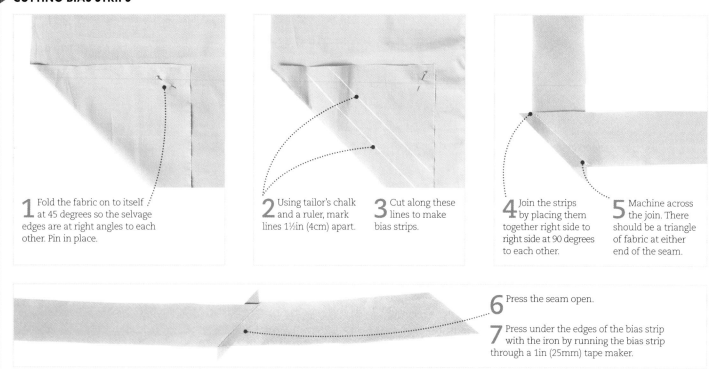

1 Fold the fabric on to itself at 45 degrees so the selvage edges are at right angles to each other. Pin in place.

2 Using tailor's chalk and a ruler, mark lines 1½in (4cm) apart.

3 Cut along these lines to make bias strips.

4 Join the strips by placing them together right side to right side at 90 degrees to each other.

5 Machine across the join. There should be a triangle of fabric at either end of the seam.

6 Press the seam open.

7 Press under the edges of the bias strip with the iron by running the bias strip through a 1in (25mm) tape maker.

▶ NEATENING THE EDGE OF A FACING WITH A BIAS STRIP

1 Making your own bias strip is easy (see above). Open out one folded edge of the bias strip and place to the outer edge of the facing, right side to right side.

2 Machine along the crease line in the bias.

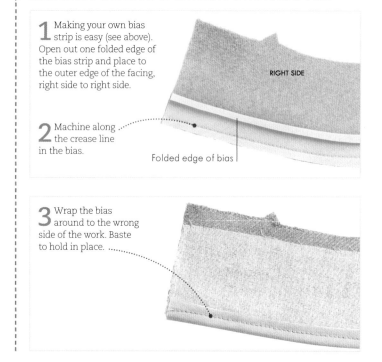

RIGHT SIDE

Folded edge of bias

3 Wrap the bias around to the wrong side of the work. Baste to hold in place.

4 Working from the right side of the facing, stitch in the ditch made by the bias-to-facing stitching.

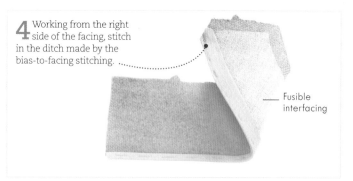

Fusible interfacing

5 On the right side of the facing, the bias-bound edge has a neat, professional finish.

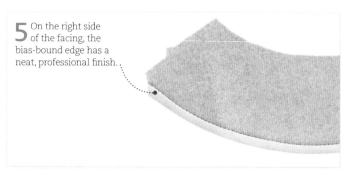

OTHER NEATENING METHODS

The following techniques are popular alternative ways to neaten the edge of a facing.
The one you choose depends upon the garment being made and the fabric used.

Level of difficulty ✱✱✱

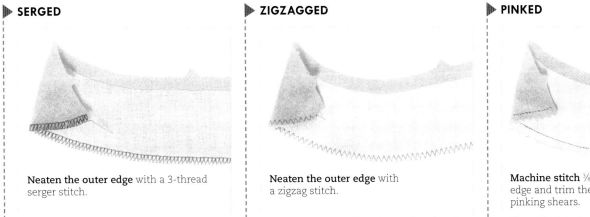

▶ **SERGED**

Neaten the outer edge with a 3-thread serger stitch.

▶ **ZIGZAGGED**

Neaten the outer edge with a zigzag stitch.

▶ **PINKED**

Machine stitch ⅜in (1cm) from the edge and trim the raw edge with pinking shears.

ATTACHING A NECK FACING

Level of difficulty ✱✱✱

This technique applies to all shapes of neckline, from round to square to sweetheart.

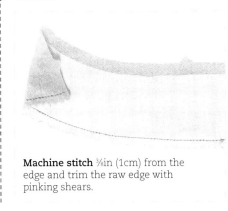

4 Pin the facing in place, matching around the neck edge.

5 Match the shoulder seams on the facing and the bodice.

Shoulder seams match

Facing and garment match at center back

6 Machine in place using a ⅝in (1.5cm) seam allowance.

7 Trim the facing down to half its width.

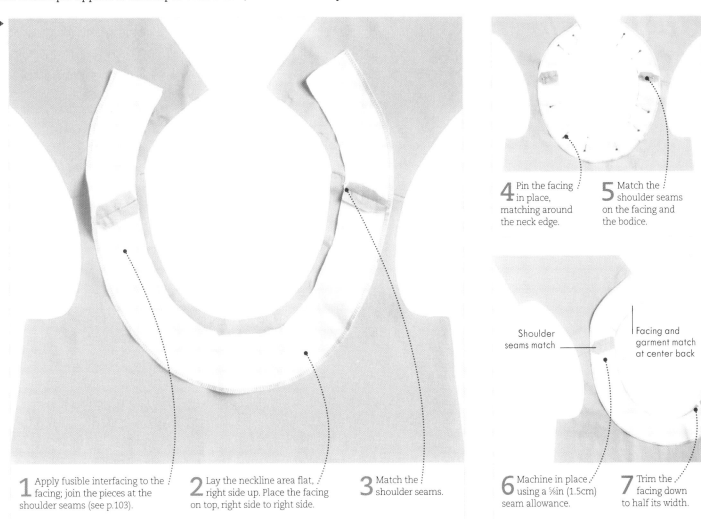

1 Apply fusible interfacing to the facing; join the pieces at the shoulder seams (see p.103).

2 Lay the neckline area flat, right side up. Place the facing on top, right side to right side.

3 Match the shoulder seams.

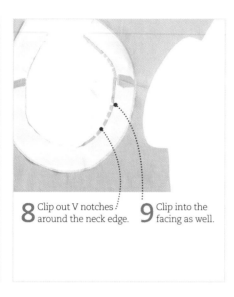

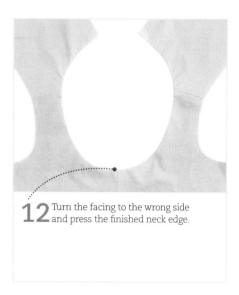

8 Clip out V notches around the neck edge.

9 Clip into the facing as well.

10 Press the seam allowance toward the facing.

11 Understitch by machining the seam allowance to the facing about ³⁄₁₆in (5mm) from the first stitching line.

12 Turn the facing to the wrong side and press the finished neck edge.

ATTACHING AN ARMHOLE FACING

Level of difficulty ✱✱✱

On sleeveless garments, a facing is an excellent way of neatening an armhole because it is not bulky. Also, as the facing is made in the same fabric as the garment, it does not show.

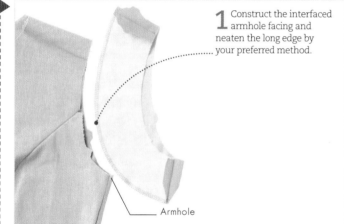

Armhole

1 Construct the interfaced armhole facing and neaten the long edge by your preferred method.

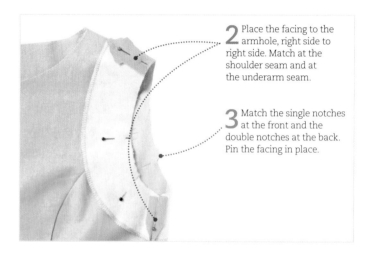

2 Place the facing to the armhole, right side to right side. Match at the shoulder seam and at the underarm seam.

3 Match the single notches at the front and the double notches at the back. Pin the facing in place.

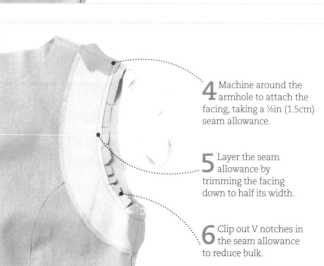

4 Machine around the armhole to attach the facing, taking a ⅝in (1.5cm) seam allowance.

5 Layer the seam allowance by trimming the facing down to half its width.

6 Clip out V notches in the seam allowance to reduce bulk.

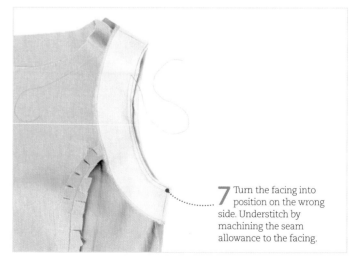

7 Turn the facing into position on the wrong side. Understitch by machining the seam allowance to the facing.

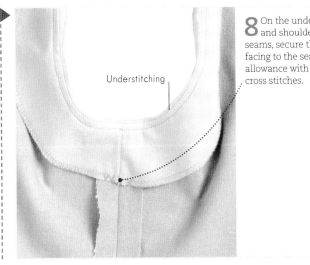

8 On the underarm and shoulder seams, secure the facing to the seam allowance with cross stitches.

Understitching

9 Press the stitched edge. On the right side the armhole will have a neat finish.

BIAS-BOUND NECK EDGE

Level of difficulty **✶✶✶**

Binding is another way to finish a raw neck edge, especially on bulkier fabrics. In this method the bias strip is cut from the same fabric as the garment.

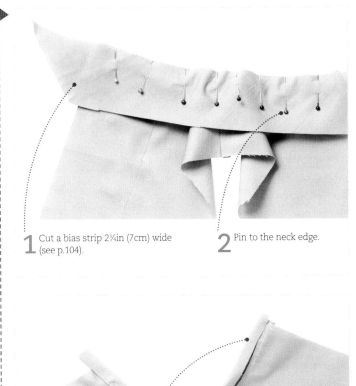

1 Cut a bias strip 2¾in (7cm) wide (see p.104).

2 Pin to the neck edge.

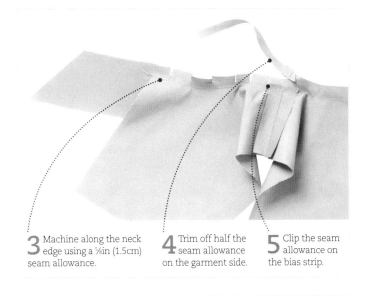

3 Machine along the neck edge using a ⅝in (1.5cm) seam allowance.

4 Trim off half the seam allowance on the garment side.

5 Clip the seam allowance on the bias strip.

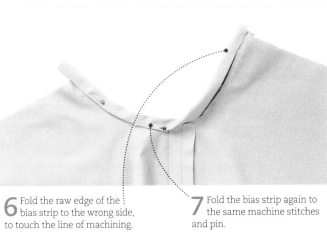

6 Fold the raw edge of the bias strip to the wrong side, to touch the line of machining.

7 Fold the bias strip again to the same machine stitches and pin.

8 Stitch permanently in position using a flat fell stitch.

A WAIST WITH A FACING

Many waistlines on skirts and pants are finished with a facing, which will follow the contours of the waist but will have had the dart shaping removed to make the facing smooth. A faced waistline always fits comfortably to the body. The facing is attached after all the main sections of the skirt or pants have been constructed.

Level of difficulty ✳✳✳

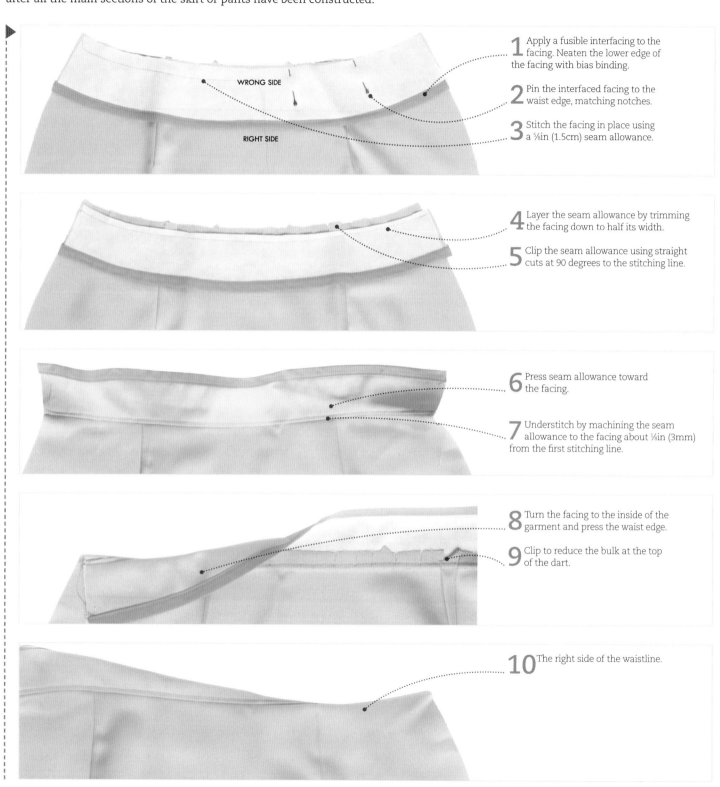

1 Apply a fusible interfacing to the facing. Neaten the lower edge of the facing with bias binding.

2 Pin the interfaced facing to the waist edge, matching notches.

3 Stitch the facing in place using a ⅝in (1.5cm) seam allowance.

WRONG SIDE

RIGHT SIDE

4 Layer the seam allowance by trimming the facing down to half its width.

5 Clip the seam allowance using straight cuts at 90 degrees to the stitching line.

6 Press seam allowance toward the facing.

7 Understitch by machining the seam allowance to the facing about ⅛in (3mm) from the first stitching line.

8 Turn the facing to the inside of the garment and press the waist edge.

9 Clip to reduce the bulk at the top of the dart.

10 The right side of the waistline.

COLLARS

All collars consist of a minimum of two pieces, the upper collar (which will be on the outside) and the under collar. Interfacing, which is required to give the collar shape and structure, is often applied to the upper collar to give a smoother appearance to the fabric.

TWO-PIECE SHIRT COLLAR

Level of difficulty ✱✱✱

A traditional-style shirt has a collar that consists of two pieces: a collar and a stand, both of which require interfacing. The stand fits close around the neck and the collar is attached to the stand. This type of collar is found on men's and ladies' shirts. On a man's shirt, the stand accommodates the tie.

1 Cut the upper and under collar. Apply interfacing to the upper collar.

2 Machine the upper and under collar together, right side to right side, stitching around the sides and the outside edge. Stitch a sharp point by pivoting at the corners.

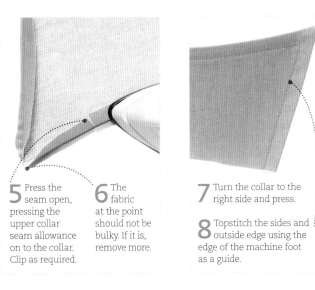

3 Trim the seam allowance from the under collar.

4 Remove surplus fabric at the point.

5 Press the seam open, pressing the upper collar seam allowance on to the collar. Clip as required.

6 The fabric at the point should not be bulky. If it is, remove more.

7 Turn the collar to the right side and press.

8 Topstitch the sides and outside edge using the edge of the machine foot as a guide.

Collar fits between the tailor's bastes

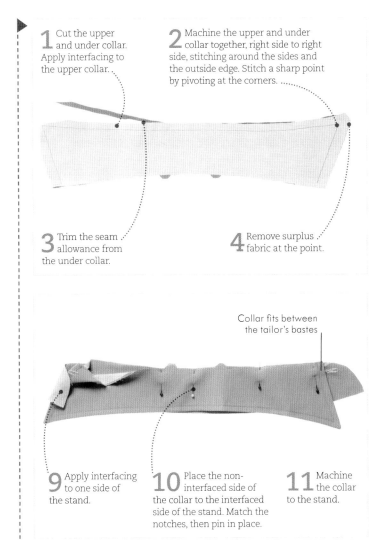

9 Apply interfacing to one side of the stand.

10 Place the non-interfaced side of the collar to the interfaced side of the stand. Match the notches, then pin in place.

11 Machine the collar to the stand.

12 Place the stand to the shirt neck, matching the notches. The seam allowance on the stand will extend at the center front. Pin and baste the stand to the shirt neck.

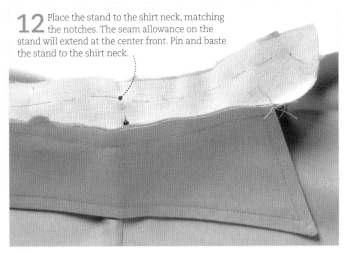

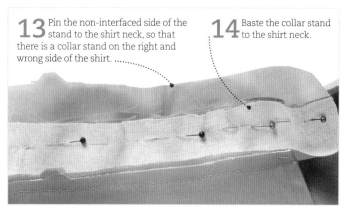

13 Pin the non-interfaced side of the stand to the shirt neck, so that there is a collar stand on the right and wrong side of the shirt.

14 Baste the collar stand to the shirt neck.

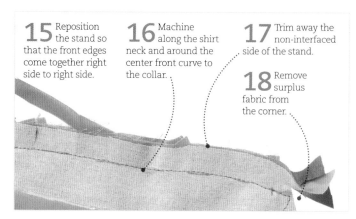

15 Reposition the stand so that the front edges come together right side to right side.

16 Machine along the shirt neck and around the center front curve to the collar.

17 Trim away the non-interfaced side of the stand.

18 Remove surplus fabric from the corner.

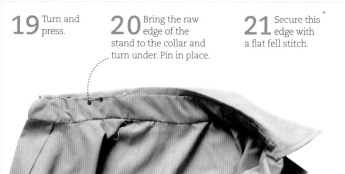

19 Turn and press.

20 Bring the raw edge of the stand to the collar and turn under. Pin in place.

21 Secure this edge with a flat fell stitch.

22 Topstitch the stand, if required. The stand fits snugly under the collar at the center front.

SIMPLE COLLAR

Level of difficulty ✲✲✲

This method of making a collar avoids pivoting on the corner, layering the seams, and clipping the edges by sewing the seams slightly differently and by folding the seams prior to turning to the right side. It can be used for collars where the under collar section is made with one piece, as for the Classic Shirt Dress (see p.212) or two pieces, as with the Classic Blazer (see p.267).

Seam allowance

1 Cut out the interfacing. Remove the seam allowance along the upper edge and the two outer edges.

WRONG SIDE

2 Apply interfacing to the WS (wrong side) of the under collar. The bottom edge of the interfacing should align with the bottom edge of the fabric.

3 With RS (right sides) facing, sew the interfacing and upper and under collars together along the upper edge.

4 Sew both short ends.

Seam line

5 To make sure there is no bulk when turned to the RS, fold the seam back along the seam line on one raw short edge and the upper edge.

6 Push the corner through to the RS. Repeat for the other corner. Press.

7 Edge stitch the collar if wished, then attach to a collar band or around the neck curve, depending on garment instructions.

RIGHT SIDE

WRONG SIDE

WAISTBANDS

A waistband is designed to fit snugly but not tightly to the waist. Whether it is shaped, straight, or slightly curved, it will be constructed and attached in a similar way. Every waistband will require a fusible interfacing to give it structure and support.

FINISHING THE EDGE OF THE WAISTBAND

Level of difficulty ✷✷✷

One long edge of the waistband will be stitched to the garment waist. The other edge will need to be finished, to prevent fraying and reduce bulk inside.

▶ **TURNING UNDER**

This method is suitable for fine fabrics only. Turn under ⅝in (1.5cm) along the edge of the waistband and press in place. After the waistband has been attached to the garment, hand stitch the pressed-under edge in place.

▶ **SERGER STITCHING**

This method is suitable for heavier fabrics, since it lies flat inside the garment after construction. Neaten one long edge of the waistband with a 3-thread serger stitch.

▶ **BIAS BINDING**

This method is ideal for fabrics that fray badly and can add a feature inside the garment. It lies flat inside the garment after construction. Apply a ¾in (2cm) bias binding to one long edge of the waistband.

ATTACHING A STRAIGHT WAISTBAND

Level of difficulty ✷✷✷

Special waistband interfacings are available, usually featuring slot lines that will guide you where to fold the fabric. Make sure the slots on the outer edge correspond to a ⅝in (1.5cm) seam allowance. If a specialized waistband fusible interfacing is not available you can use any medium-weight fusible interfacing.

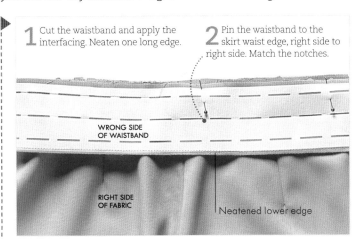

1 Cut the waistband and apply the interfacing. Neaten one long edge.

2 Pin the waistband to the skirt waist edge, right side to right side. Match the notches.

WRONG SIDE OF WAISTBAND

RIGHT SIDE OF FABRIC

Neatened lower edge

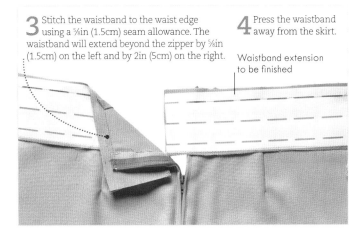

3 Stitch the waistband to the waist edge using a ⅝in (1.5cm) seam allowance. The waistband will extend beyond the zipper by ⅝in (1.5cm) on the left and by 2in (5cm) on the right.

4 Press the waistband away from the skirt.

Waistband extension to be finished

5 Fold the waistband along the crease in the interfacing, right side to right side. The neatened edge of the waistband should extend ⅝in (1.5cm) below the stitching line.

6 Pin and stitch the left-hand back of the waistband, as worn, in line with the center back.

7 On the right-hand back, as worn, extend the waist/skirt stitching line along the waistband and pivot to stitch across the end.

8 Turn the ends of the waistband to the right side. The extension on the waistband should be on the right-hand back.

9 Add your chosen fasteners.

10 To complete the waistband, stitch through the band to the skirt seam. This is known as stitching in the ditch.

11 The finished straight waistband.

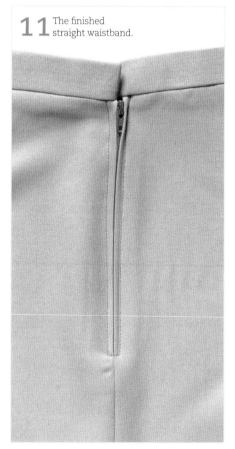

TIE BELT

Level of difficulty ✳✳✳

A tie belt is the easiest of all the belts to make. It can be any width and made with almost any fabric, from cottons for summer dresses to satin and silks for bridal wear. Most tie belts will require a light- to medium-weight interfacing for support. A fusible interfacing is the best choice, as it will stay in place when tied repeatedly. If a very long tie belt is required, the belt can be joined at the center back.

1 Cut fabric for the belt, with a point at each end. Cut a fusible interfacing the same length but half the width.

2 Place the interfacing on one half of the fabric on the wrong side and press to fuse.

3 Fold the belt in half, right side to right side so the fusible interfacing is showing. Pin.

4 Sew along all the raw edges using a ⅝in (1.5cm) seam allowance. Remember to leave a gap of about 3¼in (8cm) at the center back to turn the belt through.

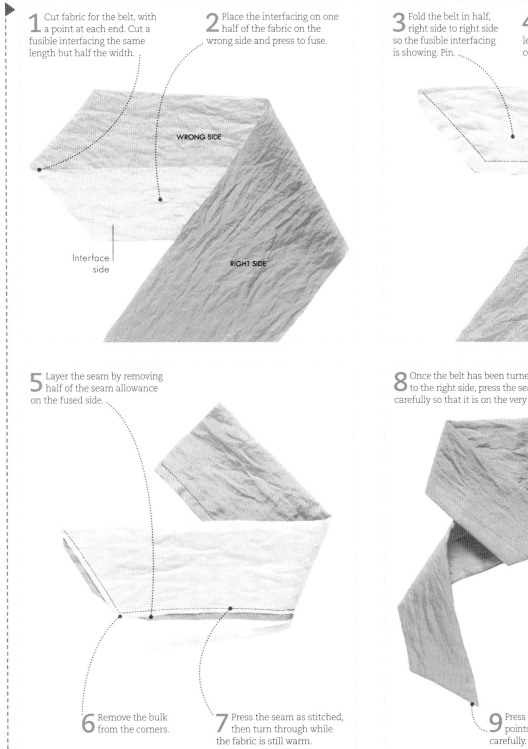

WRONG SIDE

Interface side

RIGHT SIDE

5 Layer the seam by removing half of the seam allowance on the fused side.

8 Once the belt has been turned to the right side, press the seam carefully so that it is on the very edge.

6 Remove the bulk from the corners.

7 Press the seam as stitched, then turn through while the fabric is still warm.

9 Press the points carefully.

10 Hand stitch the gap at the center back with a flat fell or blind hem stitch to close.

SLEEVES

Sleeves come in all shapes and lengths and form an important part of the design of a garment. A set-in sleeve should always hang from the end of the wearer's shoulder, without wrinkles. The lower end of the sleeve is normally finished by means of a cuff or a facing.

INSERTING A SET-IN SLEEVE

Level of difficulty ✱✱✱

A set-in sleeve should feature a smooth sleeve head that fits on the end of your shoulder accurately. This is achieved by the use of ease stitches, which are long stitches used to tighten the fabric but not gather it.

1 Machine the side seams and the shoulder seams on the garment and press them open.

Armhole with notches

Single notch denotes front of the sleeve

Double notch denotes back of the sleeve

2 Machine the sleeve seam and press open. Turn the sleeve to the right side.

3 Around the sleeve head, machine two rows of long stitches between the notches—one row at ⅜in (1cm) from the edge and the second row at ½in (1.2cm). These are the ease stitches.

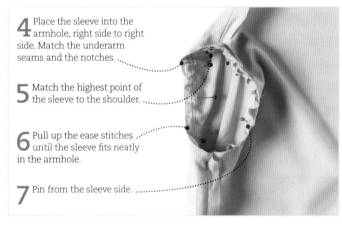

4 Place the sleeve into the armhole, right side to right side. Match the underarm seams and the notches.

5 Match the highest point of the sleeve to the shoulder.

6 Pull up the ease stitches until the sleeve fits neatly in the armhole.

7 Pin from the sleeve side.

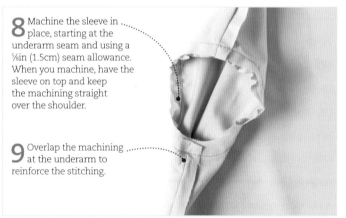

8 Machine the sleeve in place, starting at the underarm seam and using a ⅝in (1.5cm) seam allowance. When you machine, have the sleeve on top and keep the machining straight over the shoulder.

9 Overlap the machining at the underarm to reinforce the stitching.

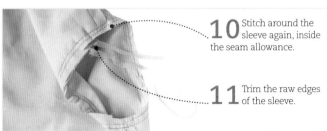

10 Stitch around the sleeve again, inside the seam allowance.

11 Trim the raw edges of the sleeve.

12 Neaten the seam with a zigzag or serger stitch, then turn the sleeve through the armhole. Do not press or you will flatten the sleeve head.

Smooth sleeve head

RIGHT SIDE OF THE GARMENT

MAKING AND INSERTING A PLEATED SLEEVE

A pleated sleeve has two or more pleats just below the shoulder at the top of the arm. These can be either inverted or box pleats.

Level of difficulty

1 Identify the pleat position on the pattern. The direction of the folds will be indicated on the pattern by arrows when viewed on the right side (RS).

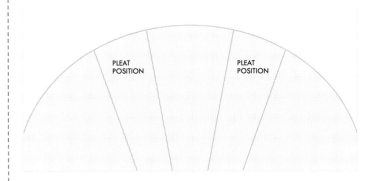

PLEAT POSITION

PLEAT POSITION

2 Mark the position of the sleeve head and pleats by clipping into the edge of the fabric.

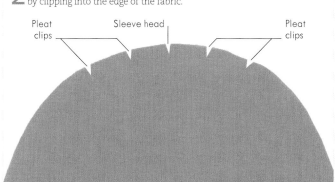

Pleat clips

Sleeve head

Pleat clips

3 On the RS, create the pleats by placing the pleat clips together on either side of the sleeve working from the innermost to outermost. Pin and tack in place along the length of the pleat for at least 1in (2.5cm).

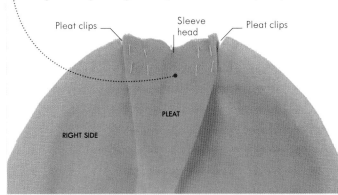

Pleat clips

Sleeve head

Pleat clips

PLEAT

RIGHT SIDE

4 With RS facing, pin the sleeve into the armhole, matching the underarm seam with the bodice side seam, and matching the sleeve head with the shoulder seam. Ease in if needed. Before sewing, turn to the RS and make sure the sleeve seam and the bodice seam line up.

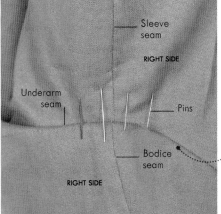

Sleeve seam

RIGHT SIDE

Underarm seam

Pins

Bodice seam

RIGHT SIDE

5 Sew the sleeve in place. Then sew a second line of stitches, approximately $1/16$in (2mm) inside the seam allowance.

6 Neaten the armhole and sleeve head seams using an overlock stitch or a small zigzag stitch.

Seam allowance

7 Turn the sleeve RS out and gently press the armhole seam and pleats.

INSERTING A PUFF SLEEVE

Level of difficulty ✷✷✷

A sleeve that has a gathered sleeve head is referred to as a puff sleeve or gathered sleeve.
It is one of the easiest sleeves to insert because the gathers take up any spare fabric.

1 Machine the sleeve seam, right side to right side, using a ⅝in (1.5cm) seam allowance. Press the seam open.

2 Machine two rows of gather stitches between the sleeve notches, one row at ⅜in (1cm) from the raw edge and the second row at ½in (1.2cm).

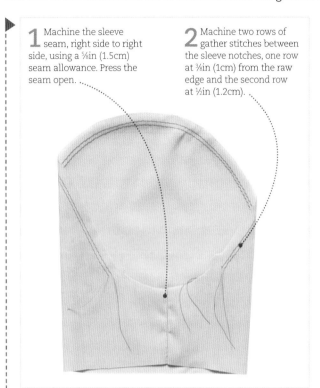

3 Place the sleeve into the armhole, right side to right side.

4 Match the underarm seams and the notches.

5 Pull up the gather stitches to make the sleeve head fit the armhole.

6 Pin from the sleeve side.

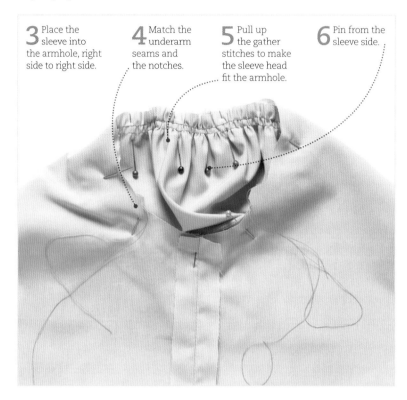

7 Working with the sleeve on top, machine the sleeve to the armhole. Use a ⅝in (1.5cm) seam allowance. Overlap the machining at the underarm.

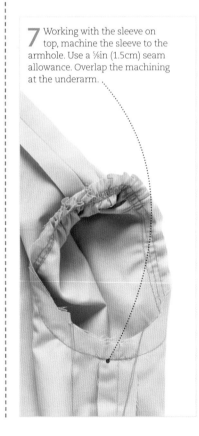

8 Stitch around the sleeve seam again between the first row of stitching and the raw edge.

9 Trim away the surplus fabric by ³⁄₁₆in (5mm).

10 Neaten the seam with a zigzag or serger stitch.

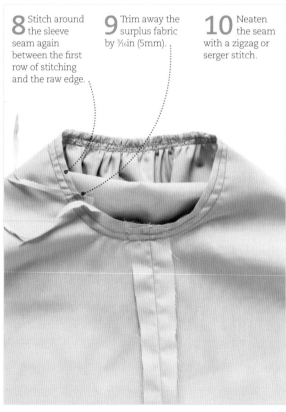

11 Turn right side out—all the gathers will be at the top of the sleeve.

SLEEVE HEMS

The simplest way to finish a sleeve is with a self hem. Here the edge of the sleeve is turned up onto itself. Alternative finishes include inserting elastic into a casing or attaching a cuff.

Level of difficulty ✳✳✳

▶ SELF HEM

1 Mark the final length of the sleeve with a row of basting stitches.

2 Remove the excess seam allowance in the hem area.

3 Turn up the hem along the basted line.

4 Match the seams. Pin in place.

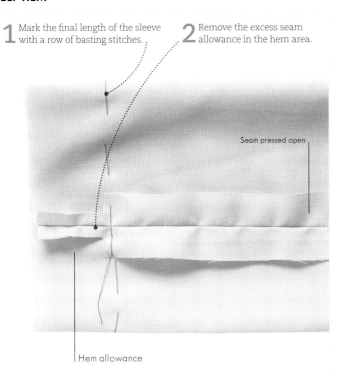

Seam pressed open

Hem allowance

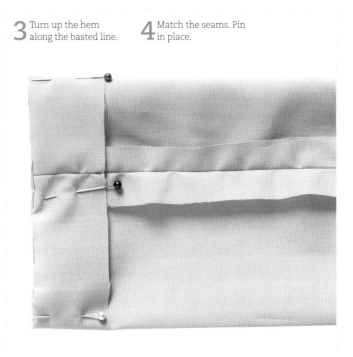

5 Turn under the top edge of the hem allowance by ⅜in (1cm) and pin.

6 Baste to secure.

7 Hand stitch the sleeve hem in place using a slip stitch.

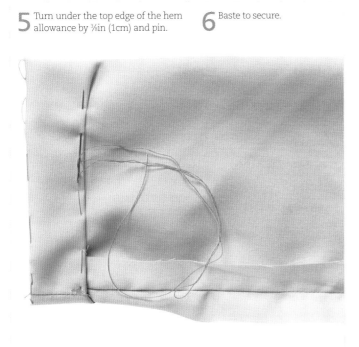

Finished hem

▶ **ELASTICATED SLEEVE EDGE**

1 Make up the sleeve and press the seam open.

2 Work a row of basting stitches on the foldline of the hem.

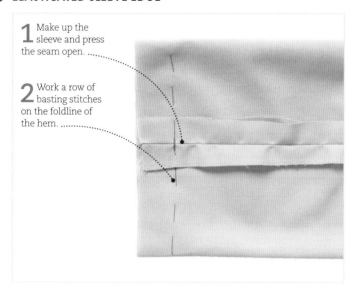

3 Turn up ³⁄₁₆in (5mm) at the raw edge and press.

4 Turn again on to the basting line.

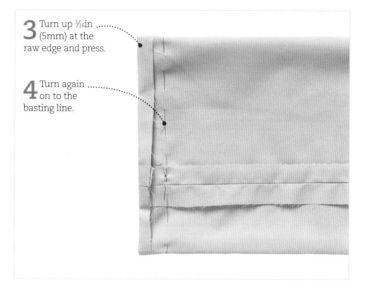

5 Machine to hold the turn-up in place, ¹⁄₁₆in (2mm) from the folded edge. Leave a gap on each side of the seam allowance through which you will insert the elastic.

Gap to insert the elastic.

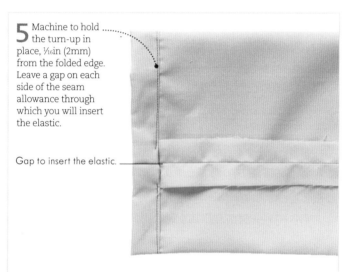

6 Machine the bottom of the sleeve ¹⁄₁₆in (2mm) from the edge, to give a neat finish. This will also help prevent the elastic from twisting.

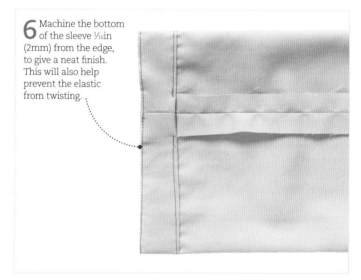

7 Cut a piece of elastic to fit the arm or wrist and insert it into the sleeve end between the two rows of machining.

8 Secure the ends of the elastic together, stitching an X for strength.

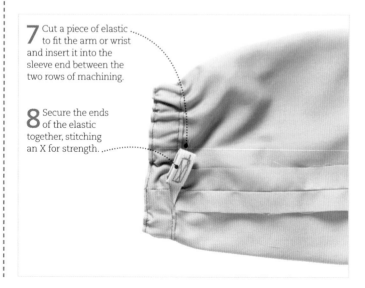

9 Turn the sleeve to the right side and check that the elasticated edge is even.

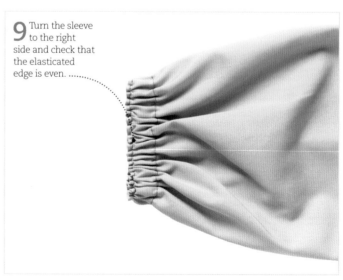

OPENINGS

The following finishes can both be used to complete the opening that accompanies a cuff. Use the bound opening on fabrics that fray easily.

Level of difficulty ✸✸✸

▶ BOUND OPENING

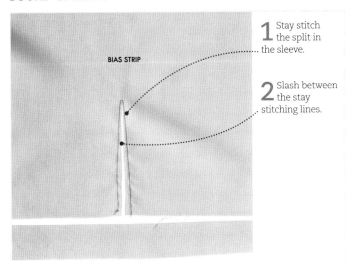

1 Stay stitch the split in the sleeve.

2 Slash between the stay stitching lines.

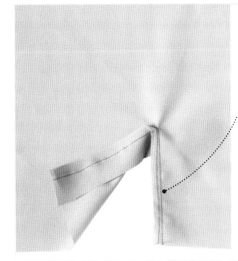

3 Working on the right side of the sleeve, pin the bias strip along the stay stitching lines. To stitch around the end of the split, open the split out into a straight line.

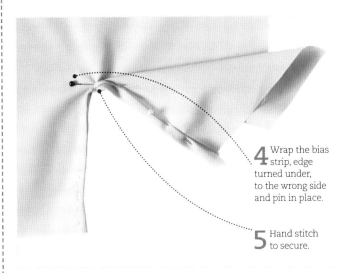

4 Wrap the bias strip, edge turned under, to the wrong side and pin in place.

5 Hand stitch to secure.

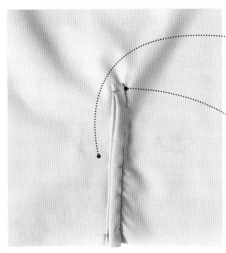

6 Allow the bias strip to close. One side of the strip will fold under and the other will extend over it.

7 Secure the top fold in the bias strip with a double stitch.

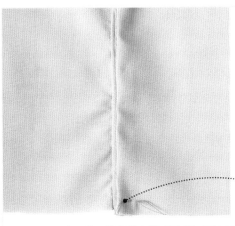

8 Tailor baste the cuff end of the bias strip to aid the placement of the cuff.

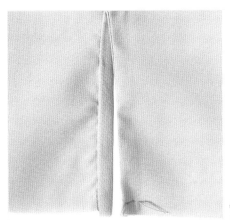

9 The finished bias-bound opening.

▶ **FACED OPENING**

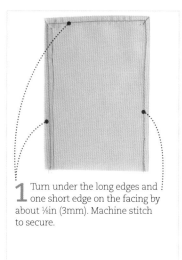

1 Turn under the long edges and one short edge on the facing by about ⅛in (3mm). Machine stitch to secure.

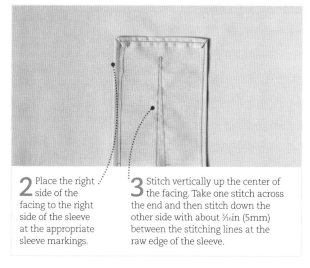

2 Place the right side of the facing to the right side of the sleeve at the appropriate sleeve markings.

3 Stitch vertically up the center of the facing. Take one stitch across the end and then stitch down the other side with about ³⁄₁₆in (5mm) between the stitching lines at the raw edge of the sleeve.

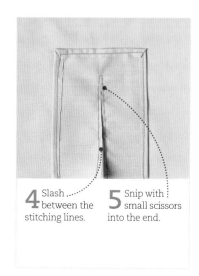

4 Slash between the stitching lines.

5 Snip with small scissors into the end.

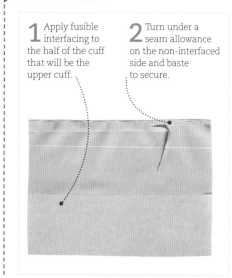

6 Turn the facing to the wrong side of the sleeve and press.

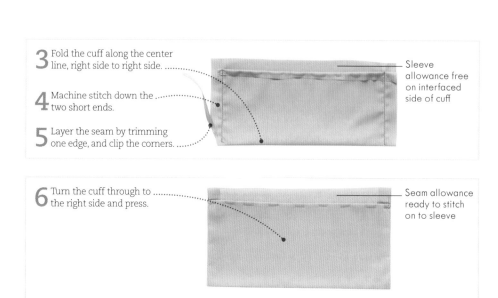

7 The finished opening on the right side.

ATTACHING A CUFF

There are various types of cuffs that can be attached to sleeve openings. The one-piece cuff and the one-piece lapped cuff are both—as their names suggest—cut from the fabric in one piece. Both work well with either a bound or faced opening.

Level of difficulty ✳✳✳

▶ **ONE-PIECE CUFF**

1 Apply fusible interfacing to the half of the cuff that will be the upper cuff.

2 Turn under a seam allowance on the non-interfaced side and baste to secure.

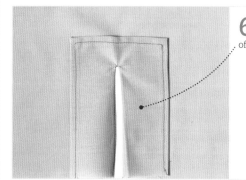

3 Fold the cuff along the center line, right side to right side.

4 Machine stitch down the two short ends.

5 Layer the seam by trimming one edge, and clip the corners.

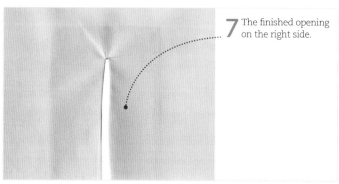

Sleeve allowance free on interfaced side of cuff

6 Turn the cuff through to the right side and press.

Seam allowance ready to stitch on to sleeve

ONE-PIECE LAPPED CUFF

1 Apply fusible interfacing to the upper half of the cuff. Pin the interfaced half of the cuff to the sleeve end, right side to right side.

2 Machine the cuff to the sleeve using a ⅝in (1.5cm) seam allowance.

3 Trim the sleeve side of the seam allowance to half its width. Press the seam toward the cuff.

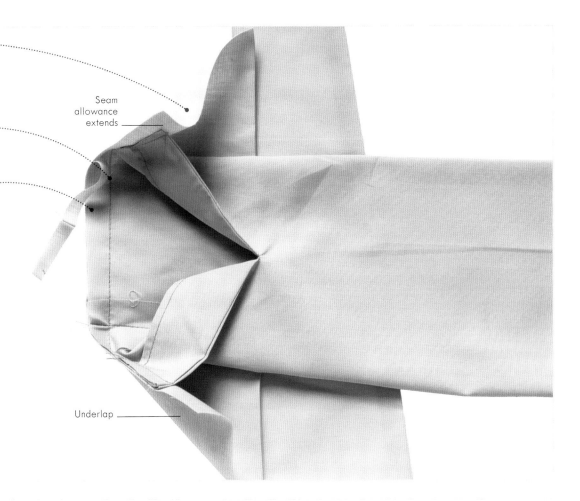

Seam allowance extends ——

Underlap ——

4 Fold the non-interfaced edge of the cuff over to the wrong side by ⅝in (1.5cm).

5 Fold the cuff to itself, right side to right side, so the folded edge of the cuff comes to the sleeve-to-cuff seam line.

6 Stitch one short end in line with the opening.

7 Stitch the other short end along from the sleeve-to-cuff seam line and then down the cuff.

8 Trim away the corners. Press the seams open.

9 Turn the cuff to the right side. Push the corners out to points.

10 On the inside, hand stitch the folded edge with a flat fell or blind hem stitch.

11 Make a buttonhole on the upper side of the cuff.

12 Sew a button on the underside of the cuff.

POCKETS

Pockets come in lots of shapes and formats. Some, such as patch pockets, are external and can be decorative, while others, including front hip pockets, are more discreet and hidden from view. You can also have a pocket flap that is purely decorative. This can be made from the same fabric as the garment or from a contrasting fabric. Whether casual or tailored, all pockets are functional.

POCKET FLAP

This pocket flap is sewn where the pocket would be, but there is no opening beneath it. This is to reduce the bulk that would arise if there were a complete pocket.

Level of difficulty ✱✱✱

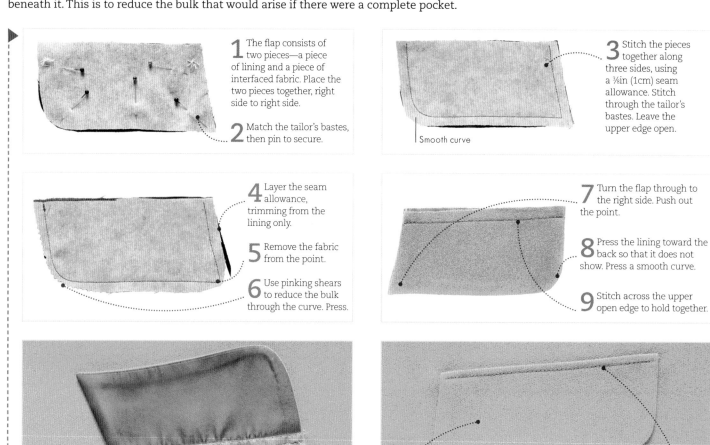

1 The flap consists of two pieces—a piece of lining and a piece of interfaced fabric. Place the two pieces together, right side to right side.

2 Match the tailor's bastes, then pin to secure.

Smooth curve

3 Stitch the pieces together along three sides, using a ⅜in (1cm) seam allowance. Stitch through the tailor's bastes. Leave the upper edge open.

4 Layer the seam allowance, trimming from the lining only.

5 Remove the fabric from the point.

6 Use pinking shears to reduce the bulk through the curve. Press.

7 Turn the flap through to the right side. Push out the point.

8 Press the lining toward the back so that it does not show. Press a smooth curve.

9 Stitch across the upper open edge to hold together.

10 Place the flap to the garment, right side to right side. Match the edges of the flap to the tailor's bastes on the garment.

11 Machine in place over the stitching line.

12 Reduce the seam allowance by half. Press.

13 Press the flap into place. Allow the fabric at the top of the flap to roll gently downward.

14 Topstitch across the upper edge to secure.

LINED PATCH POCKET

A lined patch pocket is ideal for lightweight fabrics, as it is not too bulky. It is advisable to interface the pocket fabric.

 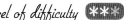

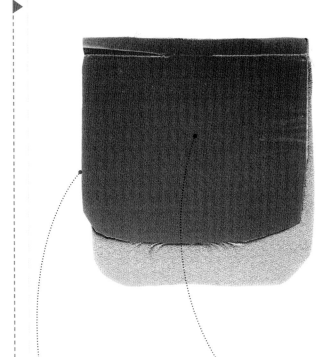

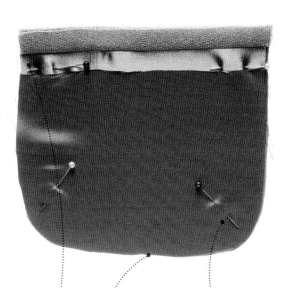

1 Cut the pocket fabric and apply interfacing. Cut the lining fabric. The lining should be shorter than the pocket.

2 Place the lining top edge to the pocket top edge and machine together. Leave a gap of about 1¼in (3cm) in the seam for turning through.

3 Press the pocket-to-lining seam open.

4 Bring the bottom edges of pocket and lining together.

5 Pin through the corners and along the sides.

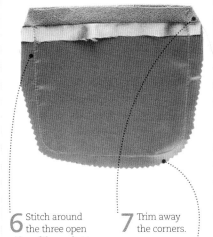

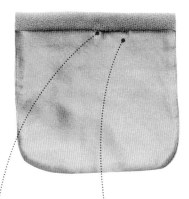

6 Stitch around the three open sides of the pocket to attach the lining to the pocket fabric.

7 Trim away the corners.

8 Use pinking shears to trim the curves.

9 Turn the pocket to the right side through the gap left in the seam. Press.

10 Hand stitch the gap with a flat fell or blind hem stitch.

11 The lined patch pocket is ready to be attached.

IN-SEAM POCKET

In pants and skirts, the pocket is sometimes disguised in the seam line. In the method below, a separate pocket is attached to the seam, but the pocket shape could also be cut as part of the main fabric.

Level of difficulty ✳✳✳

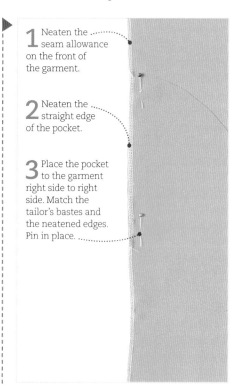

1 Neaten the seam allowance on the front of the garment.

2 Neaten the straight edge of the pocket.

3 Place the pocket to the garment right side to right side. Match the tailor's bastes and the neatened edges. Pin in place.

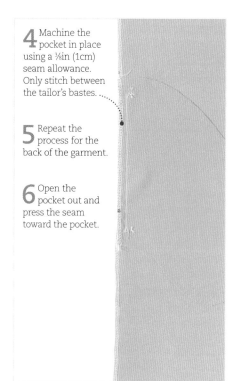

4 Machine the pocket in place using a ⅜in (1cm) seam allowance. Only stitch between the tailor's bastes.

5 Repeat the process for the back of the garment.

6 Open the pocket out and press the seam toward the pocket.

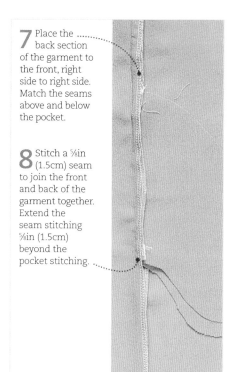

7 Place the back section of the garment to the front, right side to right side. Match the seams above and below the pocket.

8 Stitch a ⅝in (1.5cm) seam to join the front and back of the garment together. Extend the seam stitching ⅝in (1.5cm) beyond the pocket stitching.

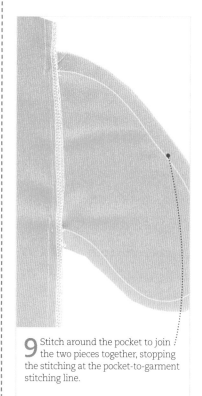

9 Stitch around the pocket to join the two pieces together, stopping the stitching at the pocket-to-garment stitching line.

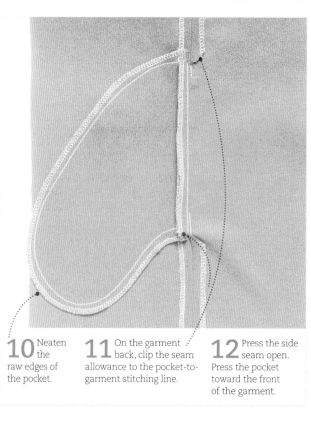

10 Neaten the raw edges of the pocket.

11 On the garment back, clip the seam allowance to the pocket-to-garment stitching line.

12 Press the side seam open. Press the pocket toward the front of the garment.

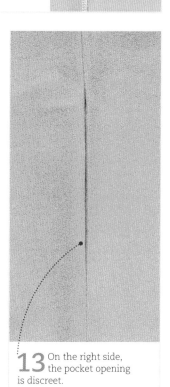

13 On the right side, the pocket opening is discreet.

FRONT HIP POCKET

On many pants and casual skirts, the pocket is placed on the hipline. It can be low on the hipline or cut quite high, as on jeans. The construction is the same for all types of hip pockets. When inserted at an angle, hip pockets can slim the figure.

Level of difficulty ❋❋❋

1 Apply a piece of fusible tape on the garment along the line of the pocket.

WRONG SIDE

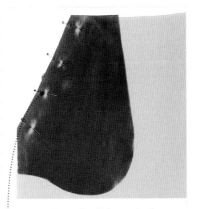

2 Place the pocket lining to the front of the garment, right side to right side. Match any notches that are on the seam. Pin in place.

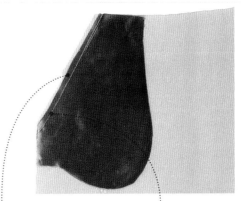

3 Machine the lining in place, taking a ⅝in (1.5cm) seam allowance.

4 Trim the lining side of the seam allowance down to half its width.

5 Open out the lining and press the seam toward it.

6 Turn the lining to the inside. Press so that the lining is not visible on the outside.

7 Topstitch ³⁄₁₆in (5mm) from the edge.

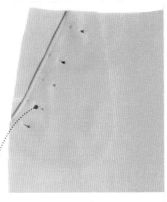

8 On the right side of the garment, pin the front to the side front along the placement lines.

WRONG SIDE

9 On the wrong side, pin the side front to the lining to create the pocket.

10 Machine the pocket and lining together using a ⅝in (1.5cm) seam allowance. Press.

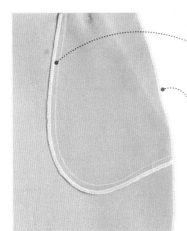

11 Neaten the raw edges of the seam allowance around the pocket.

12 Neaten the side seam allowance, stitching from the top down. Make sure that the fabric lies flat on the side seam.

13 The angled front hip pocket from the right side.

HEMLINES

The lower edge of a garment is normally finished with a hem.
Sometimes the style of the garment dictates the type of hem used, and
sometimes the fabric.

MARKING A HEMLINE

On a garment such as a skirt or a dress it is important that the hemline is level all around. Even if the fabric
has been cut straight, some styles of skirt—such as A-line or circular—will "drop," which means that the hem
edge is longer in some places. This is because the fabric can stretch where it is not on the straight of the grain.
Hang the garment for 24 hours in a warm room before hemming so you do not end up with an uneven hem.

▶ USING A RULER

1 Put on the skirt or dress but no shoes. With the end of the ruler on the floor, have a helper measure and mark.

2 Use pins to mark the crease line of the proposed hem. Make sure the measurement from floor to pin line is the same all the way around.

▶ USING A DRESSMAKER'S DUMMY

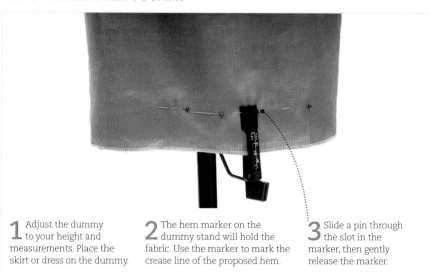

1 Adjust the dummy to your height and measurements. Place the skirt or dress on the dummy.

2 The hem marker on the dummy stand will hold the fabric. Use the marker to mark the crease line of the proposed hem.

3 Slide a pin through the slot in the marker, then gently release the marker.

HAND-STITCHED HEMS

Level of difficulty ✱✱✱

One of the most popular ways to secure a hem edge is by hand. Hand stitching is discreet
and, if a fine hand-sewing needle is used, the stitching should not show on the right side
of the work. Always finish the raw edge before stitching the hem.

TIPS FOR SEWING HEMS BY HAND

1 Always use a single thread in the needle—a polyester all-purpose thread is ideal for hemming.

2 Once the raw edge of the hem allowance has been neatened (see opposite), secure it using a slip hem stitch. Take half of the stitch into the neatened edge and the other half into the wrong side of the garment fabric.

3 Start and finish the hand stitching with a double stitch, not a knot, because knots will catch and pull the hem down.

4 It is a good idea to take a small back stitch every 4in (10cm) or so to make sure that if the hem does come loose in one place it will not all unravel.

▶ SERGED FINISH

1 Using a 3-thread serger stitch, stitch along the raw edge of the hem allowance.

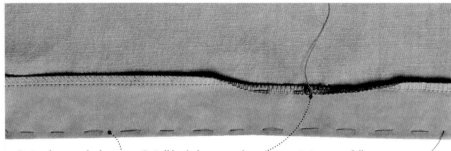

2 Gently press the hem up into position and baste close to the crease.

3 Roll back the sergered edge. Using a slip hem stitch, stitch the hem in place.

4 Press carefully to prevent the serging from being imprinted on the right side.

▶ BIAS-BOUND FINISH

1 This is a good finish for fabrics that fray or that are bulky. Turn up the hem on to the wrong side of the garment and baste close to the crease line.

2 Pin the bias binding to the raw edge of the hem allowance.

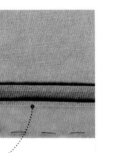

3 Open out the crease in the bias and stitch along the crease line, keeping the raw edges level.

4 Turn down the bias over the raw edge and press.

5 Using a slip hem stitch, join the edge of the bias to the wrong side of the fabric. Remove the basting and press lightly.

▶ ZIGZAG FINISH

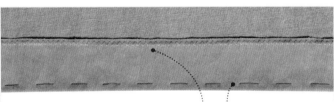

1 Use this to neaten the edge of the hem on fabrics that do not fray too badly. Set the sewing machine to a zigzag stitch, width 4.0 and length 3.0. Machine along the raw edge. Trim the fabric edge back to the zigzag stitch.

2 Turn up the hem on to the wrong side of the garment and baste in place close to the crease line.

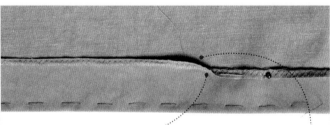

3 Fold back the zigzag-stitched edge. Using a slip hem stitch, stitch the hem into place.

4 Roll the edge back into position. Remove the basting and press lightly.

▶ PINKED FINISH

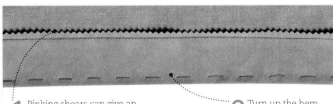

1 Pinking shears can give an excellent hem finish on difficult fabrics. Machine a row of straight stitching along the raw edge, ⅜in (1cm) from the edge. Pink the raw edge.

2 Turn up the hem on to the wrong side of the garment and baste in place close to the crease line.

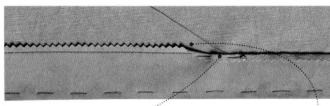

3 Fold back the edge along the machine stitching line. Using a slip hem stitch, stitch the hem in place.

4 Roll the hem edge back into position. Remove the basting and press lightly.

CURVED HEM FINISH

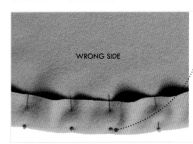

1 Fold up the hemline and pin, placing the pins vertically to keep from squashing the fullness out of the raw upper edge.

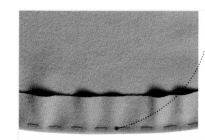

2 Baste the hem into position close to the crease line. Remove the pins.

3 Make a row of long machine stitches, length 5.0, close to the raw upper edge of the turned-up hem.

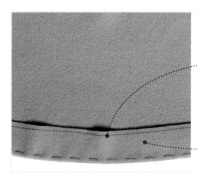

4 Pull on one of the threads of the long stitches to tighten the fabric and ease out the fullness.

5 Use the steam iron to shrink out the remainder of the fullness. The hem is now ready to be stitched in place by hand or machine.

MACHINED HEMS

Level of difficulty ✳✳✳

On many occasions, the hem or edge of a garment or other item is turned up and secured using the sewing machine. It can be stitched with a straight stitch, a zigzag stitch, or a blind hem stitch. Hems can also be made on the serger.

▷ DOUBLE-TURN HEM

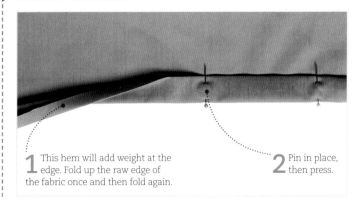

1 This hem will add weight at the edge. Fold up the raw edge of the fabric once and then fold again.

2 Pin in place, then press.

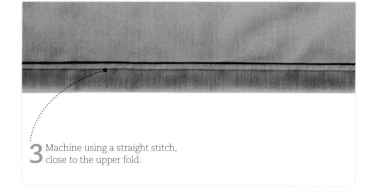

3 Machine using a straight stitch, close to the upper fold.

▷ HEMS ON DIFFICULT FABRICS

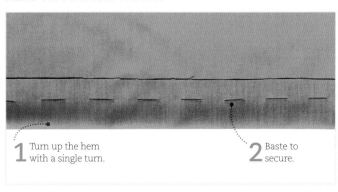

1 Turn up the hem with a single turn.

2 Baste to secure.

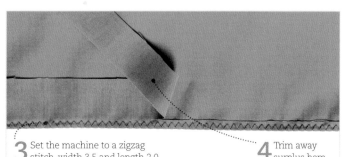

3 Set the machine to a zigzag stitch, width 3.5 and length 2.0, and zigzag close to the fold.

4 Trim away surplus hem allowance. Press.

ZIPPERS

The zipper is probably the most used of all fastenings. There are a great many types available, in a variety of lengths, colors, and materials, but they all fall into one of five categories: skirt or pant zippers, metal or jeans zippers, invisible zippers, open-ended zippers, and decorative zippers.

LAPPED ZIPPER

A skirt zipper in a skirt or a dress is usually put in by means of a lapped technique or a centered zipper technique (see p.130). For both of these techniques you will require the zipper foot on the sewing machine. A lapped zipper features one side of the seam—the left-hand side—lapping over the teeth of the zipper to conceal them.

Level of difficulty ✳✳✳

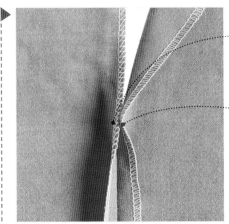

1 Stitch the seam, leaving enough of it open to accommodate the zipper.

2 Secure the end of the stitching.

3 Insert the right-hand side of the zipper first. Fold back the right-hand seam allowance by ½in (1.2cm). This folded edge will not be in line with the seam.

4 Place the folded edge against the zipper teeth. Baste.

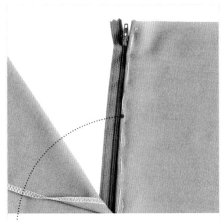

5 Using the zipper foot, stitch along the baste line to secure the zipper tape to the fabric. Stitch from the bottom of the zipper to the top.

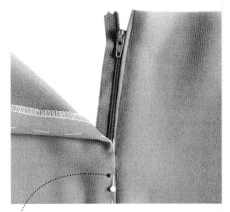

6 Fold back the left-hand seam allowance by ⅝in (1.5cm). Place the folded edge over the machine line of the other side. Pin and then baste.

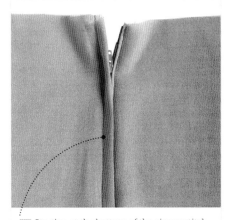

7 Starting at the bottom of the zipper, stitch across from the center seam line and then up the left side of the zipper. The finished zipper should have its teeth covered by the fabric.

GENERAL TECHNIQUES

CENTERED ZIPPER

With a centered zipper, the two folded edges of the seam allowances meet over the center of the teeth to conceal the zipper completely.

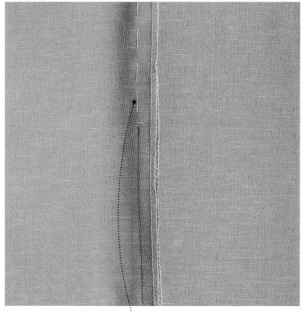

1 Stitch the seam, leaving a gap for the zipper.

2 Baste the rest of the seam.

3 Press the seam open lightly.

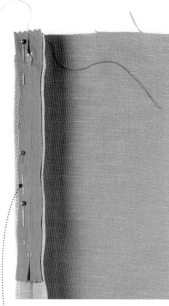

4 Center the zipper behind the basted part of the seam. Pin and then baste in place along both sides.

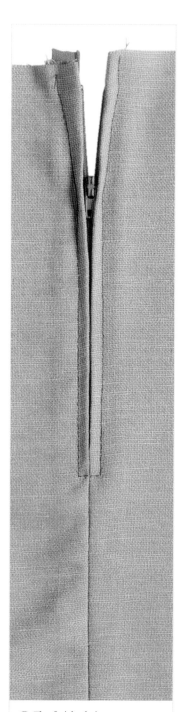

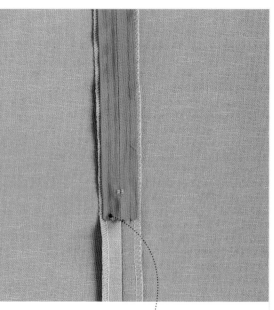

5 Machine the zipper tape to the seam allowance. Make sure both sides of the tape are secured to the seam allowances. Stitch right to the end of the zipper tape.

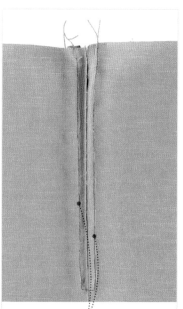

6 Working from the right side, stitch down one side of the zipper, across the bottom, and up the other side through all the layers

7 Remove the bastes.

8 The finished zipper from the right side.

INVISIBLE ZIPPER

This type of zipper looks different from other zippers because the teeth are on the reverse and nothing except the pull is seen on the front. The zipper is inserted before the seam is stitched. A special invisible zipper foot is required for stitching this zipper in position.

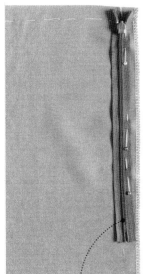

1 Mark the seam allowance with basting stitches.

2 Center the zipper over the baste line, right side of zipper to right side of fabric. Pin in place down one side.

3 Undo the zipper. Using the invisible zipper foot, stitch under the teeth from the top of the zipper. Stop when the foot hits the zipper pull and do two reverse stitches.

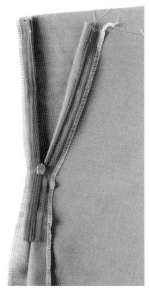

4 Pull the zipper up. Place the other side of the fabric to the zipper. Match along the upper edge. Pin the other side of the zipper tape in place.

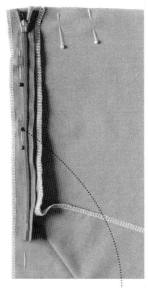

5 Open the zipper again. Using the invisible zipper foot, stitch down the other side of the zipper to attach to the other side of the fabric. Remove any basting stitches.

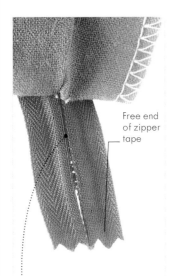

Free end of zipper tape

6 Close the zipper. On the wrong side at the bottom of the zipper the two rows of stitching that hold in the zipper should finish at the same place.

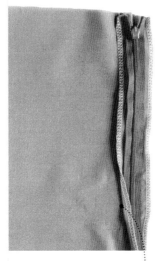

7 Stitch the seam below the zipper using the normal machine foot. There will be a small gap of about ⅛in (3mm) between the stitching line for the zipper and that for the seam.

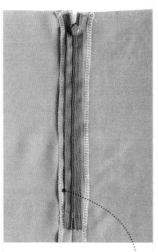

8 Stitch the last 1¼in (3cm) of the zipper tape just to the seam allowances. This will keep the zipper from pulling loose.

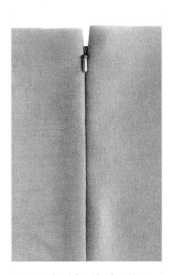

9 On the right side, the zipper is completely invisible, with only the pull visible at the top. Apply waistband or facing.

FACED FLY-FRONT ZIPPER

Level of difficulty ✳✳✳

Whether it's for a classic pair of pants or a pair of jeans, a fly front is the most common technique for inserting a pant zipper. The zipper usually has a facing behind it to prevent the zipper teeth from catching.

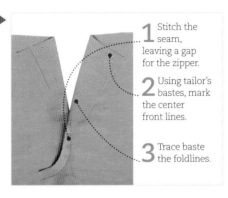

1 Stitch the seam, leaving a gap for the zipper.

2 Using tailor's bastes, mark the center front lines.

3 Trace baste the foldlines.

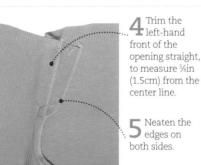

4 Trim the left-hand front of the opening straight, to measure ⅝in (1.5cm) from the center line.

5 Neaten the edges on both sides.

6 Fold the left-hand front along the foldline.

7 Place the fold adjacent to the zipper teeth and pin in place. The zipper may be too long; if so, it will extend beyond the top of the fabric.

8 Machine along the foldline using the zipper foot. Extend the machining past the seam stitching line.

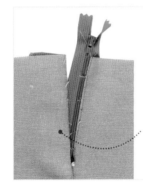

9 Fold the right-hand front along the foldline. Place the foldline over the zipper and pin to the machine stitching on the left-hand side.

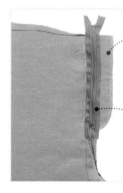

10 On the inside, pin the zipper tape to the fabric extension.

11 Machine the zipper tape to the fabric along the center of the tape.

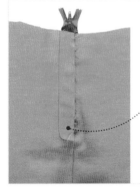

12 On the right side, topstitch around the zipper. Start stitching at the center front. Stitch a smooth curve.

13 Neaten all the edges of the fly-front facing, leaving the top edge raw.

14 On the wrong side, pin the facing to the left-hand side seam allowance. Ensure that the facing fully covers the zipper.

15 Machine to the seam allowance on the left-hand side.

16 Attach the waistband over the zipper and the facings. Trim facing and zipper.

17 Secure the lower edge of the facing on the right-hand side to the right-hand seam allowance.

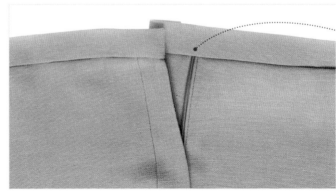

18 The waistband goes over the zipper and acts as the zipper stop. Attach a pant hook and eye.

BUTTONS

Buttons are one of the oldest forms of fastenings. They come in many shapes and sizes and can be made from a variety of materials including shell, bone, plastic, nylon, and metal. Buttons are sewn to the fabric either through holes on their face, or through a hole in a stalk called a shank, which is on the back. Buttons are normally sewn on by hand, although a two-hole button can be sewn on by machine.

SEWING ON A TWO-HOLE BUTTON

Level of difficulty ✱✱✱

This is the most popular type of button and requires a thread shank to be made when sewing in place. A toothpick on top of the button will help you to make the shank.

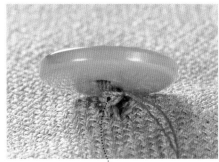

1 Position the button on the fabric. Start with a double stitch and double thread in the needle.

2 Place a toothpick on top of the button. Stitch up and down through the holes, going over the toothpick.

3 Remove the toothpick.

4 Wrap the thread around the thread loops under the button to make a shank.

5 Take the thread through to the back of the fabric.

6 Buttonhole stitch over the loop of threads on the back of the work.

SEWING ON A FOUR-HOLE BUTTON

Level of difficulty ✱✱✱

This is stitched in the same way as a two-hole button except that the threads make an X over the top of the button.

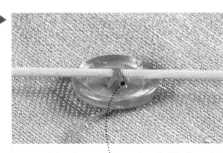

1 Position the button on the fabric. Place a toothpick on the button.

2 Using double thread, stitch diagonally between the holes of the button to make an X on top of the toothpick.

3 Remove the toothpick.

4 Wrap the thread around the thread loops under the button to make the shank.

5 On the reverse of the fabric, buttonhole stitch over the X-shaped thread loops.

SEWING ON A SHANKED BUTTON

When sewing this type of button in place, use a toothpick under the button to enable you to make a thread shank on the underside of the fabric.

Level of difficulty

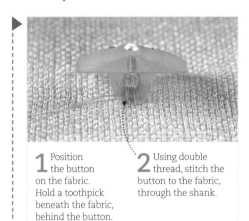

1 Position the button on the fabric. Hold a toothpick beneath the fabric, behind the button.

2 Using double thread, stitch the button to the fabric, through the shank.

3 Be sure each stitch goes around the toothpick beneath the fabric.

4 Remove the toothpick. Work buttonhole stitching over the looped thread shank beneath the fabric.

OVERSIZED AND LAYERED BUTTONS

There are some huge buttons available, many of which are really more decorative than functional. By layering buttons of varying sizes together, you can make an unusual feature on a garment.

Level of difficulty

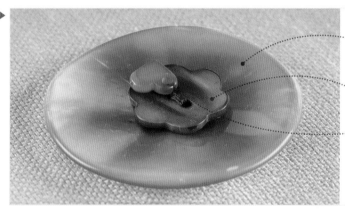

1 First position the oversized button on the fabric.

2 Top with a smaller button and stitch the two together to the fabric.

3 Place a small one-hole button on the layered buttons and attach to the thread using a buttonhole stitch.

POSITIONING BUTTONHOLES

Whether the buttonholes are to be stitched by machine or another type of buttonhole is to be made, the size of the button will need to be established in order to determine the position of the buttonhole on the fabric.

Level of difficulty ✱✱✱

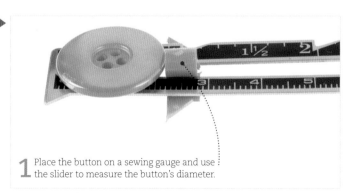

1 Place the button on a sewing gauge and use the slider to measure the button's diameter.

2 Work a row of basting stitches along the center front line of the right-hand side of the garment, as worn.

3 Work a second row of basting the diameter of the button away.

4 Lay the buttons between the baste lines. Stitch lines of basting at right angles to the first two basted rows, to mark the buttonhole positions.

VERTICAL OR HORIZONTAL?

Generally, buttonholes are only placed vertically on a garment with a placket or strip to contain the buttonhole. All other buttonholes should be horizontal. Any strain on the buttonhole will be taken by the end stop and keep the button from coming loose.

▶ HORIZONTAL BUTTONHOLES

These are positioned with the end stop on the basted center line.

▶ VERTICAL BUTTONHOLES

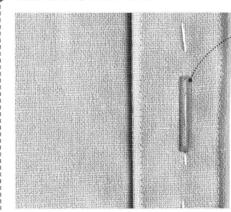

These are positioned with the buttonhole centered on the basted center line.

STAGES OF A BUTTONHOLE

A sewing machine stitches a buttonhole in three stages. The stitch can be varied slightly in width and length to suit the fabric, but the stitches need to be tight and close together.

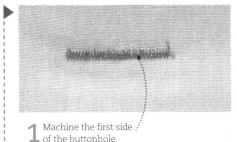

1 Machine the first side of the buttonhole.

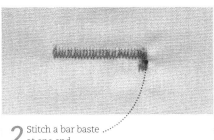

2 Stitch a bar baste at one end.

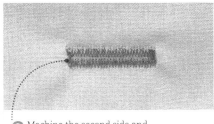

3 Machine the second side and bar baste at the other end.

MACHINE-MADE BUTTONHOLES

Level of difficulty ✱✱✱

Modern sewing machines can stitch various types of buttonholes, suitable for all kinds of garments. On many machines the button fits into a special foot, and a sensor on the machine determines the correct size of buttonhole. The width and length of the stitch can be altered to suit the fabric. Once the buttonhole has been stitched, always use a buttonhole chisel to slash through, to ensure that the cut is clean.

▶ BASIC BUTTONHOLE

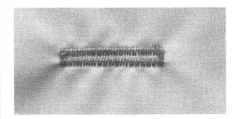

The most popular shape for a buttonhole is square on both ends.

▶ ROUND-END BUTTONHOLE

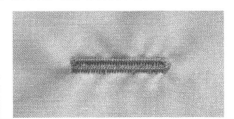

A buttonhole featuring one rounded end and one square end is used on lightweight jackets.

▶ KEYHOLE BUTTONHOLE

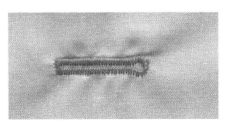

This is also called a tailor's buttonhole. It has a square end and a keyhole end and is used on jackets and coats.

GENERAL TECHNIQUES

COVERED BUTTONS

Covered buttons will add a professional finish to any jacket or other garment that you make. A purchased button-making gadget will enable you to create covered buttons very easily.

Level of difficulty **✱✱✱**

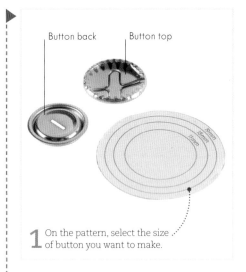

Button back   Button top

1 On the pattern, select the size of button you want to make.

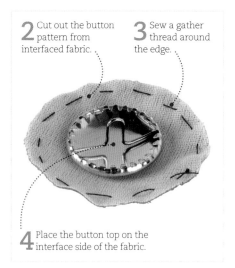

2 Cut out the button pattern from interfaced fabric.

3 Sew a gather thread around the edge.

4 Place the button top on the interface side of the fabric.

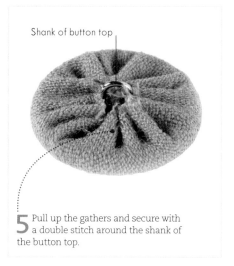

Shank of button top

5 Pull up the gathers and secure with a double stitch around the shank of the button top.

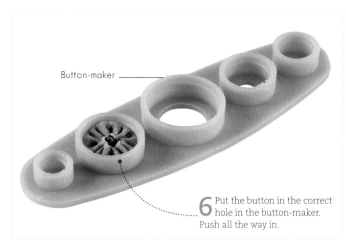

Button-maker

6 Put the button in the correct hole in the button-maker. Push all the way in.

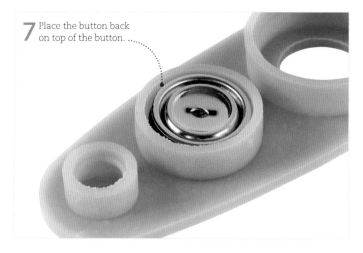

7 Place the button back on top of the button.

8 Take the other side of the button-maker and press down on the button back until it clicks into position.

9 Remove the button from the button-maker and check to be sure the back is firmly in place.

10 The finished covered button.

BUTTON PLACKET

A hidden button placket is a great addition to a shirt, a shirt dress, or a coat. It creates a discreet fastening that hides the buttons completely from view behind a fold. Topstitching the edge of the fold is optional but will produce a neat finish.

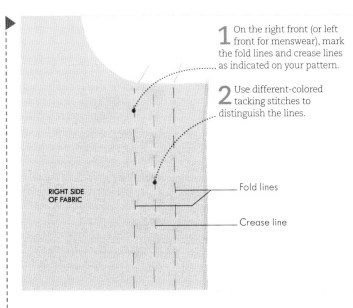

1 On the right front (or left front for menswear), mark the fold lines and crease lines as indicated on your pattern.

2 Use different-colored tacking stitches to distinguish the lines.

RIGHT SIDE OF FABRIC

Fold lines

Crease line

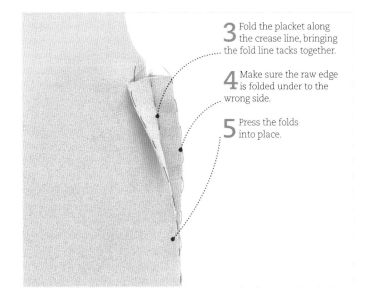

3 Fold the placket along the crease line, bringing the fold line tacks together.

4 Make sure the raw edge is folded under to the wrong side.

5 Press the folds into place.

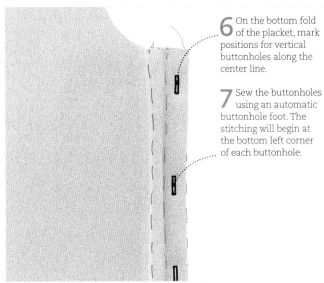

6 On the bottom fold of the placket, mark positions for vertical buttonholes along the center line.

7 Sew the buttonholes using an automatic buttonhole foot. The stitching will begin at the bottom left corner of each buttonhole.

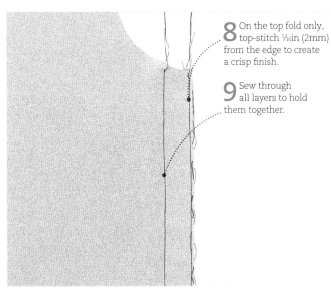

8 On the top fold only, top-stitch 1⁄16in (2mm) from the edge to create a crisp finish.

9 Sew through all layers to hold them together.

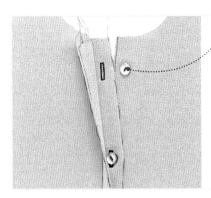

10 On the left front (or right front for menswear), attach the buttons so they align with the buttonholes.

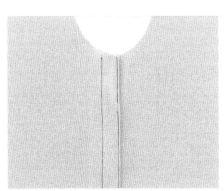

11 On the finished front, the buttons will be hidden from view behind the placket.

HOOKS AND EYES AND SNAPS

There are many alternative ways to fasten a garment. The different hooks and eyes shown below are normally used to finish the top end of a zipper to help prevent it from pulling open, but a row of hooks and eyes can also be used on its own as a decorative way of closing and opening a garment. Snap fasteners are good for children's clothing and uniforms, since they are easy to use. They are also commonly found on lightweight jackets, cardigans, and fleece jackets.

HOOKS AND EYES

Level of difficulty ✱✱✱

There are a multitude of different types of hook-and-eye fasteners. Purchased hooks and eyes are made from metal and are normally silver or black in color. Different-shaped hooks and eyes are used on different garments—large, broad hooks and eyes can be decorative and stitched to show on the outside, while tiny fasteners are meant to be discreet. A hook with a hand-worked eye produces a neat, close fastening.

▶ **ATTACHING HOOKS AND EYES**

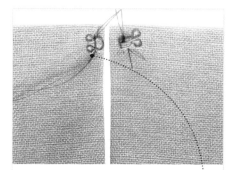

1 Secure the hook and eye in place with a basting stitch. Make sure they are in line with each other.

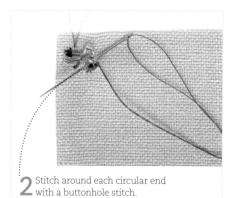

2 Stitch around each circular end with a buttonhole stitch.

3 Place a few overstitches under the hook to stop it from moving.

▶ **HAND-WORKED EYE**

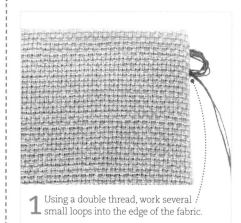

1 Using a double thread, work several small loops into the edge of the fabric.

2 Buttonhole stitch over these loops.

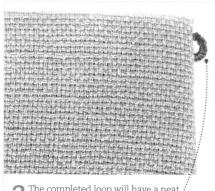

3 The completed loop will have a neat row of tight buttonhole stitches.

▶ PANT HOOK AND EYE

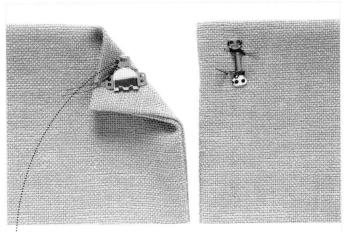

1 A hook-and-eye fastener for pant and skirt waistbands is large and flat. Baste both the hook and eye in position. Do not baste through their securing holes.

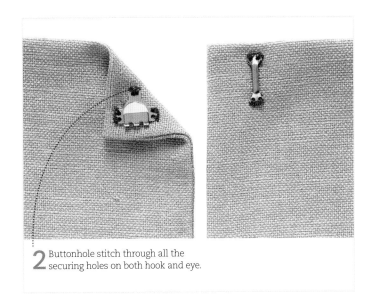

2 Buttonhole stitch through all the securing holes on both hook and eye.

SNAPS

Level of difficulty ✱✱✱

A snap is a ball-and-socket fastener that is used to hold two overlapping edges closed. The ball side goes on top and the socket side underneath. Snaps can be round or square and can be made from metal or plastic.

▶ ATTACHING SNAPS

1 Baste the ball and socket halves of the snap in place.

2 Secure permanently using a buttonhole stitch through each hole in the outer edges of the snap halves.

3 Remove the bastes.

▶ PLASTIC SNAPS

A plastic snap may be white or clear plastic and is usually square in shape. Stitch in place as for a metal snap.

GARMENTS

Page 144

CLASSIC A-LINE SKIRT

Page 148

BUTTON FRONT A-LINE SKIRT

Page 150

CLASSIC TAILORED SKIRT

Page 155

TAILORED EVENING SKIRT

Page 158

CLASSIC FLARED SKIRT

Page 163

FLARED SKIRT WITH YOKE

THE SKIRTS

This section is the perfect place for a beginner to start. It gives instructions for making three fabulous skirts and one simple variation of each. These stylish garments are straightforward and use a minimum number of pattern pieces.

SKIRT PATTERN ONE
CLASSIC A-LINE SKIRT

This A-line skirt will never go out of style and can be worn at all times of the year and on all occasions. It is also one of the easiest garments for a beginner to make. It has only three pattern pieces—a front, a back, and a waistband. The skirt needs to fit comfortably around the waist and across the tummy, so check your measurements carefully against the pattern.

YOU WILL NEED

- 51in (1.3m) x 59in (150cm) fabric
- 1 x spool matching all-purpose sewing thread
- 1 x spool contrasting all-purpose sewing thread for pattern marking
- 1 x 39in (1m) waistband interfacing
- 1 x 8½in (22cm) skirt zipper
- 1 x button

PREPARING THE PATTERN

This skirt is made using Skirt Pattern One. Follow the instructions to download the pattern in your size (see pp.10–11).

Corduroy

Linen

This skirt is made in a cotton print, but works well in a wide range of fabrics. For winter you could choose a cozy corduroy. For summer, linen will keep you cool and fresh.

A simple A-line skirt with a narrow waistband will flatter all figure types and all ages.

GARMENT CONSTRUCTION

This A-line skirt is shaped by the two darts in the front and back. There is a zipper on the left-hand side. The narrow waistband is fastened with a button and buttonhole fastening. The finished skirt should sit just above the knee.

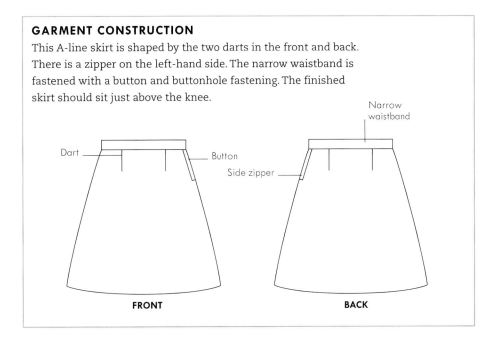

Dart — Button — Narrow waistband — Side zipper

FRONT   **BACK**

▶ HOW TO MAKE A CLASSIC A-LINE SKIRT

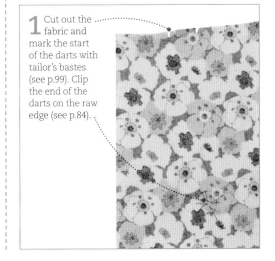

1 Cut out the fabric and mark the start of the darts with tailor's bastes (see p.99). Clip the end of the darts on the raw edge (see p.84).

2 Make the darts (see p.99) and press toward the center of the garment.

3 Neaten the side seams on the back and the front using a 3-thread serger stitch or a small zigzag stitch (see pp.92–93).

4 Stitch the LH (left-hand) side seam, leaving a gap for the zipper. Press the seam open, then insert a zipper (see p.129).

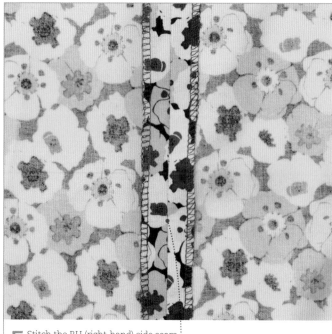

5 Stitch the RH (right-hand) side seam and press the seam open (see p.92).

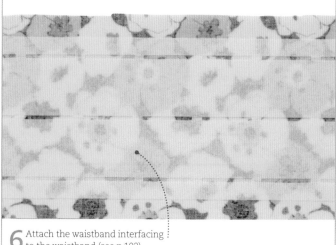

6 Attach the waistband interfacing to the waistband (see p.102).

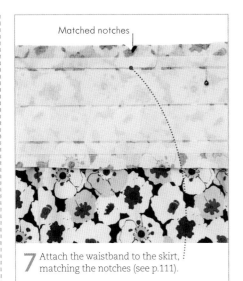

Matched notches

7 Attach the waistband to the skirt, matching the notches (see p.111).

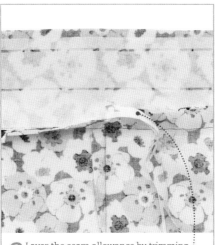

8 Layer the seam allowance by trimming the waistband side of the seam to half its width (see p.97). Press toward the waistband.

9 Fold the waistband RS (right side) to RS. Pin, then stitch the ends of the waistband.

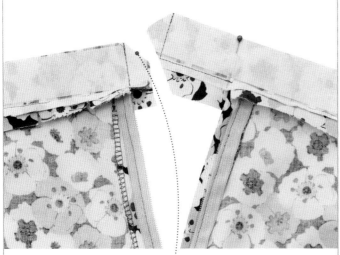

10 Clip the ends of the waistband to reduce bulk.

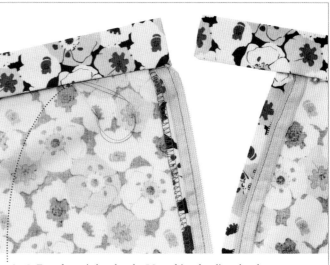

11 Turn the waistband to the RS, pushing the clipped ends out. Fold under the raw edge, then pin and hand stitch in place.

12 Neaten the hem edge by serging (see p.126). Turn up a 1½in (4cm) hem and hand stitch in place.

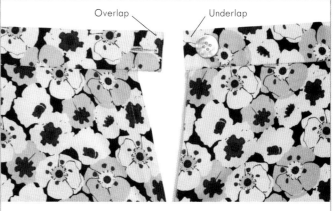

Overlap   Underlap

13 Make a buttonhole on the overlap of the waistband (see p.135). Sew a button on the underlap (see pp.133–134).

SKIRT PATTERN ONE VARIATION
BUTTON FRONT A-LINE SKIRT

This variation of the A-line skirt is a little more complicated and is the perfect next step for a novice sewer. To make it, you will shorten the basic pattern and extend the center front to create the pleat. The buttons on the pleat are purely decorative. This skirt would make a great winter or fall wardrobe staple.

YOU WILL NEED

- 48in (1.2m) x 59in (150cm) fabric
- 1 x spool matching all-purpose sewing thread
- 1 x spool contrasting all-purpose sewing thread for pattern marking
- 39 in (1m) x waistband interfacing
- 7in (18cm) skirt zipper
- 7 x buttons

PREPARING THE PATTERN

This skirt is made using Skirt Pattern One. Follow the instructions to download the pattern in your size (see pp.10–11).

Denim

Cotton twill

This skirt is made in corduroy, but denim or cotton twill also work well.

GARMENT CONSTRUCTION

This variation of the Classic A-line skirt is shorter. It has a zipper on the left-hand side and features a stitched pleat to which buttons have been sewn for decoration.

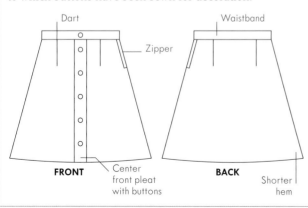

Dart · Waistband · Zipper · **FRONT** · Center front pleat with buttons · **BACK** · Shorter hem

▶ HOW TO MAKE THE BUTTON FRONT A-LINE SKIRT

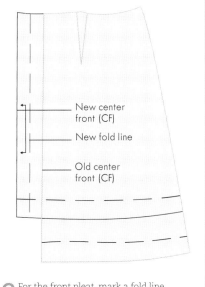

New center front (CF)

New fold line

Old center front (CF)

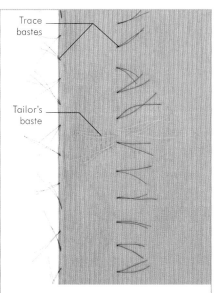

Trace bastes

Tailor's baste

1 To shorten the hem, copy the front and back pattern pieces. Mark the hemline. Mark the new hemline 4in (10cm) above the old hemline. Draw a new cutting line 1½in (4cm) below the new hemline.

New hemline
New cutting line
Old hemline

2 For the front pleat, mark a fold line 1¼in (3cm) to the left of the CF (center front). Mark the new CF 1¼in (3cm) to the left of the new fold line.

3 Cut out the fabric. On the skirt front, mark the fold line and the CF with trace bastes (see p.84). Mark a point on the fold line, 6in (15cm) from the hem edge, with a tailor's baste.

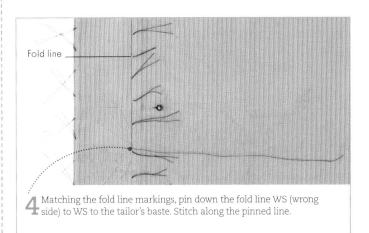

Fold line

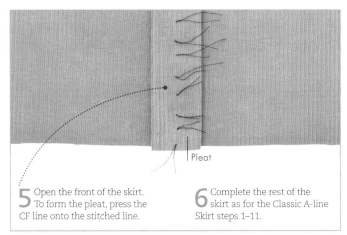

Pleat

4 Matching the fold line markings, pin down the fold line WS (wrong side) to WS to the tailor's baste. Stitch along the pinned line.

5 Open the front of the skirt. To form the pleat, press the CF line onto the stitched line.

6 Complete the rest of the skirt as for the Classic A-line Skirt steps 1–11.

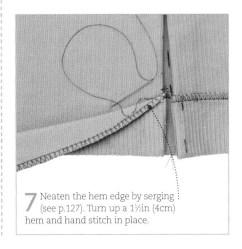

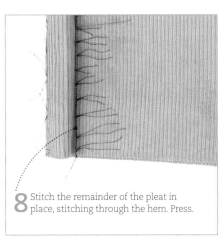

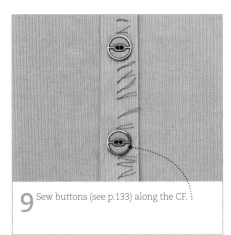

7 Neaten the hem edge by serging (see p.127). Turn up a 1½in (4cm) hem and hand stitch in place.

8 Stitch the remainder of the pleat in place, stitching through the hem. Press.

9 Sew buttons (see p.133) along the CF.

SKIRT PATTERN TWO
CLASSIC TAILORED SKIRT

A straight skirt is a staple garment in every wardrobe. Paired with the Classic Blazer (see pp.264–273) it could be the bottom half of a suit, or could just be a simple, hardworking, everyday skirt. The vent in the center back hemline ensures that you have freedom of movement to walk easily. The skirt should be close-fitting, so choose the pattern size by your hip measurement.

SKIRTS

YOU WILL NEED

- 39in (1m) x 59in (150cm) fabric
- 1 x spool matching all-purpose sewing thread
- 1 x spool contrasting all-purpose sewing thread for pattern marking
- 20in (50cm) lightweight fusible interfacing
- 1 x 7in (18cm) skirt zipper

PREPARING THE PATTERN

This skirt is made using Skirt Pattern Two. Follow the instructions to download the pattern in your size (see pp.10–11).

Wool worsted   **Matka silk**

This skirt is made in lightweight tweed, but this style would look great in many fabrics. Choose from suitings, cottons, or silks.

A must-have skirt for everyone's wardrobe, this classic straight skirt with a back vent will never go out of fashion.

GARMENT CONSTRUCTION

This close-fitting skirt narrows slightly toward the hem and has a center back vent. One dart in the front and two in the back shape the skirt to the waist and there is a zipper in the center back. The waistline is finished with a facing.

Dart

Center back zipper

Vent

FRONT   **BACK**

▶ HOW TO MAKE THE CLASSIC TAILORED SKIRT

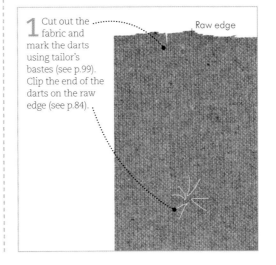

1 Cut out the fabric and mark the darts using tailor's bastes (see p.99). Clip the end of the darts on the raw edge (see p.84).

Raw edge

2 Make the darts (see p.99) and press toward the center of the garment.

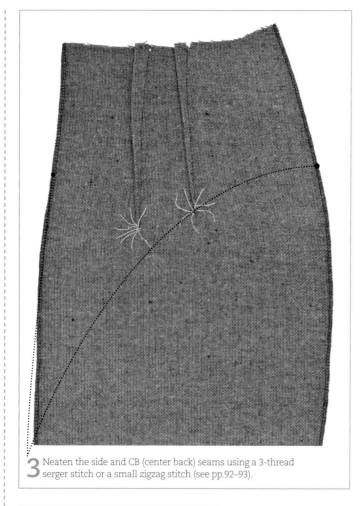

3 Neaten the side and CB (center back) seams using a 3-thread serger stitch or a small zigzag stitch (see pp.92–93).

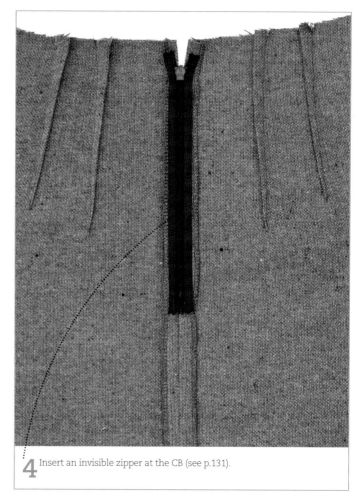

4 Insert an invisible zipper at the CB (see p.131).

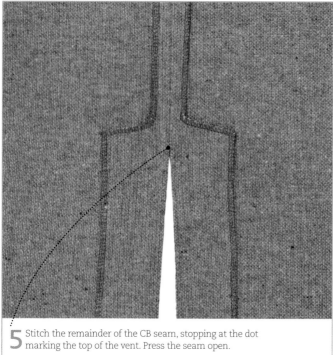

5 Stitch the remainder of the CB seam, stopping at the dot marking the top of the vent. Press the seam open.

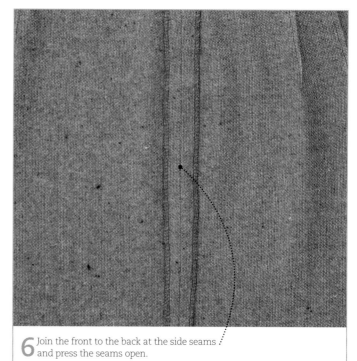

6 Join the front to the back at the side seams and press the seams open.

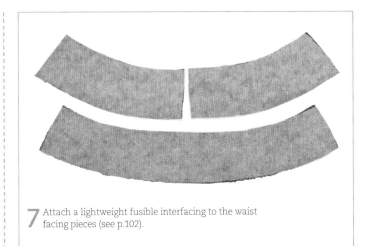

7 Attach a lightweight fusible interfacing to the waist facing pieces (see p.102).

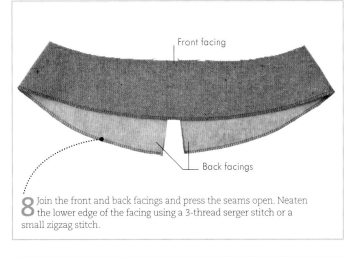

Front facing

Back facings

8 Join the front and back facings and press the seams open. Neaten the lower edge of the facing using a 3-thread serger stitch or a small zigzag stitch.

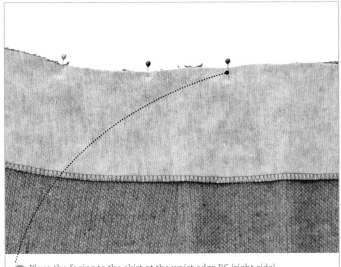

9 Place the facing to the skirt at the waist edge RS (right side) to RS, matching the side seams and matching at the top of the zipper. Pin and machine.

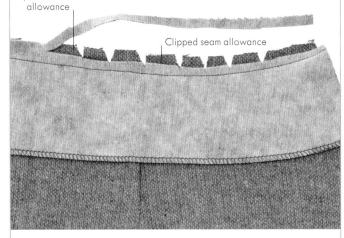

Layered seam allowance

Clipped seam allowance

10 Layer the seam allowance by trimming the facing side of the seam to half its width. Clip the seam allowance to reduce bulk (see p.97).

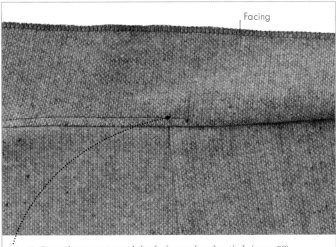

Facing

11 Press the seam toward the facing and understitch (see p.98).

12 Turn the facing to the inside then, at the CB, fold the edge of the facing in to meet the zipper tape. Pin and hand stitch in place.

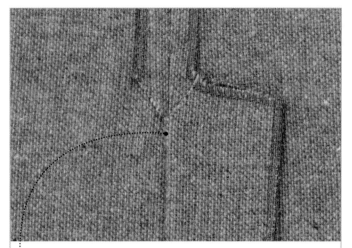

13 At the vent, snip through the seam allowance on the LH (left-hand) side and press the seam extension to the RH (right-hand) side.

14 Machine the extension in place.

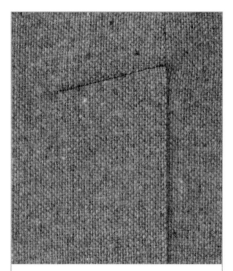

15 From the RS, the top of the vent can be seen as a line of stitching.

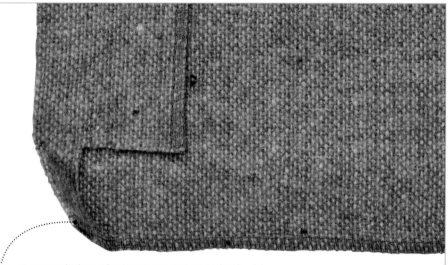

16 Neaten the hem edge (see pp.126–127) On each side of the vent, remove the surplus fabric in the hem allowance.

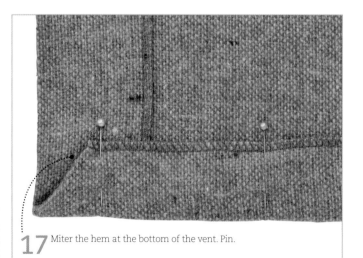

17 Miter the hem at the bottom of the vent. Pin.

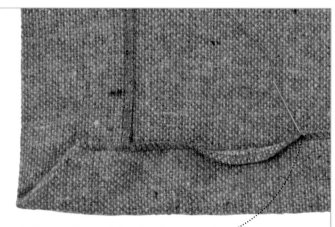

18 Turn up the remainder of the hem, pin and hand stitch in place.

SKIRT PATTERN TWO VARIATION
TAILORED EVENING SKIRT

For this version of the skirt you will add a lining for a more luxurious finish. You will also shorten the skirt, which means you no longer need a center back vent to make walking easier. This skirt has been made in silk for an evening out, but would also work well in a heavier fabric.

YOU WILL NEED

- 36in (90cm) x 59in (150cm) fabric
- 36in (90cm) x 59in (150cm) lining fabric
- 1 x spool matching all-purpose sewing thread
- 1 x spool contrasting all-purpose sewing thread for pattern marking
- 20in (50cm) lightweight fusible interfacing
- 1 x 7in (18cm) skirt zipper

PREPARING THE PATTERN

This skirt is made using Skirt Pattern Two. Follow the instructions to download the pattern in your size (see pp.10–11).

Tweed

Wool suiting

This skirt is made in silk dupioni. Other silks, such as silk brocade, tweeds, or suitings could also be used.

GARMENT CONSTRUCTION

This lined variation of the Classic Tailored Skirt is shorter without a back vent. There is a zipper in the center back. The waistline is finished with a facing. The lining is cut from the same pattern pieces as the skirt.

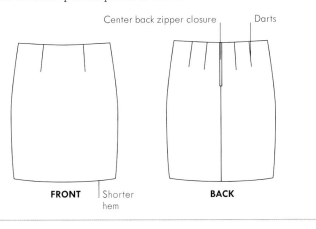

Center back zipper closure   Darts

FRONT   Shorter hem

BACK

SKIRTS

▶ **HOW TO MAKE THE TAILORED EVENING SKIRT**

New hemline

New cutting line

Old hemline

1 To shorten the front of the skirt, copy the skirt front pattern piece. Mark the hemline. Mark the new hemline 3¼in (8cm) above the old hemline. Draw a new cutting line 1½in (4cm) below the new hemline.

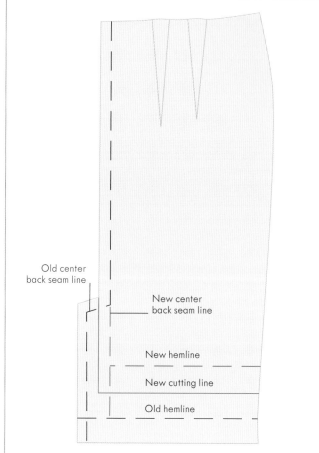

Old center
back seam line

New center
back seam line

New hemline

New cutting line

Old hemline

2 To shorten the back of the skirt, copy the skirt back pattern piece. Shorten the skirt as for step 1. To remove the vent, extend the CB (center back) seam line to the hemline.

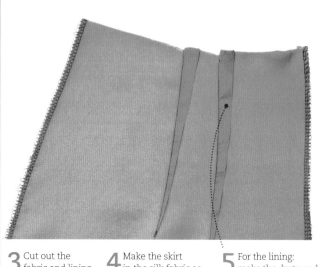

3 Cut out the fabric and lining using the new pattern pieces.

4 Make the skirt in the silk fabric as for the Classic Tailored Skirt steps 1–6.

5 For the lining: make the darts and neaten the side and CB seams as for the skirt.

6 Stitch the CB seam in the lining between the marked dots, leaving the seam above open for the zipper. Press open.

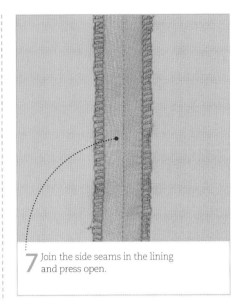

7 Join the side seams in the lining and press open.

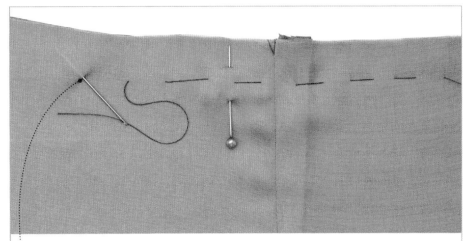

8 Pin and baste the lining to the skirt at the waist edge WS (wrong side) to WS, matching the darts and seams.

9 Attach the facing to the skirt and lining as for the Classic Tailored Skirt steps 7–11.

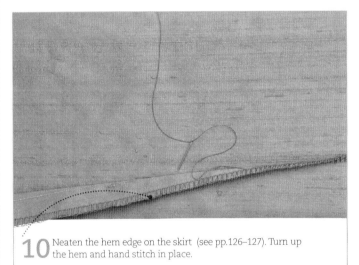

10 Neaten the hem edge on the skirt (see pp.126–127). Turn up the hem and hand stitch in place.

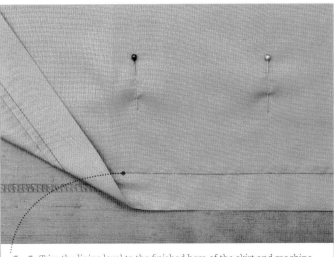

11 Trim the lining level to the finished hem of the skirt and machine a ¾in (2cm) double-turn hem (see p.128).

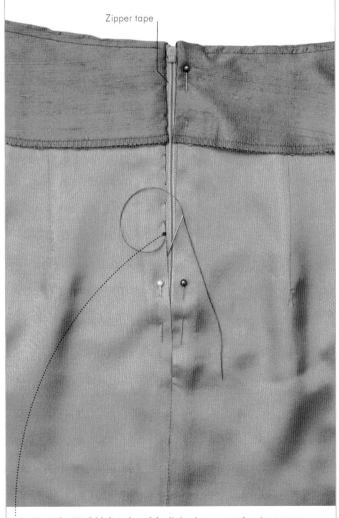

Zipper tape

12 At the CB, fold the edge of the lining in to meet the zipper tape. Pin and hand stitch in place.

SKIRT PATTERN THREE
CLASSIC FLARED SKIRT

This lined, flared skirt is flattering, versatile, and simple to create. It is cut on the bias to create the flare and is a simple shape to start with to practice sewing your own clothes. If you are making the skirt in a light, thin fabric you will need to line it, as shown here, to make sure the skirt hangs properly and to stop see-through. If you make it in a "scratchy," heavier material, you might also need a lining to make the skirt more comfortable to wear.

YOU WILL NEED

- 63in (1.6m) x 59in (150cm) skirt fabric
- 63in (1.6m) x 59in (150cm) lining fabric
- 36in (90cm) x 6in (15cm) medium-weight fusible interfacing
- 1 x spool of matching all-purpose sewing thread
- 1 x spool of contrasting all-purpose sewing thread for pattern marking
- 1 x 8in (20cm) invisible zipper

PREPARING THE PATTERN

This skirt is made from Skirt Pattern Three. Follow the instructions to download the pattern in your size (see pp.10–11).

Dupioni silk

Duchesse satin

This skirt was made in cotton but would also work well if made from dupioni silk and duchesse satin.

If made from a soft, flowing fabric this smart skirt it will become your favorite summer garment. Make it in a slightly heavier fabric for a must-have fall skirt.

GARMENT CONSTRUCTION

This bias-cut flared skirt is fully lined. It is cut in two parts so only has side seams and front and back darting at the waist. There is an invisible zipper on the left-hand side.

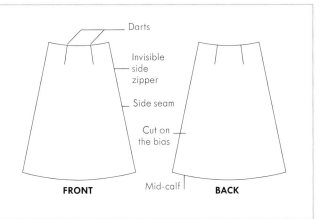

Darts

Invisible side zipper

Side seam

Cut on the bias

FRONT　　Mid-calf　　**BACK**

▶ HOW TO MAKE THE FLARED SKIRT

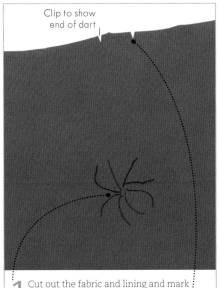

Clip to show end of dart

1 Cut out the fabric and lining and mark the start of the darts with tailor's tacks (see p.99). Clip the end of the darts on the raw edge (see p.84).

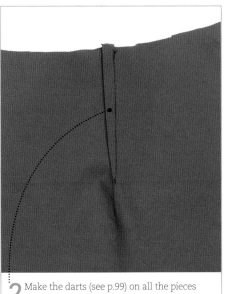

2 Make the darts (see p.99) on all the pieces and press toward the center of the garment.

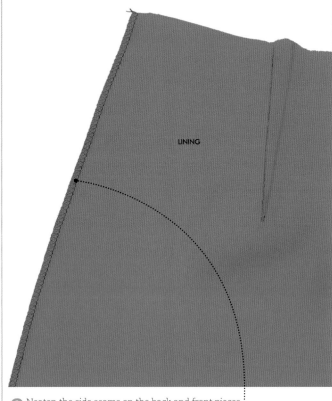

3 Neaten the side seams on the back and front pieces of the main fabric and lining using a 3-thread overlock stitch or a small zigzag stitch (see pp.92-93).

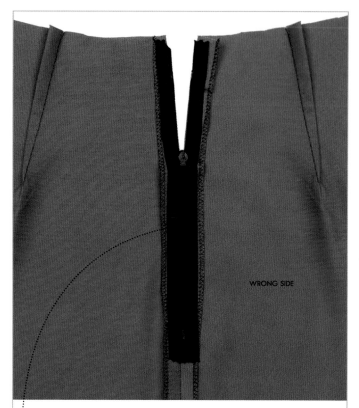

4 Sew the LH (left-hand) side seam of the main fabric, leaving a gap for the zipper. Press the seam open, then insert the zipper (see p.132).

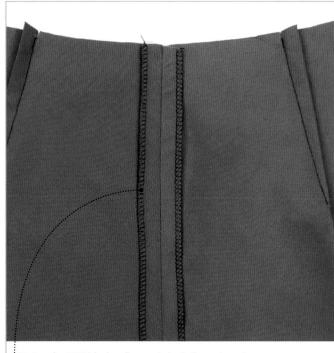

5 Sew the RH (right-hand) seam in both the main and lining fabrics. Press the seams open (see p.92).

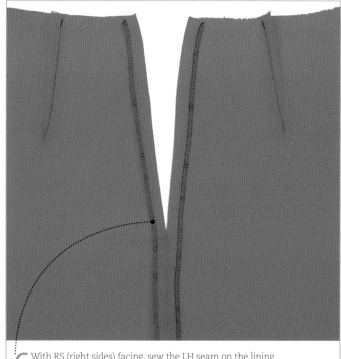

6 With RS (right sides) facing, sew the LH seam on the lining, leaving a gap for the zipper. Press seam open.

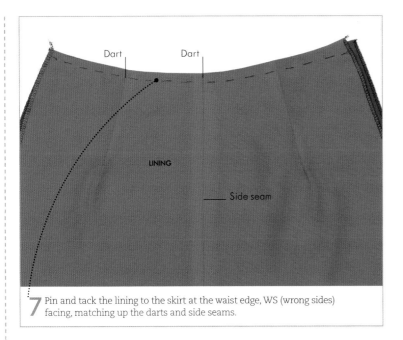

7 Pin and tack the lining to the skirt at the waist edge, WS (wrong sides) facing, matching up the darts and side seams.

8 Attach a medium-weight fusible interfacing to the WS of the waist facing pieces (see p.102).

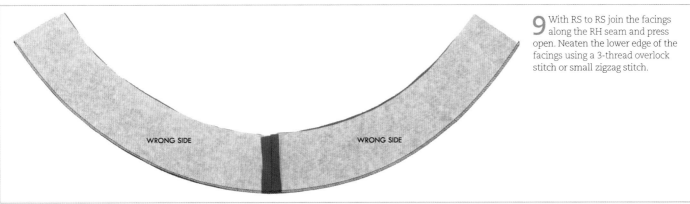

9 With RS to RS join the facings along the RH seam and press open. Neaten the lower edge of the facings using a 3-thread overlock stitch or small zigzag stitch.

10 Place the facing to the skirt at the waist edge RS to RS, matching the side seams and the top of the zipper. Fold the short ends of the facing back, so they are next to the zipper when turned. Pin and sew.

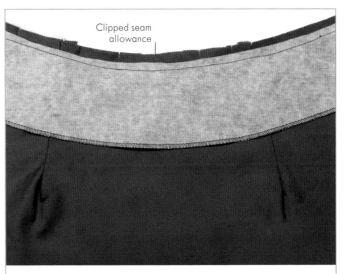

11 Layer the seam allowance by trimming the facing side of the seam to half its width. Clip the seam to reduce bulk (see p.97).

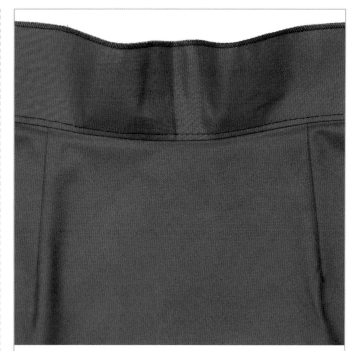

12 Press the seam toward the facing and undersew (see p.98).

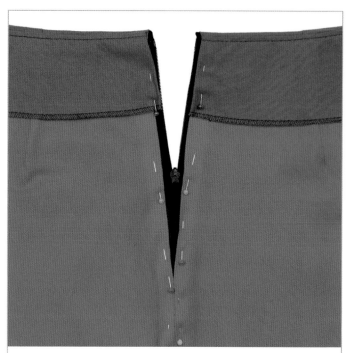

13 Turn the facing to the inside and fold the edge of the facing in to meet the zipper tape. Pin and hand stitch the lining and facing around the zipper.

14 Neaten the hem edge of the main fabric using a 3-thread overlock stitch or a small zigzag stitch. Turn up ³/₈in (1cm) following instructions for a curved hem finish (see p.128). Sew or hand stitch in place.

15 Trim the lining level to the finished hem of the skirt and sew a ³/₄in (2cm) double-turn hem (see p.128). Press. Trim the hem back to within ¹/₈in (3mm) of the sewn line without cutting the stitches.

SKIRT PATTERN THREE VARIATION
FLARED SKIRT WITH YOKE

A yoke has been added to this skirt pattern to create a more formal, fitted look. The lower section of the skirt is cut on the bias which means it drapes well and creates movement when you walk. To determine the length required, measure down your outside leg to just below the knee. The topstitching can be done in a matching thread or you can use a contrasting-colored thread for an added feature.

YOU WILL NEED
- 63in (1.6m) x 59in (150cm) fabric
- 1 x spool of matching all-purpose sewing thread
- 1 x spool of matching or contrasting sewing thread for topstitch
- 1 x spool of contrasting all-purpose sewing thread for pattern marking
- 16in (40cm) x 20in (50cm) lightweight fusible interfacing
- 1 x 8in (20cm) invisible zipper

PREPARING THE PATTERN
The skirt is made by altering Skirt Pattern Three. Follow the instructions to download the pattern in your size (see pp.10–11).

This skirt was made in cotton but eco-viscose or bio-linen would also work well.

Eco-viscose   **Bio-linen**

GARMENT CONSTRUCTION
This skirt has a topstitched yoke, a bias-cut flared lower section that ends just below the knee, and an invisible side zipper.

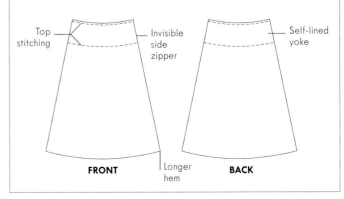

Top stitching · Invisible side zipper · Self-lined yoke

FRONT   Longer hem   **BACK**

▶ **HOW TO MAKE THE FLARED SKIRT WITH YOKE**

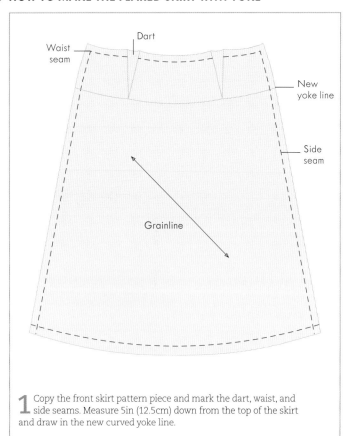

1 Copy the front skirt pattern piece and mark the dart, waist, and side seams. Measure 5in (12.5cm) down from the top of the skirt and draw in the new curved yoke line.

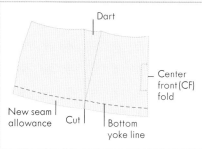

2 Copy the yoke pattern piece and add a ⅝in (1.5cm) seam allowance along the bottom edge. Cut out this new pattern piece.

3 Working on the new pattern piece, cut through the seam allowance from the bottom yoke line to the point of the dart.

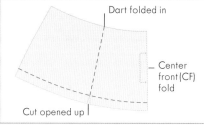

4 Join together the RH (right-hand) line of the dart to the LH (left-hand) line of the dart. The cut made in step 4 will open out to form a V-shape. This gives a curve to the yoke.

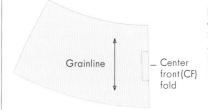

5 Copy the yoke with the V shape to make a new pattern piece. Add the pattern markings for the grainline and CF (center front).

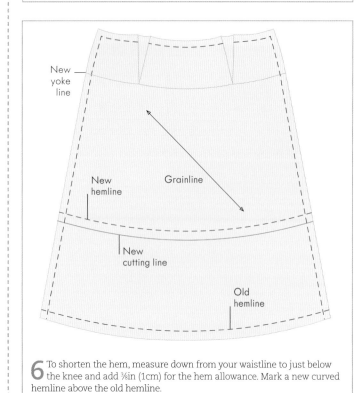

6 To shorten the hem, measure down from your waistline to just below the knee and add ⅜in (1cm) for the hem allowance. Mark a new curved hemline above the old hemline.

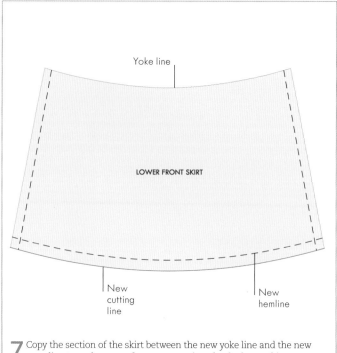

7 Copy the section of the skirt between the new yoke line and the new seamline to make a new front pattern piece for the lower skirt.

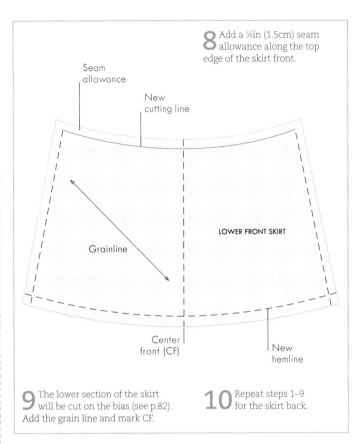

Seam allowance

New cutting line

8 Add a ⅝in (1.5cm) seam allowance along the top edge of the skirt front.

Grainline

LOWER FRONT SKIRT

Center front (CF)

New hemline

9 The lower section of the skirt will be cut on the bias (see p.82). Add the grain line and mark CF.

10 Repeat steps 1–9 for the skirt back.

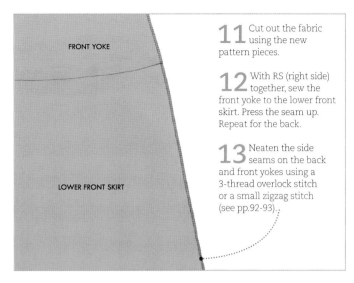

FRONT YOKE

LOWER FRONT SKIRT

11 Cut out the fabric using the new pattern pieces.

12 With RS (right side) together, sew the front yoke to the lower front skirt. Press the seam up. Repeat for the back.

13 Neaten the side seams on the back and front yokes using a 3-thread overlock stitch or a small zigzag stitch (see pp.92-93).

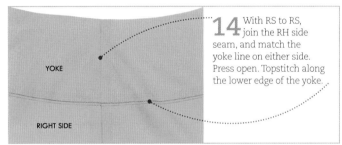

YOKE

RIGHT SIDE

14 With RS to RS, join the RH side seam, and match the yoke line on either side. Press open. Topstitch along the lower edge of the yoke.

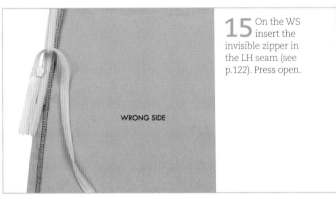

WRONG SIDE

15 On the WS insert the invisible zipper in the LH seam (see p.122). Press open.

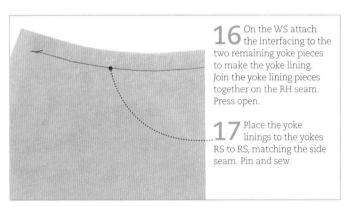

16 On the WS attach the interfacing to the two remaining yoke pieces to make the yoke lining. Join the yoke lining pieces together on the RH seam. Press open.

17 Place the yoke linings to the yokes RS to RS, matching the side seam. Pin and sew.

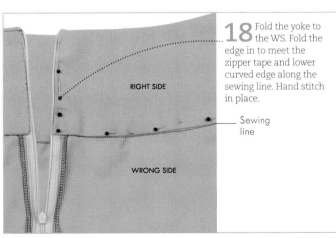

RIGHT SIDE

WRONG SIDE

18 Fold the yoke to the WS. Fold the edge in to meet the zipper tape and lower curved edge along the sewing line. Hand stitch in place.

Sewing line

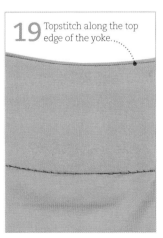

19 Topstitch along the top edge of the yoke.

20 Neaten the hem edge (see pp.126-127). Turn up ⅜in (1cm) following instructions for a curved hem finish (see p.118). Machine or hand stitch in place.

DRESS PATTERN ONE

VARIATIONS

Page 168

CLASSIC SHIFT DRESS

Page 173

SHORT-SLEEVED SHIFT DRESS

Page 177

SLEEVELESS SHIFT DRESS

DRESS PATTERN TWO

VARIATIONS

Page 180

CLASSIC WAISTED DRESS

Page 185

SHORT-SLEEVED WAISTED DRESS

Page 187

SLEEVELESS WAISTED DRESS

Page 191

WAISTED COCKTAIL DRESS

DRESS PATTERN THREE

VARIATIONS

Page 196

CLASSIC EMPIRE WAIST DRESS

Page 201

SLEEVELESS EMPIRE WAIST DRESS

Page 204

LONG EMPIRE WAIST DRESS

DRESS PATTERN FOUR

VARIATION

Page 208

CLASSIC SHIRTDRESS

Page 214

SHIRTDRESS WITH ROLL-TAB SLEEVES

THE DRESSES

The four classic dresses in this section can be adapted to make a total of twelve styles, some unlined and some lined. The dresses suit all ages and can take you to any occasion at any time of the year, depending on the fabric you choose.

DRESS PATTERN ONE
CLASSIC SHIFT DRESS

A classic fitted dress like this never goes out of fashion and you can make it in almost any fabric. In fact, you'll love it so much that you'll want it in several different ones. The dress must fit well across the bust and in the hip area, so choose your pattern by your bust measurement and alter the waist and hip as required. As with any fitted style, it's best to make the pattern in muslin first and try it out.

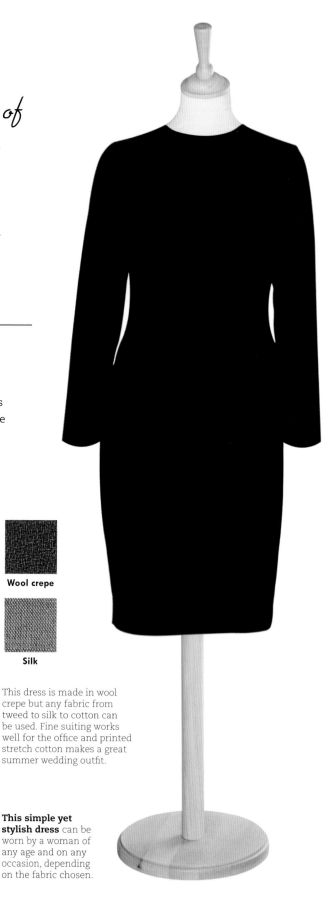

YOU WILL NEED

- 67in (1.7m) x 59in (150cm) fabric
- 1 x spool matching all-purpose sewing thread
- 1 x spool contrasting all-purpose sewing thread for pattern marking
- 20in (50cm) lightweight interfacing
- 1 x 22in (56cm) zipper

PREPARING THE PATTERN

This dress is made using Dress Pattern One. Follow the instructions to download the pattern in your size (see pp.10–11).

GARMENT CONSTRUCTION

This unlined one-piece fitted dress has darts at the bust and waist to ensure a fitted silhouette. It also has a zipper in the center back and a center-back vent. It features a high round neck and long set-in sleeves. The hemline just brushes the knee.

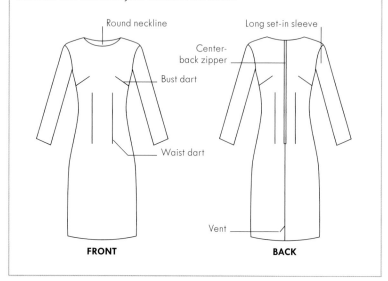

Round neckline
Long set-in sleeve
Center-back zipper
Bust dart
Waist dart
Vent

FRONT   **BACK**

Wool crepe

Silk

This dress is made in wool crepe but any fabric from tweed to silk to cotton can be used. Fine suiting works well for the office and printed stretch cotton makes a great summer wedding outfit.

This simple yet stylish dress can be worn by a woman of any age and on any occasion, depending on the fabric chosen.

▶ **HOW TO MAKE THE CLASSIC SHIFT DRESS**

1 Cut out the fabric and mark the darts using tailor's bastes (see p.85).

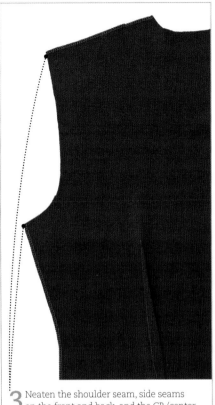

2 Make the plain and the contour darts (see pp.99–100).

3 Neaten the shoulder seam, side seams on the front and back, and the CB (center back) seams, using either a 3-thread serger stitch or a small zigzag stitch (see pp.92–93).

4 Insert a zipper of your choice in the CB. A concealed zipper is used here (see p.131).

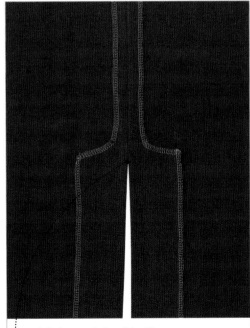

5 Stitch the remainder of the CB seam stopping at the dot marking the top of the vent. Press the seam open.

6 Join the front to the back at the shoulder and side seams. Press the seams open.

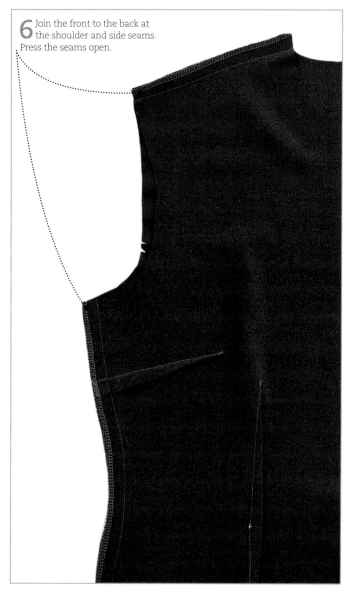

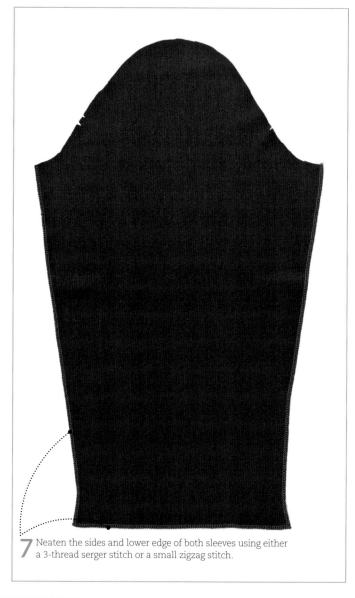

7 Neaten the sides and lower edge of both sleeves using either a 3-thread serger stitch or a small zigzag stitch.

8 Machine the sleeve seam and press it open.

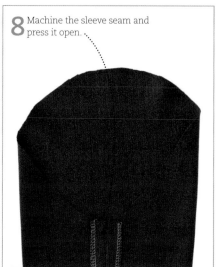

9 Using the longest stitch available, machine two rows of ease stitches through the sleeve head (see p.114).

Ease stitches

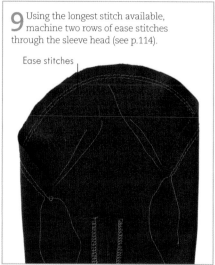

10 Insert the sleeve into the armhole, RS (right side) to RS, remembering to pin and stitch from the sleeve side (see p.114).

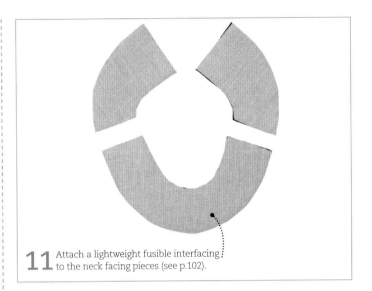

11 Attach a lightweight fusible interfacing to the neck facing pieces (see p.102).

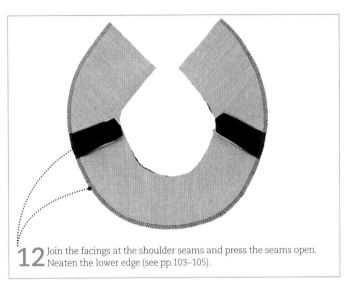

12 Join the facings at the shoulder seams and press the seams open. Neaten the lower edge (see pp.103–105).

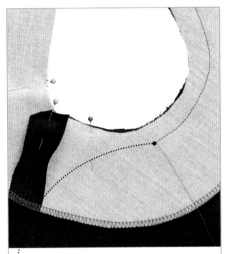

13 Place the facings to the neck edge of the dress RS to RS, matching the seams. Pin and machine.

14 Layer the seam allowance by trimming the facing side of the seam to half its width. Clip the seam allowance to reduce bulk (see p.97).

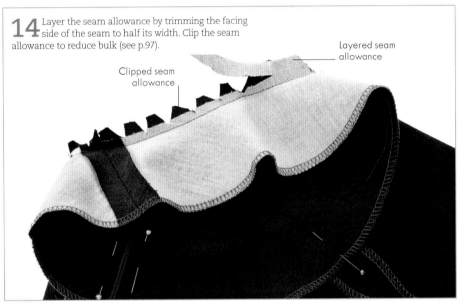

Layered seam allowance

Clipped seam allowance

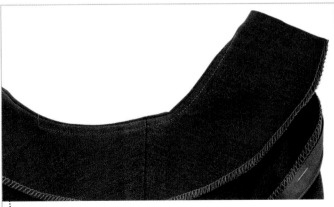

15 Press the seam toward the facing and understitch (see p.98).

16 Pin and hand stitch the facing to the seam allowance at the shoulder seams.

17 At the CB, fold the edge of the facing in to meet the zipper tape. Pin and hand stitch in place.

18 From the RS, the back neck edge should now look neatly finished.

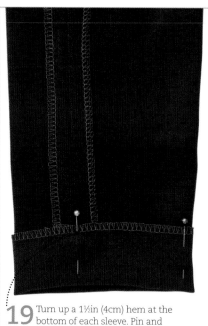

19 Turn up a 1½in (4cm) hem at the bottom of each sleeve. Pin and hand stitch in place.

20 Neaten the hem edge (see pp.126–127). On each side of the vent, remove a square of surplus fabric in the hem allowance.

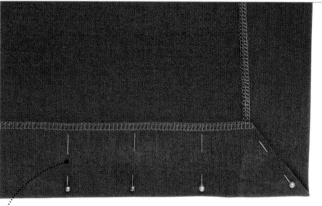

21 Miter the hem at the bottom of the vent and pin. Turn up the remainder of the hem and pin.

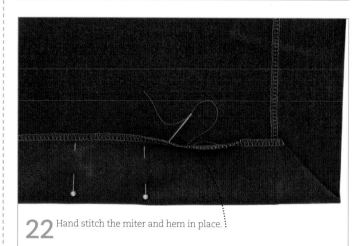

22 Hand stitch the miter and hem in place.

23 Machine through all layers at the top of the vent to secure.

DRESS PATTERN ONE VARIATION
SHORT-SLEEVED SHIFT DRESS

With this garment you'll be introduced to the techniques of lining a dress and shortening a sleeve. A lined dress is a pleasure to wear. The lining also helps prevent fabrics with a looser weave from stretching. With fine cottons or linens, the lining will keep the dress from being see-through.

YOU WILL NEED

- 67in (1.7m) x 59in (150cm) fabric
- 67in (1.7m) lining fabric
- 1 x spool matching all-purpose sewing thread
- 1 x spool contrasting all-purpose sewing thread for pattern marking
- 20in (50cm) lightweight interfacing
- 1 x 22in (56cm) zipper

PREPARING THE PATTERN

This dress is made using Dress Pattern One. Follow the instructions to download the pattern in your size (see pp.10–11).

GARMENT CONSTRUCTION

This lined variation of the Classic Shift Dress has a lower neckline and a short set-in sleeve. It has a zipper in the center back and a center-back vent. The lining is cut from the same pattern pieces as the dress.

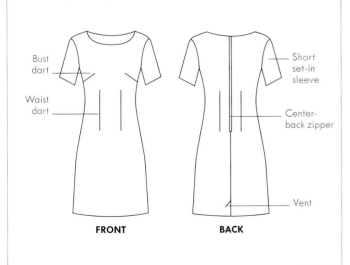

FRONT

Bust dart

Waist dart

BACK

Short set-in sleeve

Center-back zipper

Vent

Wool suiting

Dress-weight linen

This dress is made in tweed, but bouclé wools, suiting or linen and cotton would also work well.

▶ **HOW TO MAKE THE SHORT-SLEEVED SHIFT DRESS**

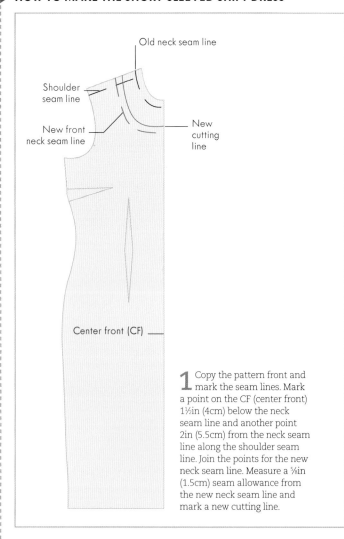

Old neck seam line

Shoulder seam line

New front neck seam line

New cutting line

Center front (CF)

1 Copy the pattern front and mark the seam lines. Mark a point on the CF (center front) 1½in (4cm) below the neck seam line and another point 2in (5.5cm) from the neck seam line along the shoulder seam line. Join the points for the new neck seam line. Measure a ⅝in (1.5cm) seam allowance from the new neck seam line and mark a new cutting line.

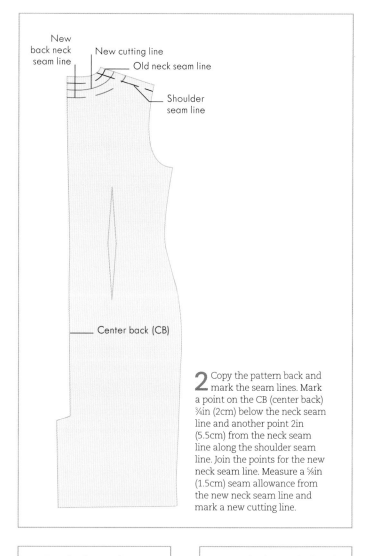

New back neck seam line

New cutting line

Old neck seam line

Shoulder seam line

Center back (CB)

2 Copy the pattern back and mark the seam lines. Mark a point on the CB (center back) ¾in (2cm) below the neck seam line and another point 2in (5.5cm) from the neck seam line along the shoulder seam line. Join the points for the new neck seam line. Measure a ⅝in (1.5cm) seam allowance from the new neck seam line and mark a new cutting line.

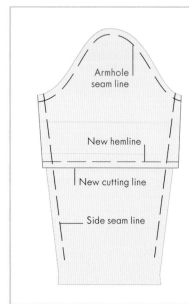

Armhole seam line

New hemline

New cutting line

Side seam line

3 To shorten the sleeve, copy the sleeve and mark the seam lines. Mark a point either side of the sleeve, 6in (15cm) below the armhole seam lines. Join these points together to make a new hemline. Draw a new cutting line ⅝in (1.5cm) below the new hemline. (If you have a slightly fuller arm you may need to extend the new hemline by ⅝in [1.5cm] on each side. Draw new cutting lines, allowing a ⅝in [1.5cm] seam allowance.)

4 To make the new front neck facing pattern piece, copy the new front neck seam line and cutting line from step 1 onto a piece of paper. Measure points 2in (5cm) from the seam line. Join these points together to create a new cutting line. Cut out along these lines.

New front neck seam line

New cutting lines

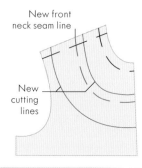

5 To make the new back neck facing pattern piece, copy the new back neck seam line and cutting line from step 2 onto a piece of paper. Measure points 2in (5cm) from the seam line. Join these points together to create a new cutting line. Cut out along these lines.

New cutting lines

New back neck seam line

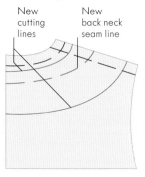

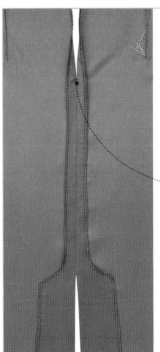

6 Cut out the dress fabric using the new pattern pieces and cut the lining using the front, back, and sleeve pieces. Mark the darts in both fabrics with tailor's bastes (see p.85).

7 Make up the dress fabric as for the Classic Shift Dress steps 2–10.

8 Make up the lining as for the Classic Shift Dress steps 2–3.

9 Stitch the lining together at the CB seam leaving a gap for the zipper and another for the vent as marked on the pattern. Press the seam open.

10 Make up the remaining lining as for the Classic Shift Dress steps 6–10.

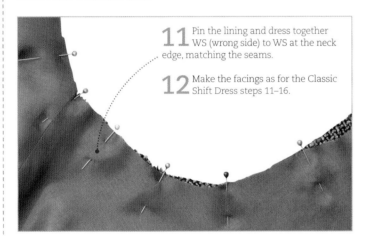

11 Pin the lining and dress together WS (wrong side) to WS at the neck edge, matching the seams.

12 Make the facings as for the Classic Shift Dress steps 11–16.

13 Hand stitch the lining to the dress on the shoulder seam and side seam, adjacent to the armhole.

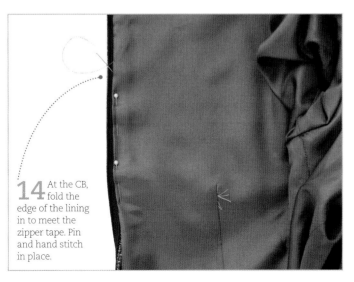

14 At the CB, fold the edge of the lining in to meet the zipper tape. Pin and hand stitch in place.

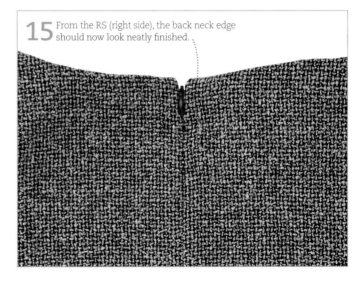

15 From the RS (right side), the back neck edge should now look neatly finished.

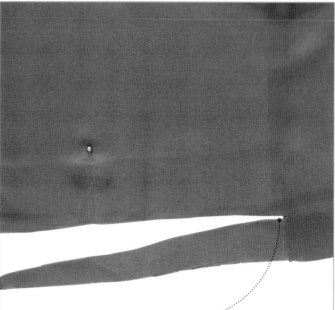

16 Turn up a ⅝in (1.5cm) hem at the bottom of each sleeve. Pin and hand stitch in place. Turn up the hem of the sleeve lining by ⅝in (1.5cm) and place the fold ⅜in (1cm) above the fold of the sleeve hem. Hand stitch in place.

17 Turn up the dress hem 1½in (4cm) and hand stitch in place. Trim the lining level to the hem of the skirt.

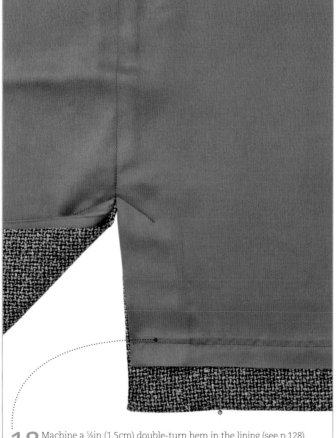

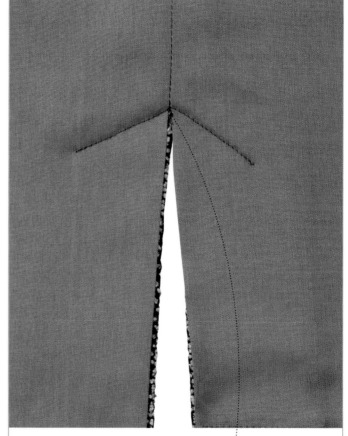

18 Machine a ⅝in (1.5cm) double-turn hem in the lining (see p.128). Fold the lining under around the vent and hand stitch in place.

19 Machine through all layers at the top of the vent to secure the lining to the dress.

DRESS PATTERN ONE VARIATION
SLEEVELESS SHIFT DRESS

This sleeveless, lined dress with its topstitched neck and armholes will easily take you from the office straight to a summer's evening party. Its simple lines can quickly be dressed up with clever accessorizing. A really easy way to insert a lining in this style of garment is shown here.

YOU WILL NEED
- 59in (1.5m) x 59in (150cm) fabric
- 59in (1.5m) x 59in (150cm) lining fabric
- 1 x spool matching all-purpose sewing thread
- 1 x spool contrasting all-purpose sewing thread for pattern marking
- 1 x 22in (56cm) zipper

PREPARING THE PATTERN
This dress is made using Dress Pattern One. Follow the instructions to download the pattern in your size (see pp.10–11).

GARMENT CONSTRUCTION
This third, lined variation of the Classic Shift Dress is shorter so there is no need for a back vent. This dress has a zipper in the center back and features topstitching at the neck and armhole edges. The lining is cut from the same pattern as the dress.

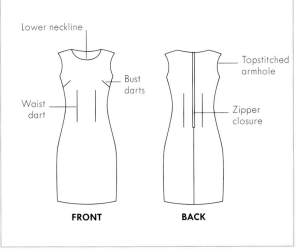

FRONT — Lower neckline, Bust darts, Waist dart

BACK — Topstitched armhole, Zipper closure

Patterned linen

Wool worsted

This dress is made in wool crepe. Lightweight suitings, cottons, and linens all work well.

DRESSES

▶ **HOW TO MAKE THE SLEEVELESS SHIFT DRESS**

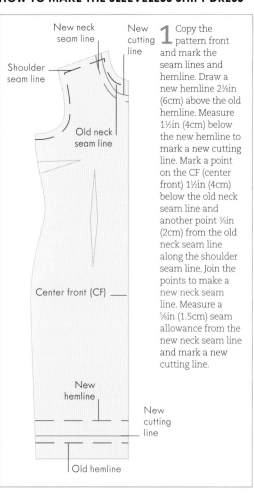

New neck seam line
New cutting line
Shoulder seam line
Old neck seam line
Center front (CF)
New hemline
New cutting line
Old hemline

1 Copy the pattern front and mark the seam lines and hemline. Draw a new hemline 2⅜in (6cm) above the old hemline. Measure 1½in (4cm) below the new hemline to mark a new cutting line. Mark a point on the CF (center front) 1½in (4cm) below the old neck seam line and another point ¾in (2cm) from the old neck seam line along the shoulder seam line. Join the points to make a new neck seam line. Measure a ⅝in (1.5cm) seam allowance from the new neck seam line and mark a new cutting line.

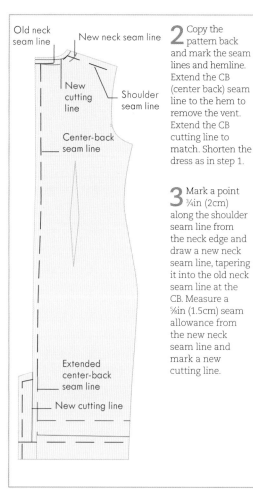

Old neck seam line
New neck seam line
New cutting line
Shoulder seam line
Center-back seam line
Extended center-back seam line
New cutting line

2 Copy the pattern back and mark the seam lines and hemline. Extend the CB (center back) seam line to the hem to remove the vent. Extend the CB cutting line to match. Shorten the dress as in step 1.

3 Mark a point ¾in (2cm) along the shoulder seam line from the neck edge and draw a new neck seam line, tapering it into the old neck seam line at the CB. Measure a ⅝in (1.5cm) seam allowance from the new neck seam line and mark a new cutting line.

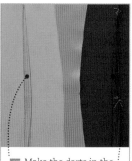

4 Cut out the dress fabric and the lining using the new pattern pieces. Mark the darts on the fabric using tailor's bastes (see pp.84–85).

5 Make the darts in the dress fabric and lining (see pp.99–100) and press toward the center of the garment.

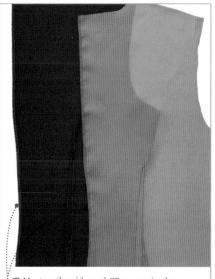

6 Neaten the side and CB seams in the dress fabric and lining using either a 3-thread serger stitch or a small zigzag stitch (see pp.92–93).

7 Join the front to the back at the shoulders in both the dress fabric and the lining. Press open.

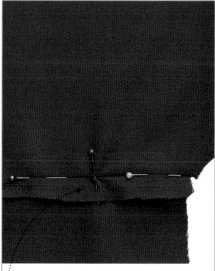

8 On the shoulder seam of the dress fabric make a ⅟₁₆in (2mm) tuck and pin in place. This slightly shortens the shoulder seam and prevents the lining from showing on the finished dress.

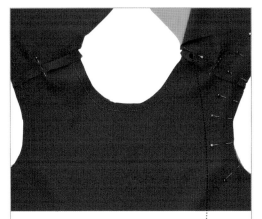

9 Place the lining to the dress fabric at the neck and armholes, RS (right side) to RS, and matching at the shoulder seams. Pin and machine.

10 Clip and trim the neck and armhole seams as for the Classic Shift Dress step 14. To turn through to the right side, pull the back of the dress through the shoulders to the front.

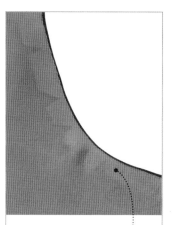

11 Roll the lining to the inside and press.

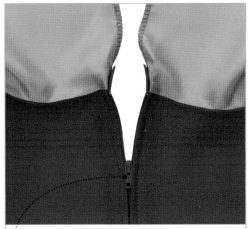

12 Insert a zipper of your choice in the CB of just the dress fabric (see pp.129–132). Stitch the remainder of the CB seam. Stitch the CB seam in the lining leaving a gap for the zipper.

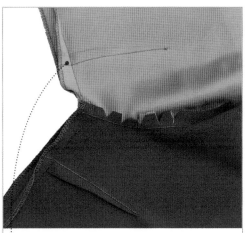

13 With RS to RS place the front to the back. Join the side seams by stitching through the fabric and lining in one continuous seam. Press the seams open.

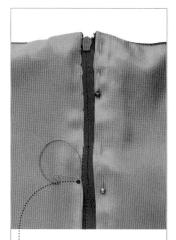

14 At the CB, fold the edge of the lining in to meet the zipper tape. Pin and hand stitch in place.

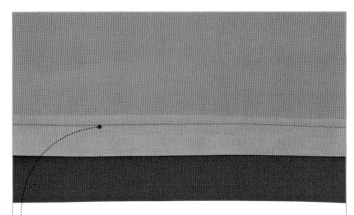

15 Neaten the hem edge of the dress (see pp.126–127). Turn up a 1½in (4cm) hem and hand stitch in place. Trim the lining level to the finished hem of the dress and machine a ⅝in (1.5cm) double-turn hem (see p.128).

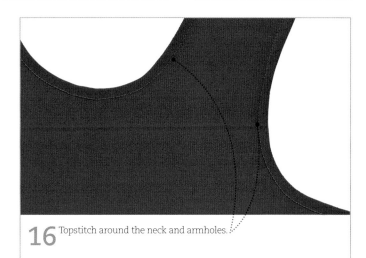

16 Topstitch around the neck and armholes.

DRESS PATTERN TWO
CLASSIC WAISTED DRESS

This dress has a darted bodice fitted into the waist for a smooth, flattering line at the waist and hips. Choose your pattern by your bust measurement and adjust the waist and hips if necessary. It is recommended to make the pattern in muslin first to ensure a good fit through the bust and waist, and to check the fit of the sleeve in the shoulder area. Lightweight fabrics work well for this dress and will ensure that the slightly A-line skirt moves with a nice swirl as you walk.

YOU WILL NEED

- 98in (2.5m) x 59in (150cm) fabric
- 1 x spool matching all-purpose sewing thread
- 1 x spool contrasting all-purpose sewing thread for pattern marking
- 20in (50cm) lightweight interfacing
- 1 x 22in (56cm) zipper

PREPARING THE PATTERN

This dress is made using Dress Pattern Two. Follow the instructions to download the pattern in your size (see pp.10–11).

GARMENT CONSTRUCTION

This unlined two-piece dress has waist darts in the bodice and in the skirt. It has long, fitted set-in sleeves and a lower neckline finished with a facing. There is a zipper in the center back and the A-line skirt sits just on the knee.

Silk

Wool crepe

This dress is made in polyester brocade, but this style of dress could be made in a variety of fabrics from cotton prints to lightweight wools, or silk.

Lower neckline

Bodice waist dart

Skirt waist dart

Long set-in sleeve

Center-back zipper

A-line skirt

FRONT

BACK

The gently flaring A-line skirt adds volume and fluidity to this long-sleeved dress.

▶ HOW TO MAKE THE CLASSIC WAISTED DRESS

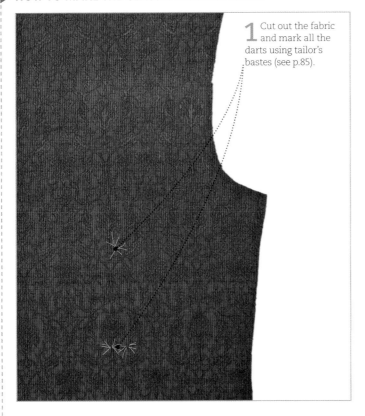

1 Cut out the fabric and mark all the darts using tailor's bastes (see p.85).

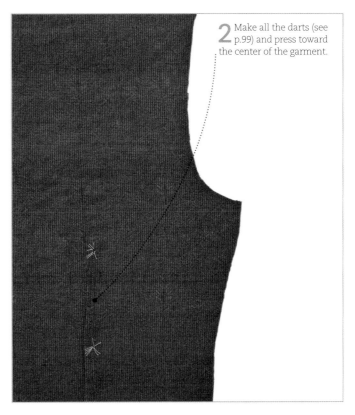

2 Make all the darts (see p.99) and press toward the center of the garment.

3 Join the front and back skirts to the front and back bodices, matching the darts. To ensure they match, you may have to ease the skirt to the bodice by stretching the bodice slightly. Press the seam allowances together.

4 Neaten the seam allowances together using either a 3-thread serger stitch or a small zigzag stitch (see pp.92–93). Press up toward the bodice.

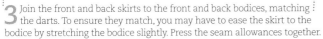

5 Using either a 3-thread serger stitch or a small zigzag stitch, neaten the CB (center back) seam, the side seams, and the shoulder seams on both the front and the back.

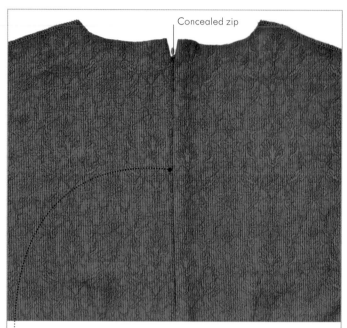

Concealed zip

6 Making sure the waist seams match on either side, insert a zipper of your choice in the CB (see pp.129–132). Stitch the remainder of the CB seam and press open.

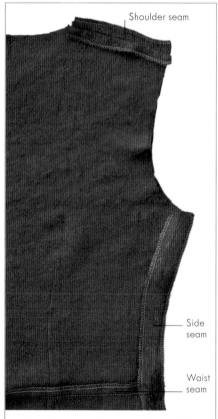

Shoulder seam

Side seam

Waist seam

7 Join the front to the back at the shoulder and side seams, matching at the waist seam. Press the seams open.

8 Neaten the sides and lower edge of both sleeves using either a 3-thread serger stitch or a small zigzag stitch.

Ease stitches

9 Machine the sleeve seam and press open. Using stitch length 5, machine two rows of ease stitches through the sleeve head (see p.114).

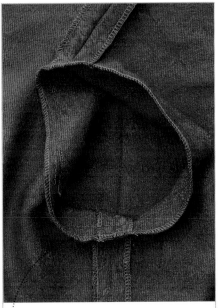

10 Insert the sleeve (see p.114) and neaten the raw edges using either a 3-thread serger stitch or a small zigzag stitch.

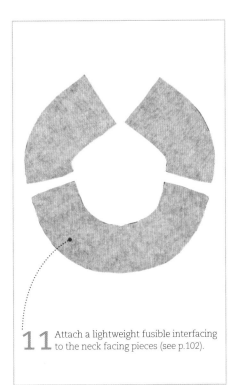

11 Attach a lightweight fusible interfacing to the neck facing pieces (see p.102).

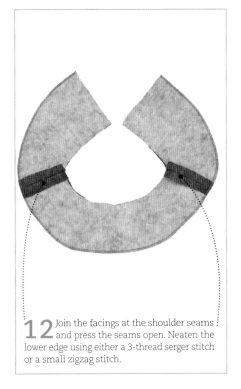

12 Join the facings at the shoulder seams and press the seams open. Neaten the lower edge using either a 3-thread serger stitch or a small zigzag stitch.

13 Place the facings to the neck edge of the dress RS (right side) to RS, matching the seams. Pin and machine.

14 Layer the seam allowance by trimming the facing side of the seam to half its width. Clip the seam allowance to reduce bulk (see p.97).

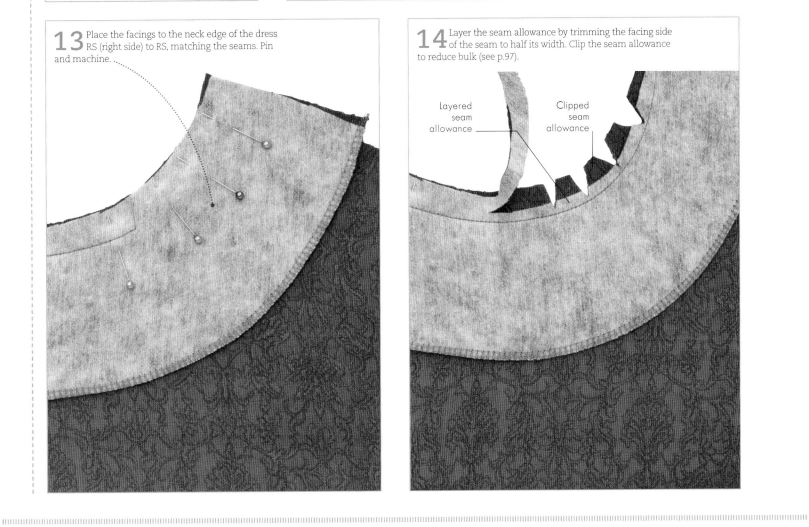

Layered seam allowance

Clipped seam allowance

15 Understitch the seam allowances to the facing (see p.98).

16 Turn the facing to the inside, then, at the CB, fold the edge of the facing in to meet the zipper tape. Pin and hand stitch in place.

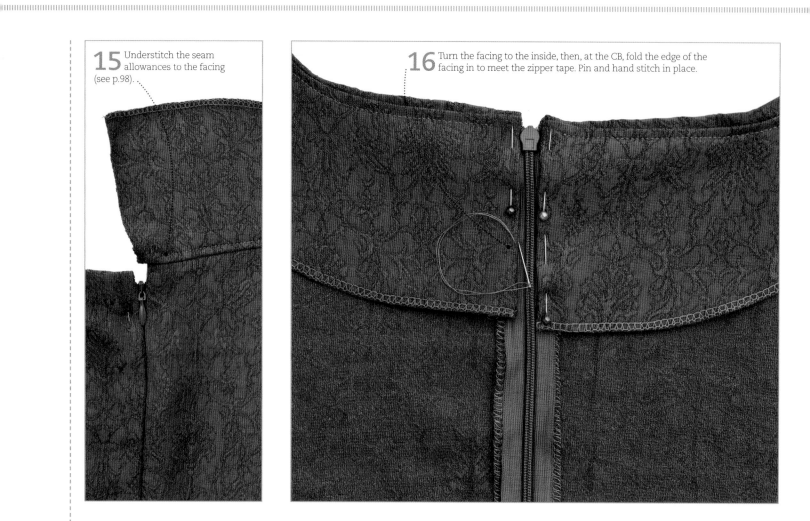

17 Neaten the hem edge (see pp.126–127) and turn up by 1½in (4cm). To ease the fullness out of the hem, make a row of running stitches close to the neatened edge (see p.89). Pull the thread to tighten the fabric. Hand stitch, then remove the running stitches.

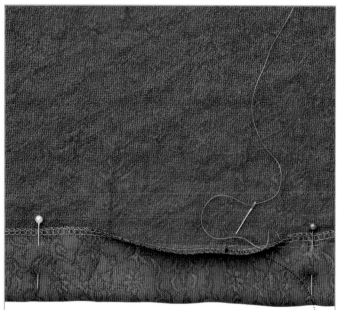

18 Turn up a 1in (2.5cm) hem at the bottom of each sleeve. Pin and hand stitch in place.

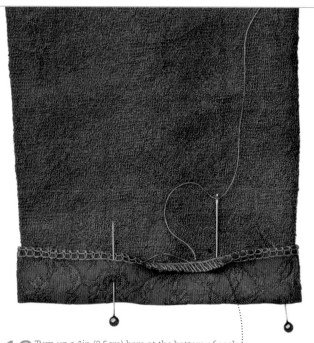

DRESS PATTERN TWO VARIATION
SHORT-SLEEVED WAISTED DRESS

For a dress with a gathered skirt, your choice of fabric is key. Don't go for anything too heavy: it won't gather evenly and could be very bulky at the waist. The skirt should sit neatly into the fitted darted bodice.

YOU WILL NEED

- 87in (2.2m) x 59in (150cm) fabric
- 1 x spool matching all-purpose sewing thread
- 1 x spool contrasting all-purpose sewing thread for pattern marking
- 20in (50cm) lightweight interfacing
- 1 x 22in (56cm) zipper

PREPARING THE PATTERN

This dress is made using Dress Pattern Two. Follow the instructions to download the pattern in your size (see pp.10–11).

Wool crepe

Tweed

This dress is made in a cotton tweed mix, but lightweight wools such as tweed or wool crepe are also suitable, as are cottons and silks.

GARMENT CONSTRUCTION

In this variation of the Classic Waisted Dress, a gathered skirt is attached to the fitted darted bodice. It has short set-in sleeves, a scoop neck, and a zipper in the center back.

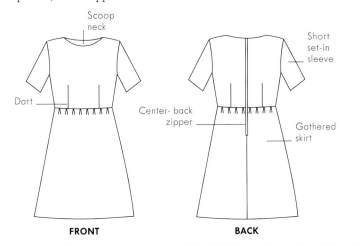

FRONT — Scoop neck, Dart

BACK — Short set-in sleeve, Center-back zipper, Gathered skirt

▶ **HOW TO MAKE THE SHORT-SLEEVED WAISTED DRESS**

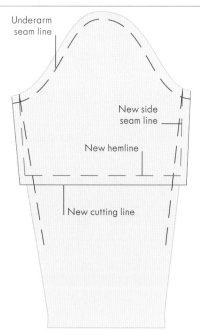

1 Copy the sleeve and mark the seam lines. Mark a point on each side of the sleeve and 6½in (17cm) below the underarm seam lines. Join these points together to make a new hemline. Draw a new cutting line ⅝in (1.5cm) below the new hemline. (If you have a slightly fuller arm you may need to extend the new hemline by ⅝in (1.5cm) on each side. Draw new side seam lines and cutting lines allowing a ⅝in (1.5cm) seam allowance.)

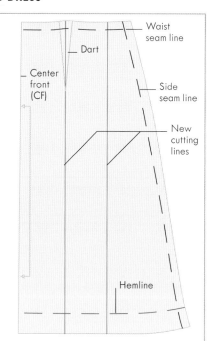

2 Copy the front skirt piece and mark the waist and side seam seam lines. Draw a vertical line parallel to the CF (center front) through the dart from waist to hem. Draw a second line 3½in (9cm) away from this line (solid red lines). Repeat on the back skirt piece, drawing the vertical line parallel to the CB (center back) seam.

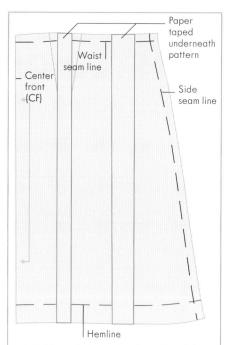

3 Cut through the vertical lines. Spread the pattern pieces apart at the dart by 1½in (3cm) at the waist and ¾in (2cm) at the hem, and at the second cut by 2in (5cm) at the waist, and 1½in (4cm) at the hem. Place paper behind the pattern pieces and tape them down. Repeat on the back.

4 Cut out the fabric using the new pattern pieces and mark and stitch the bodice darts as for the Classic Waisted Dress steps 1 and 2.

5 Stitch two rows of long machine stitches at the waist edge of the front and back skirt pieces (see p.101). Start and finish the stitching 1in (2.5cm) from the CB and side seams.

6 Place the front skirt to the front bodice RS (right side) to RS, and the back bodice pieces to the back skirts, RS to RS. Match the notches, pull up the two rows of stitches, and pin (see p.101).

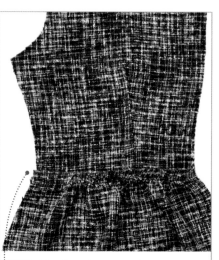

7 Machine the waist seam and neaten the seam allowances together using either a 3-thread serger stitch or a small zigzag stitch (see pp.92–93).

8 Complete the dress as for the Classic Waisted Dress steps 5–17.

DRESS PATTERN TWO VARIATION
SLEEVELESS WAISTED DRESS

In this version of the Classic Waisted Dress

the sleeves have been removed and a lining added. The dress
has the same skirt as the Short-Sleeved Waisted Dress. In a
patterned fabric, it would be lovely for a summer wedding or even
an evening function; in plain it would be ideal for office wear.

YOU WILL NEED

- 87in (2.2m) x 59in (150cm) fabric
- 87in (2.2m) x 59in (150cm) lining fabric
- 1 x spool matching all-purpose sewing thread
- 1 x spool contrasting all-purpose
  sewing thread for pattern marking
- 1 x 22in (56cm) zipper

PREPARING THE PATTERN

This dress is made using Dress Pattern
Two. Follow the instructions to download
the pattern in your size (see pp.10–11).

GARMENT CONSTRUCTION

This lined dress has a gathered A-line skirt and a fitted bodice
with waist darts. The dress is sleeveless and has a scoop neck.
There is a CB (center back) zipper.

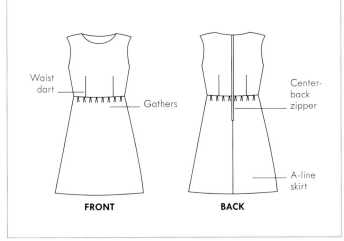

Waist dart — Gathers

FRONT

Center-back zipper

A-line skirt

BACK

Linen

Polyester

This dress is made
in a linen ikat weave,
but heavy cotton, linen,
polyester, and poly-viscose
fabrics are all suitable.

DRESSES

▶ HOW TO MAKE THE SLEEVELESS WAISTED DRESS

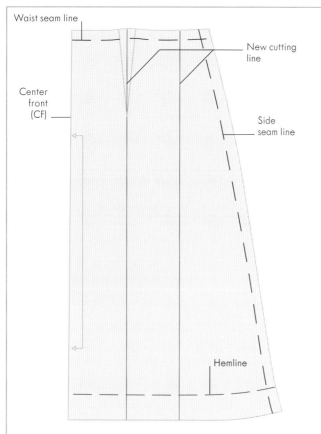

1 Copy the front skirt piece and mark the waist and side seam lines. Draw a vertical line parallel to the CF (center front) through the dart from waist to hem. Draw a second line 3½in (9cm) away from this line (solid red lines). Repeat on the back skirt piece, drawing the vertical line parallel to the CB (center back) seam.

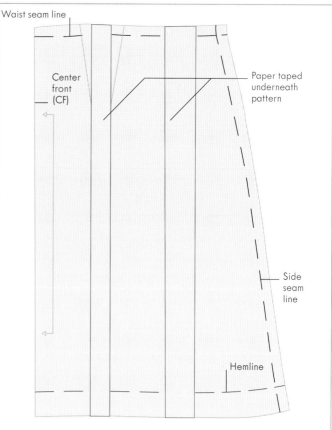

2 Cut through the vertical lines. Spread the cut pattern pieces apart through the dart by 1½in (3cm) at the waist and 1¼in (2cm) at the hem, and at the second cut by 2in (5cm) at the waist and 1½in (4cm) at the hem. Place paper behind the pattern pieces and tape them down. (For sizes over a size 10 or for more fullness, double these measurements.) Repeat on the back.

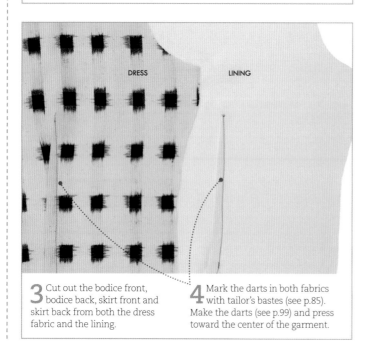

3 Cut out the bodice front, bodice back, skirt front and skirt back from both the dress fabric and the lining.

4 Mark the darts in both fabrics with tailor's bastes (see p.85). Make the darts (see p.99) and press toward the center of the garment.

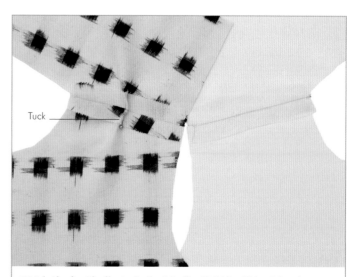

5 Join the front bodice to the back bodice RS (right side) to RS at the shoulder seam in both the dress fabric and the lining. Press the seams open. On the shoulder seam of the dress fabric make a ¹⁄₁₆in (2mm) tuck and pin in place.

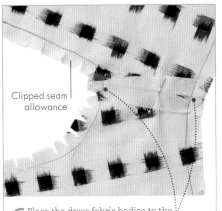

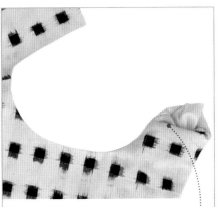

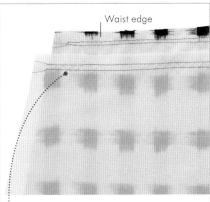

6 Place the dress fabric bodice to the lining bodice RS to RS matching at the shoulder seams. Pin and machine around the armholes and the neck. Clip the seam allowance.

Clipped seam allowance

7 Remove the pin in each shoulder. To turn through to the right side, pull the back of the dress through the shoulders to the front. Roll the lining to the inside and press.

8 Stitch two rows of long machine stitches, length 5, at the waist edge of the front and back skirt pieces in both the dress fabric and the lining (see p.101). Start and finish the stitching 1in (2.5cm) from the CB and side seams.

Waist edge

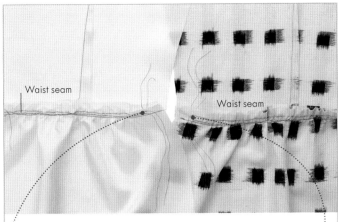

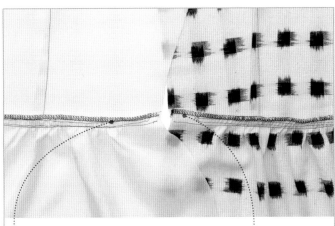

Waist seam

Waist seam

9 In both the dress fabric and the lining place the front skirt to the front bodice RS to RS, and the back bodice pieces to the back skirts, RS to RS. Match the notches, pull up the two rows of stitches, and pin (see p.101). Machine the waist seam.

10 Neaten the seam allowances together using either a 3-thread serger stitch or a small zigzag stitch (see pp.92–93). Press the seam toward the bodice.

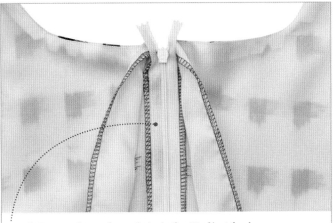

11 Using either a 3-thread serger stitch or a small zigzag stitch, neaten the CB seam and the side seam allowances in both the dress fabric and the lining.

12 Insert a zipper of your choice in the CB of just the dress fabric (see pp.129–132). Stitch the remainder of the CB seam in the dress fabric.

13 Stitch the CB seam in the lining, leaving a gap for the zipper.

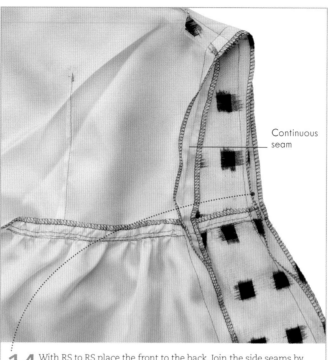
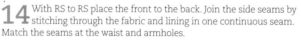

Continuous seam

14 With RS to RS place the front to the back. Join the side seams by stitching through the fabric and lining in one continuous seam. Match the seams at the waist and armholes.

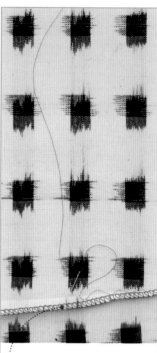

15 Neaten the hem edge of the dress (see pp.126–127). Turn up a 1½in (4cm) hem and hand stitch in place.

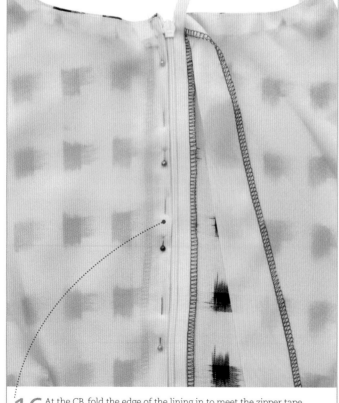

16 At the CB, fold the edge of the lining in to meet the zipper tape. Pin and hand stitch in place.

17 Trim the lining level to the finished hem of the dress and machine a ⅝in (1.5cm) double-turn hem (see p.128).

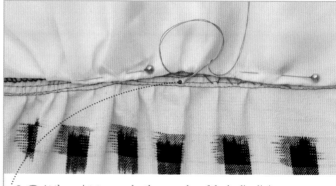

18 At the waist, turn under the raw edge of the bodice lining. Pin and hand stitch to the waist seam.

DRESS PATTERN TWO VARIATION

WAISTED COCKTAIL DRESS

This great little dress could be a cocktail or prom dress or just a sundress. If you like a vintage look you can wear a crinoline underneath. The dress requires some complex pattern alterations. The skirt has been widened to accommodate more gathers and the bodice has been reshaped.

YOU WILL NEED

- 39in (1m) x 59in (150cm) bodice fabric
- 59in (1.5m) x 59in (150cm) skirt fabric
- 36in (60cm) x 59in (150cm) lining fabric
- 1 x spool matching all-purpose sewing thread
- 1 x spool contrasting all-purpose sewing thread for pattern marking
- 39in (1m) x 46in (115cm) woven medium-weight interfacing
- 1 x 16in (40cm) zipper
- 1 x hook and eye fastener

PREPARING THE PATTERN

This dress is made using Dress Pattern Two. Follow the instructions to download the pattern in your size (see pp.10–11).

GARMENT CONSTRUCTION

This dress in two contrasting fabrics has a full, gathered skirt, a sweetheart neckline and straps. The darted bodice with center back (CB) zipper is lined and trimmed around its upper edge with the skirt fabic.

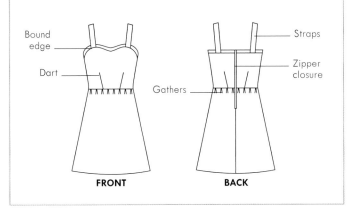

FRONT   BACK

Bound edge
Dart
Gathers
Straps
Zipper closure

Silk

Taffeta

This dress is made in polyester crinkle taffeta, but this pattern suits any lightweight taffeta, satin, silk dupioni, or crepe.

DRESSES

▶ **HOW TO MAKE THE WAISTED COCKTAIL DRESS**

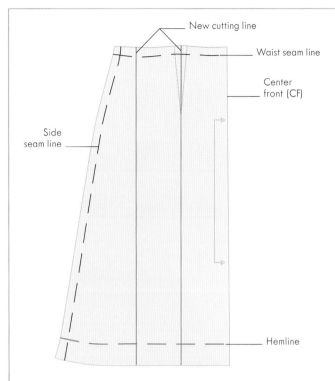

1 Copy the front skirt piece and mark the waist and side seam lines. Draw a vertical line parallel to the CF (center front) through the dart from waist to hem. Draw a second line 3½in (9cm) away from this line. Repeat on the back skirt piece, drawing the vertical line parallel to the CB (center back).

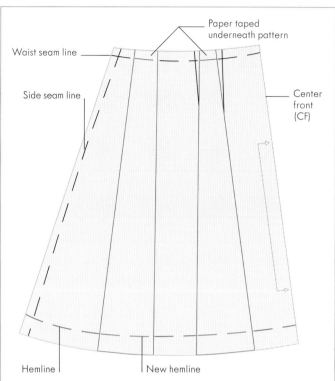

2 Cut through the vertical lines. Spread the cut pattern pieces apart through the dart by 1¼in (3cm) at the waist and by 5in (12cm) at the hem, and at the second cut by 2⅜in (6cm) at the waist and 5in (12cm) at the hem. Place paper behind the pattern pieces and tape them down. (For sizes over a size 10 or for more fullness, double these measurements.) Repeat on the back skirt piece.

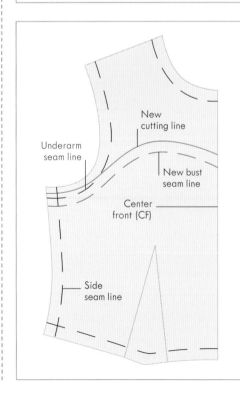

3 Copy the bodice front pattern and mark the seam lines. At the side seam line mark a point ½in (1cm) below the underarm seam line. At the CF line mark a point approx 3½in (9cm) below the neck seam line. Join these two points together to make the new bust seam line in a curve over the top of the bust. Measure a ⅝in (1.5cm) seam allowance from this line and mark a new cutting line.

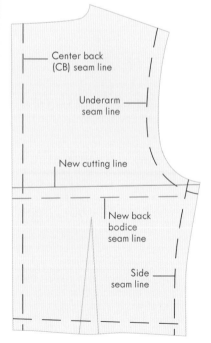

4 Copy the bodice back pattern and mark the seam lines. At the side seam line mark a point ½in (1cm) below the underarm seam line. Draw a horizontal line across the back to the CB seam line to make a new back bodice seam line. Measure a ⅝in (1.5cm) seam allowance from this line and mark a new cutting line.

5 Cut out the dress fabric using the new pattern pieces. Cut out the lining fabric using the bodice pattern pieces.

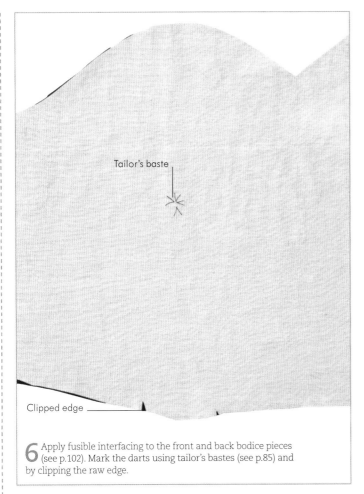

Tailor's baste

Clipped edge

6 Apply fusible interfacing to the front and back bodice pieces (see p.102). Mark the darts using tailor's bastes (see p.85) and by clipping the raw edge.

7 Make the darts in the in the front and back bodice pieces (see p.99) and press toward the center of the garment.

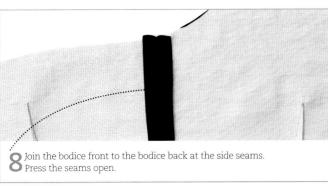

8 Join the bodice front to the bodice back at the side seams. Press the seams open.

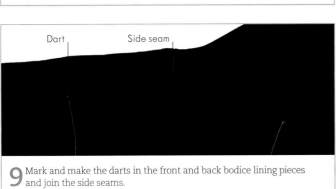

Dart   Side seam

9 Mark and make the darts in the front and back bodice lining pieces and join the side seams.

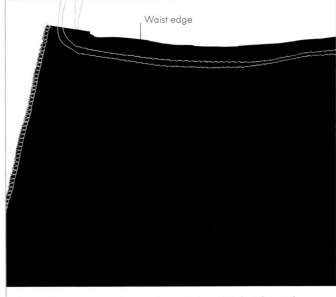

Waist edge

10 Stitch two rows of long machine stitches, stitch length 5, at the waist edge of the front and back skirt pieces (see p.101). Start and finish the stitching 1in (2.5cm) from the CB and side seams. Neaten the side seams on the skirt using either a 3-thread serger stitch or a small zigzag stitch (see pp.92–93).

DRESSES

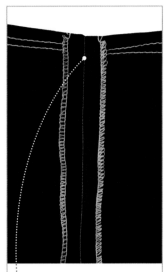

11 Machine the skirt sections together at the side seams and press open.

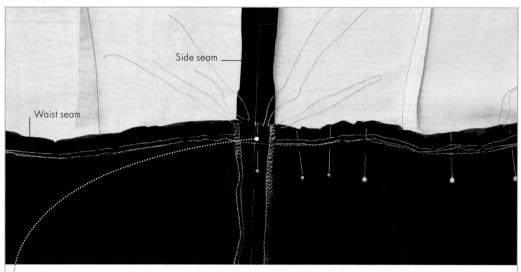

Side seam

Waist seam

12 Place the skirt to the bodice RS (right side) to RS. Match the side seams, pull up the two rows of stitches and pin (see p.101). Machine the waist seam and neaten the seam allowances together using either a 3-thread serger stitch or a small zigzag stitch. Neaten the CB seams.

13 Insert a zipper of your choice in the CB (see pp.129–132). Stitch the remainder of the CB seam. Press the seam open.

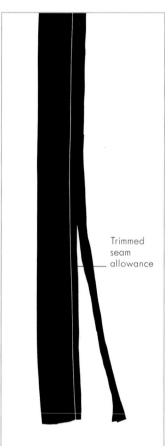

Trimmed seam allowance

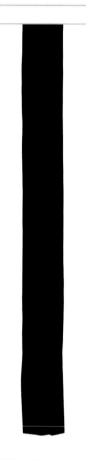

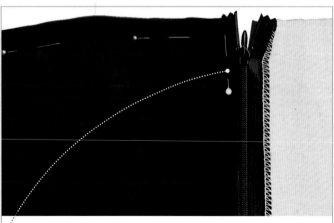

14 Place the lining to the bodice WS (wrong side) to WS and pin then baste around the top edge. At the CB, fold the edge of the lining in to meet the zipper tape. Pin in place.

15 To make the straps, cut two pieces of fabric 17¾in x 4in (45cm x 10cm). Fold each in half lengthwise RS to RS and machine along the long edge. Trim the seam allowance close to the seamline.

16 Turn the straps to the RS using a loop turner (see p.27). Press flat ensuring that the seam is at the CB of the strap.

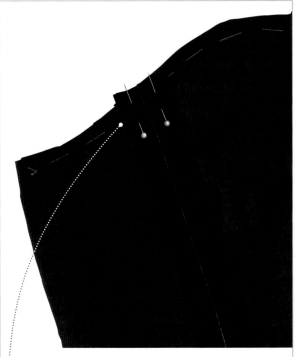

17 Pin one end of each strap to the front bodice, just to the armhole side of the dart. Try the dress on to make sure that the strap will cover your bra strap. Reposition if necessary.

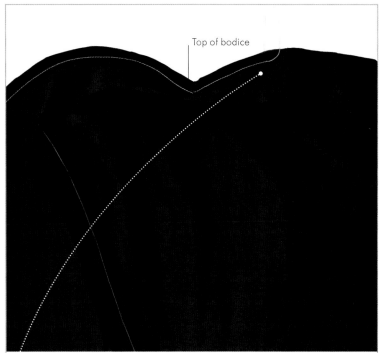

Top of bodice

18 To finish the top edge of the dress, cut 2½in (6cm) wide bias strips from the skirt fabric (see p.104). Make a strip that is long enough to go around the top of the bodice. Pin the bias strip RS (right side) to RS to the top edge of the bodice and baste down. Machine using the edge of the presser foot as a guide. Pivot (see p.95) and clip the seam allowance at the CF. Remove the basting stitches.

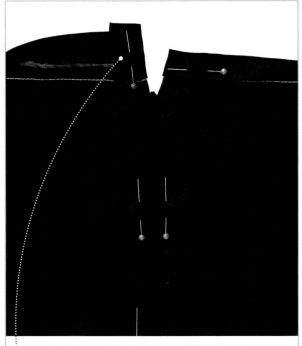

19 Trim the top of the zipper tape. Fold the bias strip to the WS of the bodice and fold the raw edge under. At the CB, trim the top of the zipper tape, and fold the end of the strip in line with the folded edge of the lining. Pin and hand stitch. Attach a hook and eye to the bias strip.

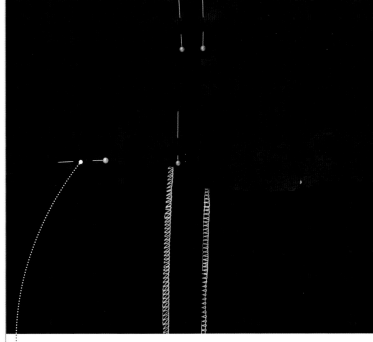

20 To finish the bodice, turn under the raw edge of the bodice lining. Pin and hand stitch to the waist seam. Hand stitch the lining to the zipper tape.

21 Finish the hem as for the Classic Waisted Dress step 17. Try the dress on and attach the straps to the back of the bodice to fit. Hand stitch the straps to the binding.

DRESS PATTERN THREE

CLASSIC EMPIRE WAIST DRESS

Those ladies of The First French Empire

certainly knew a thing or two about how to flatter the figure. The high waist of an Empire Waist Dress helps to conceal a fuller waistline and the low neck of this version sets off the face and neck. Choose your pattern size by your bust measurement and check for fit in the hip and waist areas. This is an easy-to-wear day dress that can take you from work to dinner.

YOU WILL NEED

- 100in (2.5m) x 59in (150cm) fabric
- 1 x spool matching all-purpose sewing thread
- 1 x spool contrasting all-purpose sewing thread for pattern marking
- 20in (50cm) lightweight interfacing
- 22in (56cm) zipper

PREPARING THE PATTERN

This dress is made using Dress Pattern Three. Follow the instructions to download the pattern in your size (see pp.10–11).

GARMENT CONSTRUCTION

This unlined dress has wrist-length sleeves and a wide, low neckline finished with a facing. The waist darts of the bodice meet the skirt darts at an under-bust seamline. There is a center back (CB) zipper and a vent in the gently shaped A-line skirt.

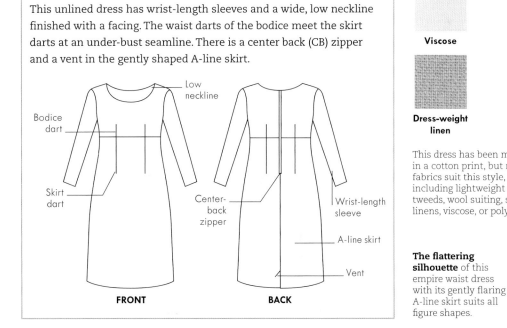

FRONT

BACK

Low neckline

Bodice dart

Skirt dart

Center-back zipper

Wrist-length sleeve

A-line skirt

Vent

Viscose

Dress-weight linen

This dress has been made in a cotton print, but many fabrics suit this style, including lightweight tweeds, wool suiting, silks, linens, viscose, or polyester.

The flattering silhouette of this empire waist dress with its gently flaring A-line skirt suits all figure shapes.

▶ HOW TO MAKE THE CLASSIC EMPIRE WAIST DRESS

1 Cut out the fabric and mark the darts using tailor's tacks (see p.85).

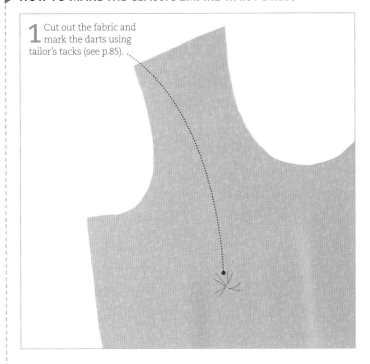

2 Make the darts (see p.99) in the bodice and skirt and press toward the center of the garment.

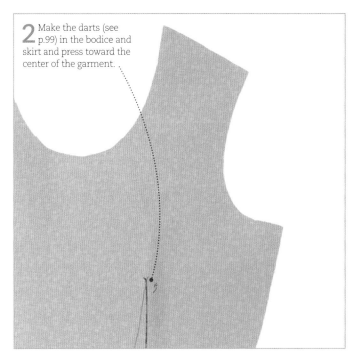

3 Neaten the waist seams on all the bodice and skirt pieces using a 3-thread serger stitch or a small zigzag stitch (see pp.92–93).

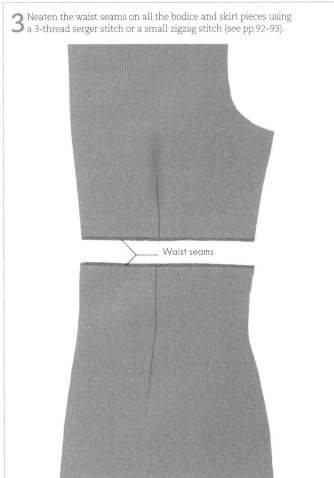

Waist seams

4 Join the front bodice to the front skirt and the back bodice pieces to the back skirts at the waist. Press the seams open.

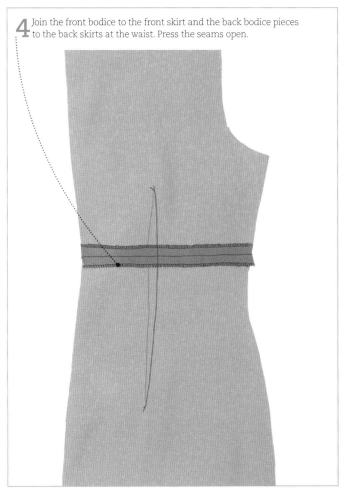

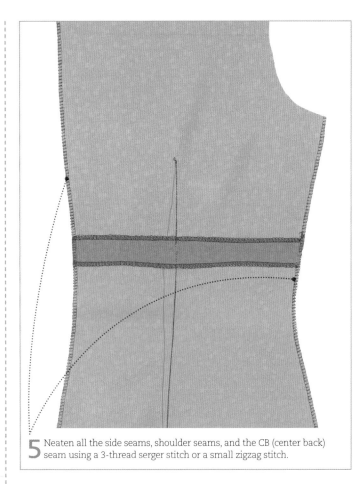

5 Neaten all the side seams, shoulder seams, and the CB (center back) seam using a 3-thread serger stitch or a small zigzag stitch.

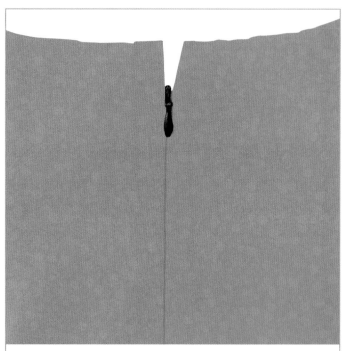

6 Insert a zip of your choice in the CB (see pp.129–132). Stitch the remainder of the CB seam, stopping at the dot marking the top of the vent.

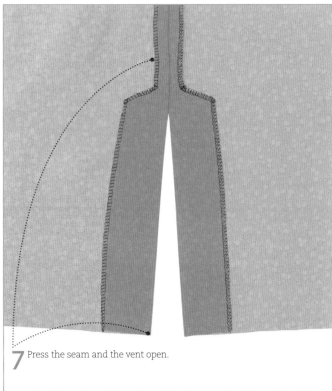

7 Press the seam and the vent open.

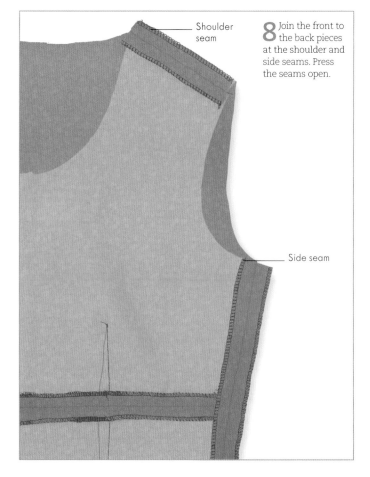

Shoulder seam

Side seam

8 Join the front to the back pieces at the shoulder and side seams. Press the seams open.

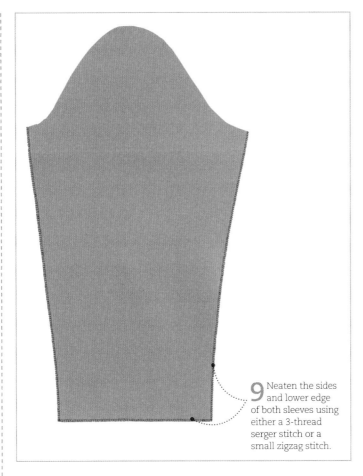

9 Neaten the sides and lower edge of both sleeves using either a 3-thread serger stitch or a small zigzag stitch.

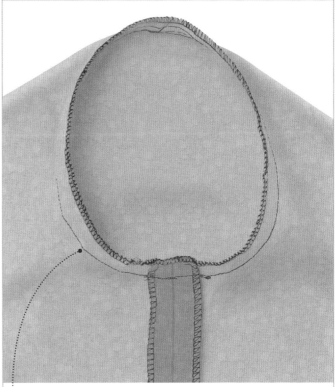

10 Machine the sleeve side seam and press it open. Using the longest stitch available, machine two rows of ease stitches through the sleeve head (see p.114). Fit the sleeve into the armhole, RS (right side) to RS. Pin, then stitch the sleeve into place from the sleeve side (see p.114).

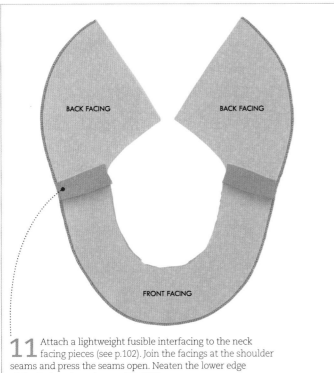

BACK FACING

BACK FACING

FRONT FACING

11 Attach a lightweight fusible interfacing to the neck facing pieces (see p.102). Join the facings at the shoulder seams and press the seams open. Neaten the lower edge of the facing pieces (see pp.103–105).

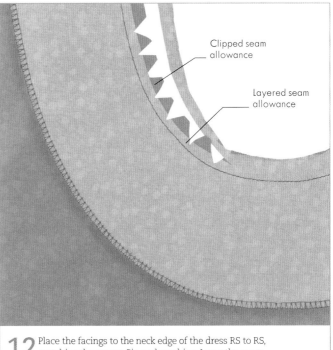

Clipped seam allowance

Layered seam allowance

12 Place the facings to the neck edge of the dress RS to RS, matching the seams. Pin and machine. Layer the seam allowance by trimming the facing side of the seam to half its width. Clip the seam allowance to reduce bulk (see p.97).

13 Turn the facing to the WS (wrong side), press and topstitch to hold in place.

Topstitching

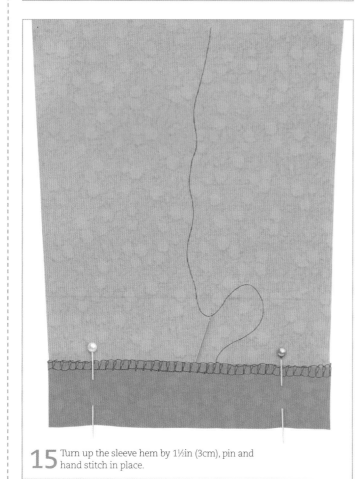

15 Turn up the sleeve hem by 1½in (3cm), pin and hand stitch in place.

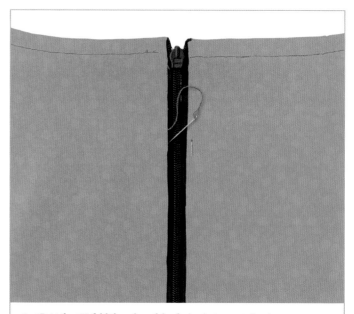

Hem edge | Mitre

14 Neaten the hem edge (see pp.126–127). On each side of the vent, remove the surplus fabric in the hem allowance. Miter the hem at the bottom of the vent and pin. Turn up the remainder of the hem and pin. Hand stitch the miter and hem in place.

16 At the CB, fold the edge of the facing in to meet the zipper tape. Pin and hand stitch in place.

DRESS PATTERN THREE VARIATION
SLEEVELESS EMPIRE WAIST DRESS

This version of the Classic Empire waist Dress
features tucks in the skirt, which give a full yet sleek line. The dress is lined but also has facings in order to show an alternative way of inserting a lining into a sleeveless dress. Made in silk, this dress is ideal for a party, or try a poly-cotton mix for everyday.

YOU WILL NEED

- 69in (1.75m) x 59in (150cm) fabric
- 69in (1.75m) x 59in (150cm) lining fabric
- 1 x spool matching all-purpose sewing thread
- 1 x spool contrasting all-purpose sewing thread for pattern marking
- 20in (50cm) x lightweight fusible interfacing
- 22in (56cm) zipper

PREPARING THE PATTERN

This dress is made using Dress Pattern Three. Follow the instructions to download the pattern in your size (see pp.10–11).

GARMENT CONSTRUCTION

This sleeveless empire waist dress has front and back bodice darts at the waist that line up with tucks in the skirt. The tucks give a fuller skirt. The dress is lined and the neckline is faced.

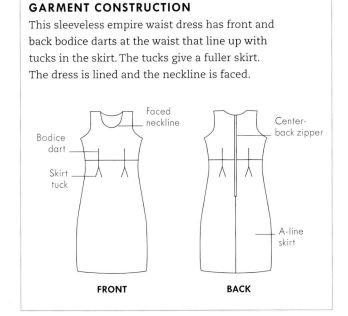

Bodice dart
Faced neckline
Skirt tuck

Center-back zipper
A-line skirt

FRONT

BACK

Wool suiting

Viscose

This dress is silk dupioni but it could also be made in poly-cotton, viscose, or wool suiting.

▶ **HOW TO MAKE THE SLEEVELESS EMPIRE LINE DRESS**

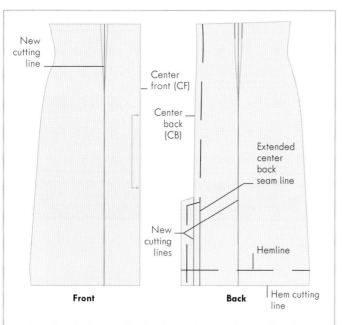

New cutting line

Center front (CF)

Center back (CB)

Extended center back seam line

New cutting lines

Hemline

Front   **Back**

Hem cutting line

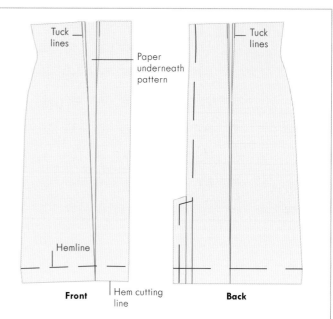

Tuck lines

Paper underneath pattern

Tuck lines

Hemline

Front   **Back**

Hem cutting line

1 Copy the skirt front and back and mark the seam lines and hemlines. On the front, draw a vertical line parallel to the CF (center front). On the back, draw a vertical line parallel to the CB (center back) seam through the dart to the hem cutting line. To remove the vent, extend the CB seam line to the hemline. Draw a new cutting line ⅝in (1.5cm) to the left of it.

2 Cut through the vertical lines to within ⅛in (3mm) of the hem cutting line. Place paper underneath, and spread the cut pattern pieces apart through the front waist by 1¼in (3cm) and through the back waist by ⅝in (1.5cm). Tape the pattern pieces to the paper. Mark the tuck lines at points 1½in (4cm) below the waist, following the original dart seam lines.

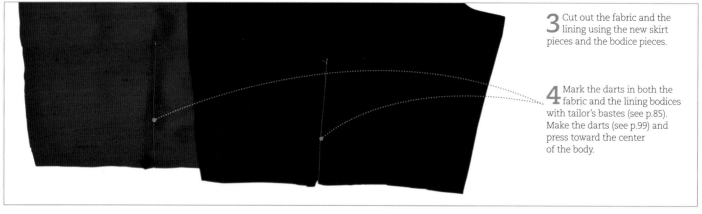

3 Cut out the fabric and the lining using the new skirt pieces and the bodice pieces.

4 Mark the darts in both the fabric and the lining bodices with tailor's bastes (see p.85). Make the darts (see p.99) and press toward the center of the body.

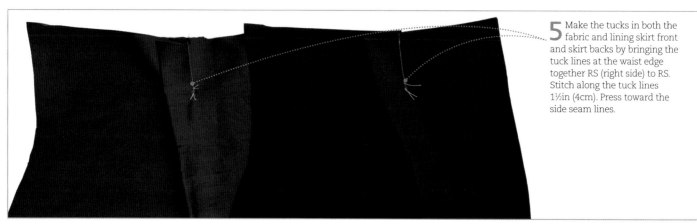

5 Make the tucks in both the fabric and lining skirt front and skirt backs by bringing the tuck lines at the waist edge together RS (right side) to RS. Stitch along the tuck lines 1½in (4cm). Press toward the side seam lines.

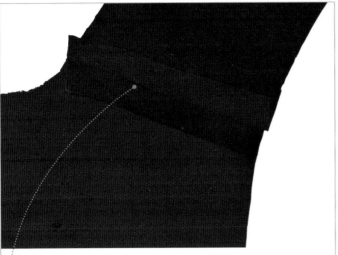

6 Join the front to the back at the shoulder seams in both the fabric and the lining bodices. Press the seams open.

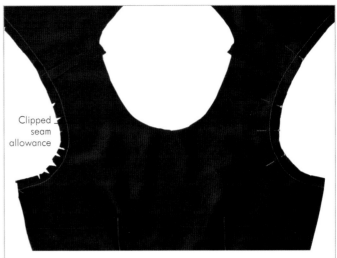

Clipped seam allowance

7 Place the fabric bodice to the lining bodice RS to RS and matching at the shoulder seams. Pin and machine just around the armholes. Clip the seam.

8 Turn through to the right side, roll the lining to the inside and press. Baste the raw edges together around the neck.

9 Working separately on the fabric and the lining, follow steps 3–7 of the Classic Empire Line Dress, leaving a gap corresponding to the zipper in the lining. Do not neaten the bodice seams and ignore the reference to the CB vent.

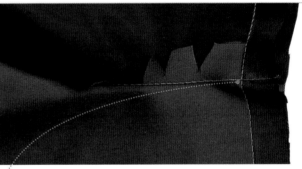

10 With RS to RS place the front to the back. Join the side seams by stitching through the fabric and lining in one continuous seam. Press the seams open.

11 Make and attach the neck facing to the basted raw neck edge as for the Classic Empire Line Dress steps 11–12.

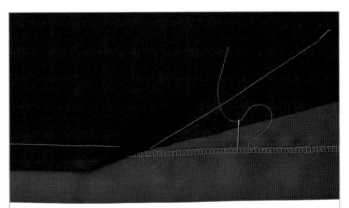

12 Neaten the hem edge of the dress(see pp.126–127). Turn up a 1½in (4cm) hem and hand stitch in place. Trim the lining level to the finished hem of the dress and machine a ¾in (2cm) double-turn hem (see p.128).

DRESS PATTERN THREE VARIATION
LONG EMPIRE LINE DRESS

Here the strapless bodice has been interlined and boned, and the skirt extended to floor length with a small "puddle" train. The bodice requires a snug fit, so you should definitely test your pattern in muslin first. Try this dress in a crepe or satin for evening wear or a prom, or in silk and lace for a wedding.

YOU WILL NEED

- 138in (3.5m) x 59in (150cm) fabric
- 138in (3.5m) x 59in (150cm) lining fabric
- 30in (75cm) x 59in (150cm) muslin
- 2 x spools matching all-purpose sewing thread
- 1 x spool contrasting all-purpose sewing thread for pattern marking
- 30in (75cm) x medium-weight fusible woven interfacing
- 79in (2m) sew-in polyester boning ½in (12mm) wide
- 16in (40cm) invisible zipper

PREPARING THE PATTERN

This dress is made using Dress Pattern Three. Follow the instructions to download the pattern in your size (see pp.10–11).

GARMENT CONSTRUCTION

The high-waisted, strapless, fitted bodice is boned, interfaced, and interlined. The full-length skirt has been widened and falls into a small "puddle" train. The dress has a center-back (CB) zipper.

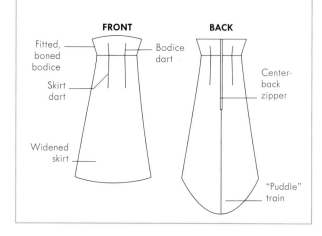

FRONT — Fitted, boned bodice; Skirt dart; Widened skirt; Bodice dart

BACK — Center-back zipper; "Puddle" train

Taffeta

Satin

This dress is made in polyester crepe, but satin, silk, taffeta, and satin-backed crepe are all good fabric choices.

▶ HOW TO MAKE THE LONG EMPIRE WAIST DRESS

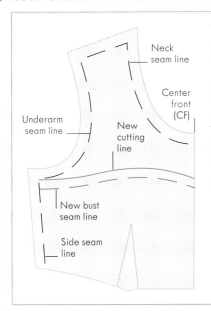

1 Copy the bodice front pattern and mark the seam lines. At the side seam line mark a point ⅝in (1.5cm) below the underarm seam line. At the CF (center front) line mark a point 2¾in (7cm) below the neck seam line. Join these two points together to make the new bust seam line in a curve over the top of the bust. Measure a ⅝in (1.5cm) seam allowance from this line and mark a new cutting line.

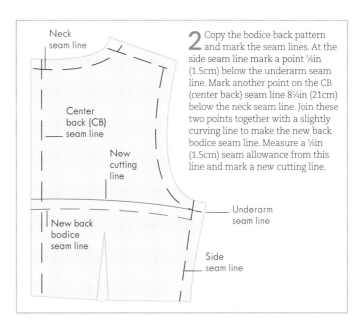

2 Copy the bodice back pattern and mark the seam lines. At the side seam line mark a point ⅝in (1.5cm) below the underarm seam line. Mark another point on the CB (center back) seam line 8¼in (21cm) below the neck seam line. Join these two points together with a slightly curving line to make the new back bodice seam line. Measure a ⅝in (1.5cm) seam allowance from this line and mark a new cutting line.

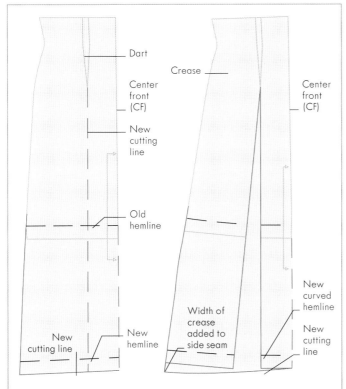

3 Copy the front skirt piece. See p.58 to extend the pattern by 18in (46cm) to make the skirt floor length. Add a 1¼in (4cm) hem allowance and mark a new cutting line. Draw a vertical line parallel to the CF through the dart from the waist to the new hem cutting line. Slash along this line and spread the pattern at the hem by 3½in (9cm). Measure the width of the crease that forms on the side seam line in the hip area and add this amount to the hem on the side seam. Draw in a new curved hemline and cutting line.

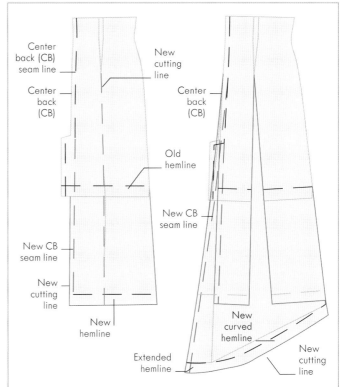

4 Copy the back skirt pieces and mark the CB seam lines and the hemlines. Extend the pattern at the hemline as in step 3. Remove the vent by extending the CB seam line to the new hemline. Slash and spread the pattern as in step 3. To create the train, extend the CB seam line by 12in (30cm). At the hemline extend the hemline horizontally by 2⅜in (6cm). Join this point with a straight line to the CB seam line in the hip area and extend the other way by at least 12in (30cm). On the extended hem, join these new points with straight lines and then draw in curved lines to create the train. Draw in a new cutting line 1½in (4cm) below this line.

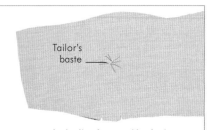

5 Cut out the bodice front and back pieces from fabric, muslin, medium-weight interfacing, and lining. Cut the skirt front and back pieces from fabric and lining. Mark the darts with tailor's bastes (see p.85).

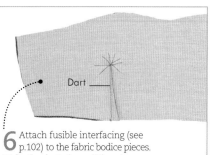

6 Attach fusible interfacing (see p.102) to the fabric bodice pieces. Make the darts (see p.99) and press toward the center of the body.

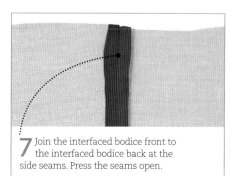

7 Join the interfaced bodice front to the interfaced bodice back at the side seams. Press the seams open.

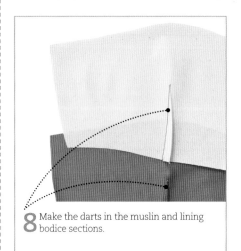

8 Make the darts in the muslin and lining bodice sections.

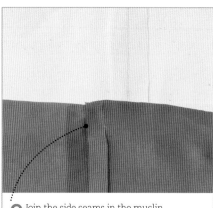

9 Join the side seams in the muslin bodice and in the lining bodice sections. Press open.

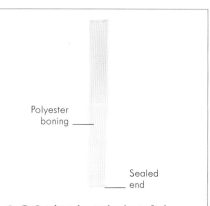

10 Cut the polyester boning to fit the bodice (see step 11) and seal the ends if required.

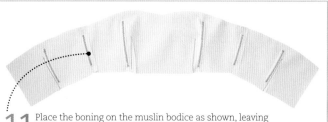

11 Place the boning on the muslin bodice as shown, leaving ¾in (2cm) clearance at the top and bottom. Attach with a zigzag stitch (see p.90).

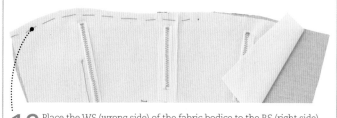

12 Place the WS (wrong side) of the fabric bodice to the RS (right side) of the boned bodice. Baste around the edges.

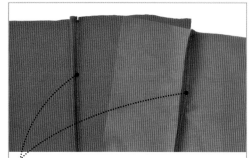

13 Cut out the skirt front and back pieces from fabric and lining. Mark and make the darts in both.

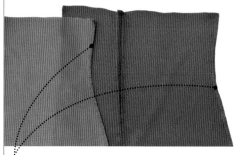

14 Neaten the side and CB seams in the fabric and the lining skirt pieces using either a 3-thread serger stitch or a small zigzag stitch (see pp.92–93).

15 Join the side seams in both the fabric and the lining skirt pieces. Press the seams open.

16 Attach just the fabric skirt to the boned bodice. Cut away the muslin from the seam and press the seam allowances up toward bodice.

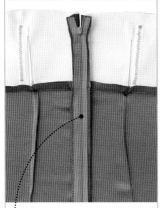

17 Insert a 16in (40cm) invisible zipper in the CB (see p.132). Stitch the remainder of the CB seam.

18 Machine the lining skirt to the skirt-to-bodice seam allowances, stopping 1¼in (3cm) from the zipper.

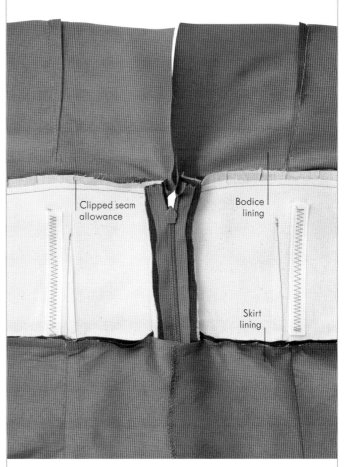

19 Attach the bodice lining to the top edge of the boned bodice RS to RS. Cut away the muslin from the seam and clip the seam allowance.

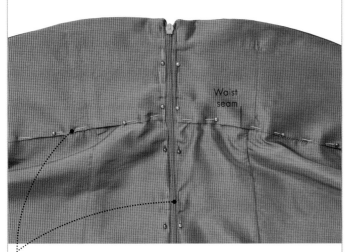

20 Turn the lining bodice to the inside and press. At the CB, fold the edge of the lining in to meet the zipper tape. Pin and hand stitch in place. At the waist, turn under the raw edge of the bodice lining. Pin and hand stitch to the waist seam.

21 Neaten the hem edge of the dress (see pp.126–127) and turn up a 1½in (4cm) hem, placing the pins vertically in the area of the train to ease out any fullness. Hand stitch in place.

22 Trim the lining level to the finished hem of the dress and machine a ¾in (2cm) double-turn hem (see p.128).

DRESS PATTERN FOUR
CLASSIC SHIRTDRESS

This classic shirtdress never goes out of fashion. Choose a fabric in a bold, bright color to make a statement, and dress it up or down with accessories. Making this dress will teach you some advanced sewing techniques, such as how to apply a yoke, collar, and cuffs with a single button fastening. It can be worn with a sash belt as shown here, or with a buckle belt for a more formal look.

YOU WILL NEED

- 134in (3.4m) x 59in (150cm) fabric
- 1 x spool of matching all-purpose sewing thread
- 1 x spool of contrasting all-purpose sewing thread for pattern marking
- 13 x ½in (13mm) buttons
- 47in x 8in (1.2m x 20cm) fusible interfacing

PREPARING THE PATTERN

This dress is made using Dress Pattern Four. Follow the instructions to download the pattern in your size (see pp.10–11).

GARMENT CONSTRUCTION

This dress has a button front opening, shirt collar, shoulder yoke, cuffed sleeves with pleats and a button fastening, and a pleat at the top of the back yoke. One half of each band is interfaced. The bodice is shaped by waist darts front and back. It is worn with a matching sash (see p.113).

FRONT — Collar, Darts, Sash, Full-length buttonband, Mid-calf length

BACK — Inverted pleat, Sleeve cuffs

Dupioni silk

Polyester satin

This dress is made from cotton but other suitable fabrics include dupioni silk or recycled polyester satin.

This stylish dress is ideal for the office or more formal occasions. The sash belt can be worn in a bow at the front or tied at the side.

▶ **HOW TO MAKE THE CLASSIC SHIRTDRESS**

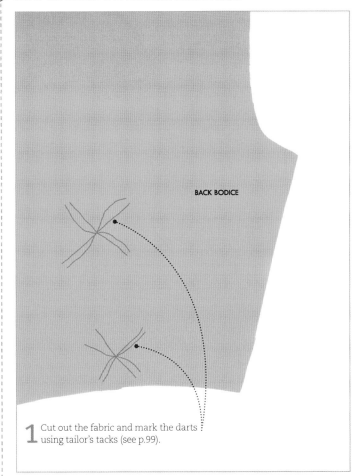

1 Cut out the fabric and mark the darts using tailor's tacks (see p.99).

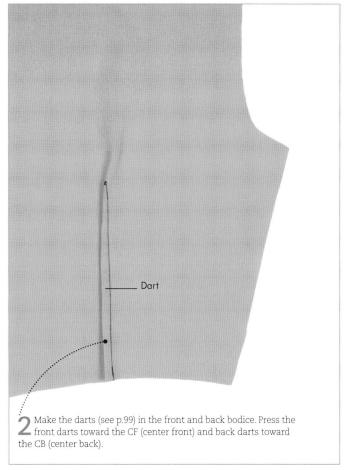

2 Make the darts (see p.99) in the front and back bodice. Press the front darts toward the CF (center front) and back darts toward the CB (center back).

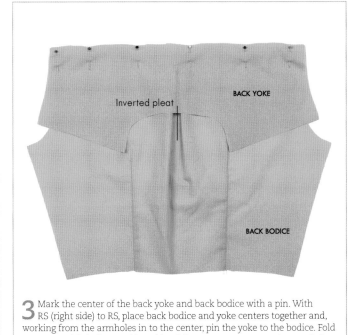

3 Mark the center of the back yoke and back bodice with a pin. With RS (right side) to RS, place back bodice and yoke centers together and, working from the armholes in to the center, pin the yoke to the bodice. Fold any excess fabric flat on either side of the center to create an inverted pleat.

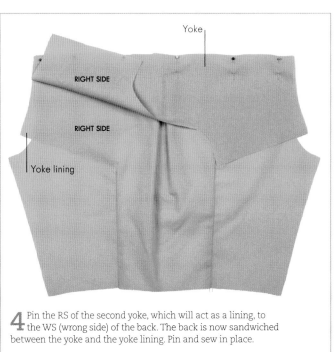

4 Pin the RS of the second yoke, which will act as a lining, to the WS (wrong side) of the back. The back is now sandwiched between the yoke and the yoke lining. Pin and sew in place.

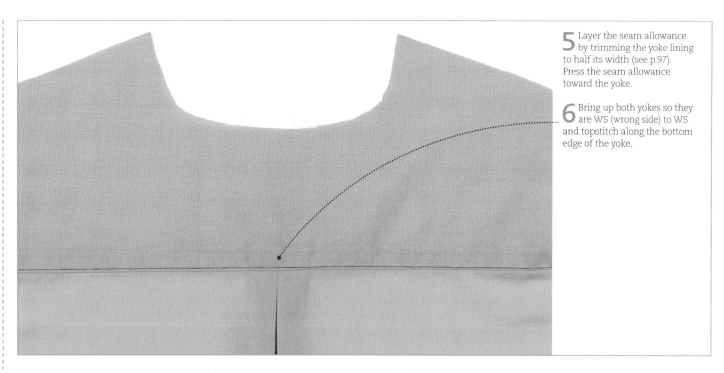

5 Layer the seam allowance by trimming the yoke lining to half its width (see p.97). Press the seam allowance toward the yoke.

6 Bring up both yokes so they are WS (wrong side) to WS and topstitch along the bottom edge of the yoke.

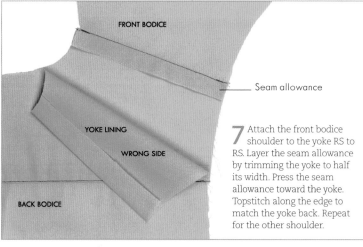

FRONT BODICE

Seam allowance

YOKE LINING

WRONG SIDE

BACK BODICE

7 Attach the front bodice shoulder to the yoke RS to RS. Layer the seam allowance by trimming the yoke to half its width. Press the seam allowance toward the yoke. Topstitch along the edge to match the yoke back. Repeat for the other shoulder.

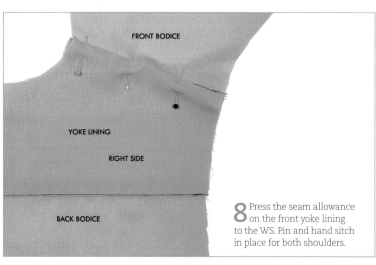

FRONT BODICE

YOKE LINING

RIGHT SIDE

BACK BODICE

8 Press the seam allowance on the front yoke lining to the WS. Pin and hand sitch in place for both shoulders.

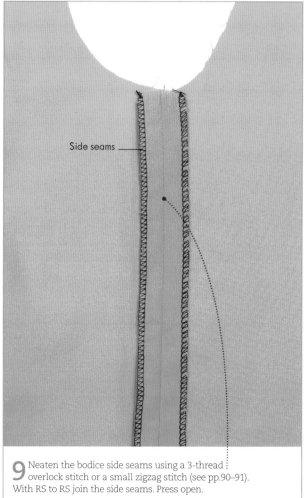

Side seams

9 Neaten the bodice side seams using a 3-thread overlock stitch or a small zigzag stitch (see pp.90–91). With RS to RS join the side seams. Press open.

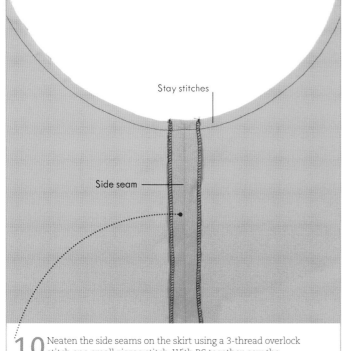

Stay stitches

Side seam

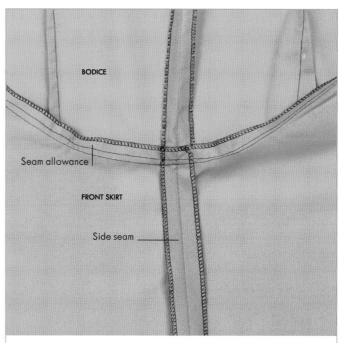

BODICE

Seam allowance

FRONT SKIRT

Side seam

10 Neaten the side seams on the skirt using a 3-thread overlock stitch or a small zigzag stitch. With RS together, sew the skirt sections together at the side seams and press open. Sew a row of stay stitches ½in (1.3cm) inside the waist seam.

11 Place the front and back skirts to the front and back bodices, RS to RS, matching the side seams. To make sure they match, you may have to fit the skirt to the bodice by easing in the bodice slightly. Press the seam allowances together. Neaten the seam allowances together using either a 3-thead overlock stitch or a small zigzag stitch. Press seam allowance up toward the bodice.

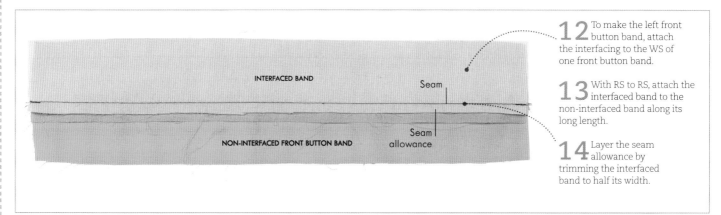

INTERFACED BAND

Seam

NON-INTERFACED FRONT BUTTON BAND

Seam allowance

12 To make the left front button band, attach the interfacing to the WS of one front button band.

13 With RS to RS, attach the interfaced band to the non-interfaced band along its long length.

14 Layer the seam allowance by trimming the interfaced band to half its width.

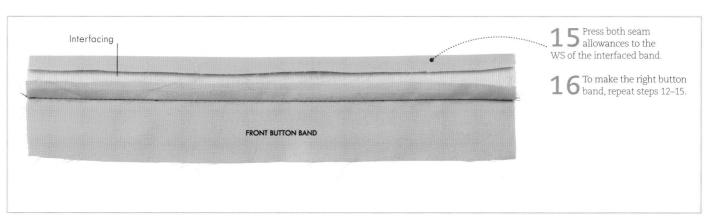

Interfacing

FRONT BUTTON BAND

15 Press both seam allowances to the WS of the interfaced band.

16 To make the right button band, repeat steps 12–15.

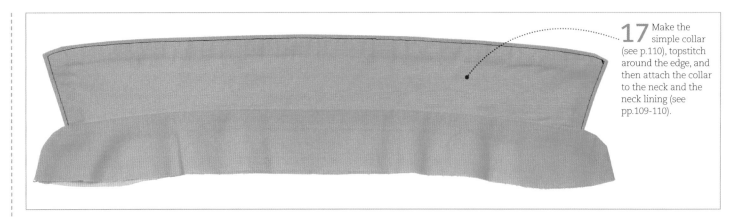

17 Make the simple collar (see p.110), topstitch around the edge, and then attach the collar to the neck and the neck lining (see pp.109-110).

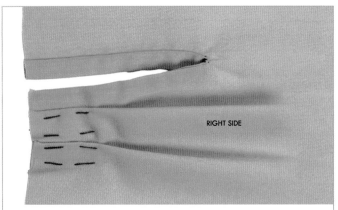

RIGHT SIDE

18 Make a bound opening at the wrist of the sleeve as marked (see p.119). Pleat the sleeve on the RS following the arrows on the pattern, creasing along the pattern marks, and tack in place.

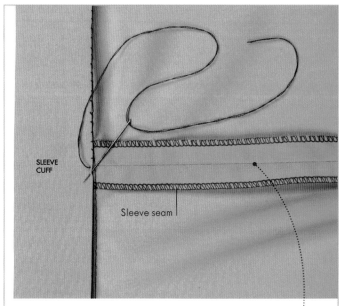

SLEEVE CUFF

Sleeve seam

19 Sew the one-piece cuffs (see p.120). Neaten the sleeve seams using a 3-thread overlock stitch or a small zigzag stitch. Sew the seams and press open. Attach the cuffs (see p.120).

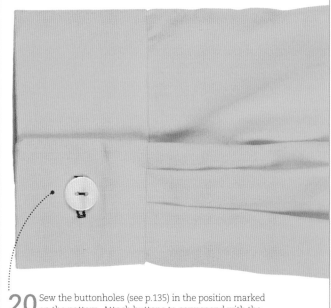

20 Sew the buttonholes (see p.135) in the position marked on the pattern. Attach buttons to correspond with the buttonholes (see p.133).

21 Create the pleats in the sleeve head and insert the sleeves into the armholes (see p.125).

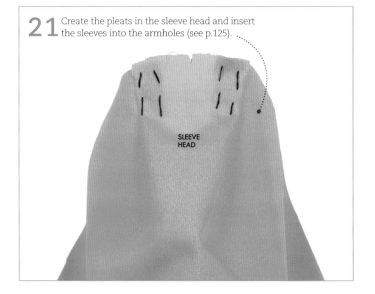

SLEEVE HEAD

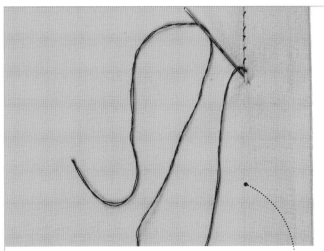

22 With RS (right side) to RS, sew the interfaced section of the band to the CF (center front) opening. Press the seam toward the band. Fold the band back along the seam that was pressed open in step 9. Hand stitch in place, stopping 3in (7.5cm) from the hem. Repeat this for second CF opening.

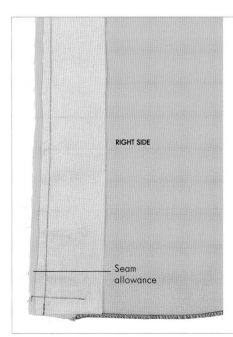

RIGHT SIDE

Seam allowance

23 For both front button bands, turn the bottom of the facing RS to RS, making sure the folded seam allowance is flat. Sew along the bottom of the front bands from the raw edge to the seam allowance fold. Neaten the hem edge using a 3-thread overlocker or a small zigzag stitch just beyond the button band seam.

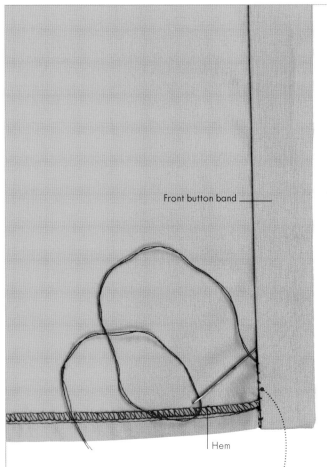

Front button band

Hem

24 Turn up ½in (1.3cm) following instructions for a curved hem finish (see p.128). Sew in place. Fold the two seams as for the simple collar and turn the front band to the WS (wrong side) and sew in place along the line of machine stitching.

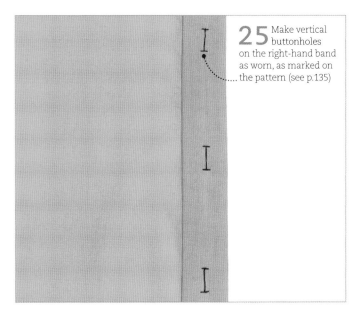

25 Make vertical buttonholes on the right-hand band as worn, as marked on the pattern (see p.135)

26 Attach buttons to correspond with the buttonholes (see p.133).

DRESS PATTERN FOUR VARIATION
SHIRTDRESS WITH ROLL-TAB SLEEVES

This shorter shirtdress comes to just below the knee. It has roll-up three-quarter length sleeves that are held in place by tabs with buttons. There is added detailing in the form of top-stitching. The sleeve strap buttons can be self-covered, as shown here, or use a contrasting color for an extra feature.

YOU WILL NEED
- 98in (2.5m) x 59in (150cm) fabric
- 1 x spool of matching all-purpose sewing thread
- 1 x spool of contrasting all-purpose sewing thread for pattern marking
- 10 x ⅜in (10mm) buttons
- 2 x ⅝in (15mm) self-cover buttons
- 39in x 8in (1m x 20cm) fusible interfacing

PREPARING THE PATTERN
This dress is made using Dress Pattern Four. Follow the instructions to download the pattern in your size (see pp.10–11).

GARMENT CONSTRUCTION
This dress has a full-length button band opening at the front, a classic shirt collar, and a shoulder yoke. The bodice is shaped by waist darts at the front and back, and the dress has a full skirt that reaches to just below the knee.

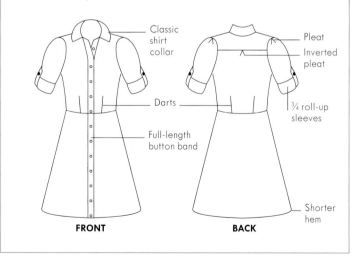

Classic shirt collar

Pleat

Inverted pleat

¾ roll-up sleeves

Darts

Full-length button band

Shorter hem

FRONT

BACK

Rayon

Double gauze

This shirtdress was made from striped linen but would also look great if made from rayon or double gauze.

▶ **HOW TO MAKE THE SHIRTDRESS WITH ROLL-TAB SLEEVES**

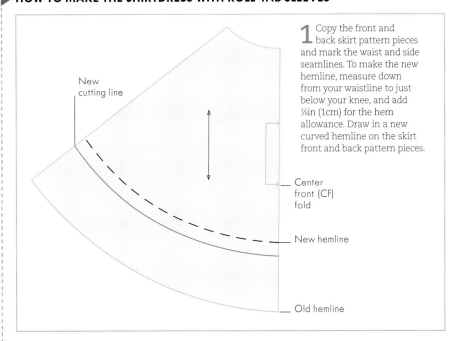

1 Copy the front and back skirt pattern pieces and mark the waist and side seamlines. To make the new hemline, measure down from your waistline to just below your knee, and add ⅜in (1cm) for the hem allowance. Draw in a new curved hemline on the skirt front and back pattern pieces.

New cutting line

Center front (CF) fold

New hemline

Old hemline

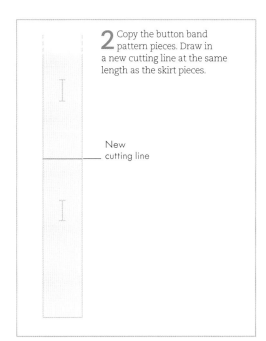

2 Copy the button band pattern pieces. Draw in a new cutting line at the same length as the skirt pieces.

New cutting line

3 Copy the sleeve and mark the seamlines. Measure 5½in (14cm) up from the bottom of the sleeve and draw in the new cutting line. Measure 9in (22.5cm) down from the center of the sleeve head. Mark the position for the button and the reinforcing patch. Repeat on the other sleeve.

4 Continue making up as for Classic Shirtdress steps 1–11 (see pp.208–213).

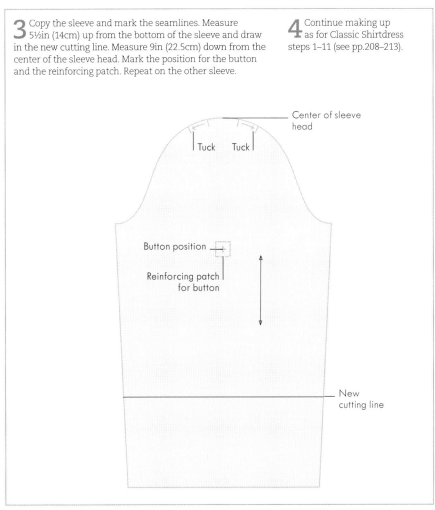

Center of sleeve head

Tuck   Tuck

Button position

Reinforcing patch for button

New cutting line

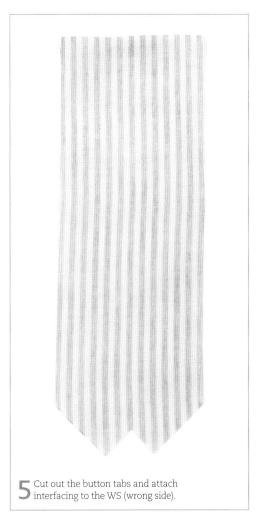

5 Cut out the button tabs and attach interfacing to the WS (wrong side).

Seam
allowance

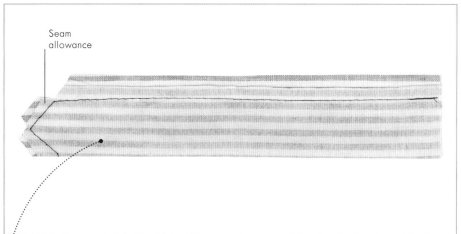

6 Fold the button tabs in half RS (right side) to RS and sew around the edges, leaving the straight short edge open. Layer the seam allowance to half its width and across the points. Turn RS out and press. Topstitch the edges and neaten the raw edge.

7 Cut two pieces of fabric 1¼in (3cm) square to make the reinforcing patches for the button tabs. Neaten the edges.

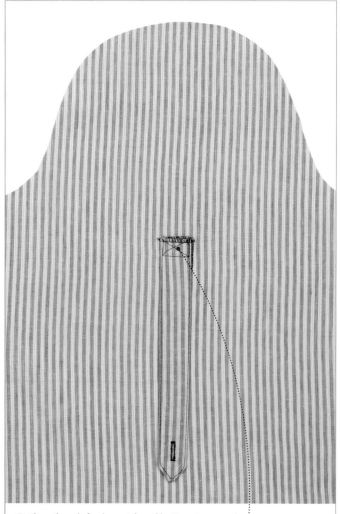

8 Place the reinforcing patch and button straps on the WS of the sleeve, in the position marked on the pattern. Sew in place, creating a cross within a rectangle for strength.

9 Neaten the sleeve seams and lower edge of the sleeves using a 3-thread overcast stitch or a small zigzag stitch.

10 Cover the buttons (see p.136) and sew them in place to the RS of the sleeve.

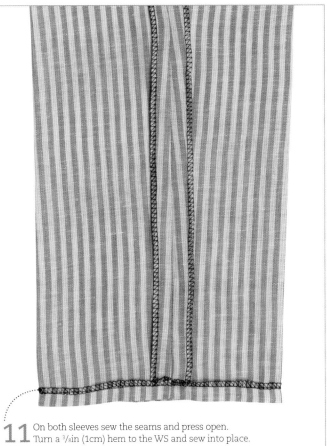

11 On both sleeves sew the seams and press open. Turn a ⅜in (1cm) hem to the WS and sew into place.

12 Continue making up following the Classic Shirtdress steps 14–17 (see pp.208–213).

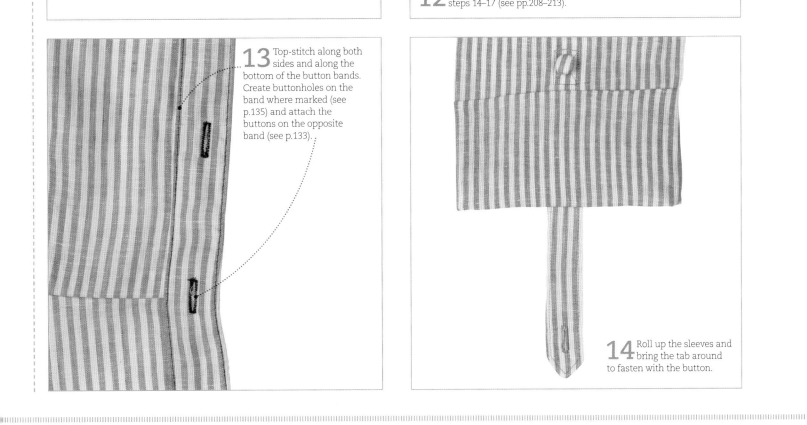

13 Top-stitch along both sides and along the bottom of the button bands. Create buttonholes on the band where marked (see p.135) and attach the buttons on the opposite band (see p.133).

14 Roll up the sleeves and bring the tab around to fasten with the button.

Page 220

CLASSIC CIGARETTE PANTS

Page 224

CROPPED CIGARETTE PANTS

Page 226

CLASSIC PALAZZO PANTS

Page 232

PALAZZO SHORTS

THE PANTS

Pants in different styles and fabrics are a wardrobe staple that can be dressed up or down. Here are two basic styles and a variation of each that will work well for most occasions. Making pants may appear daunting, but the steps are all clearly explained.

PANTS PATTERN ONE
CLASSIC CIGARETTE PANTS

These simple but elegant pants are designed to finish just above the ankle. They can be dressed up or down and teamed with a wide choice of tops. Choose your pattern according to your full hip measurement (see pp.10–11). To ensure the pants fit well, carefully measure your inside leg and crotch measurements against the pattern before cutting. It is recommended that you make the pants in muslin first to make sure of a good fit. By altering your choice of color and fabric, these pants can be adapted for casual or work wear.

YOU WILL NEED
- 49in (1.25m) x 59in (150cm) fabric
- 36in x 10in (90cm x 25cm) medium-weight fusible interfacing
- 1 x spool of matching all-purpose sewing thread
- 1 x spool of contrasting all-purpose sewing thread for pattern marking
- 1 x 8in (20cm) invisible zipper

PREPARING THE PATTERN
These pants are made using Pants Pattern One. Follow the instructions to download the pattern in your size (see pp.10–11).

Scuba

Gabardine

These pants were made in worsted wool suiting fabric, but you could also try scuba or gabardine.

These slim-fitting pants can be worn with heels or flats depending on the occasion. Wear them with a short cropped top, or a tunic for a different look.

GARMENT CONSTRUCTION
These pants have an invisible side zipper, front and back waist darts, and a narrow leg that finishes just above the ankle. They are close-fitting with a self-lined waistband.

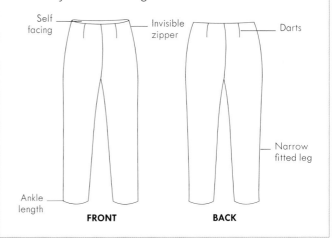

Self facing — Invisible zipper — Darts — Narrow fitted leg — Ankle length

FRONT   **BACK**

▶ HOW TO MAKE THE CIGARETTE PANTS

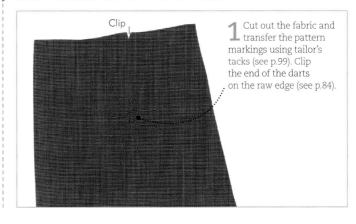

Clip

1 Cut out the fabric and transfer the pattern markings using tailor's tacks (see p.99). Clip the end of the darts on the raw edge (see p.84).

2 Make the waist darts (see p.99) in the pant front and back. Press the front darts toward the CF (center front) and toward the CB (center back).

3 Neaten the side, crotch, and inside leg seams using a 3-thread overlock stitch or a small zigzag stitch.

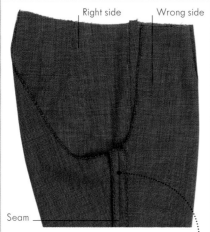

Right side   Wrong side

Seam

4 To make the right leg, join a front leg to a back leg, RS (right sides) facing, at the outside and inside seams. Press the seam open.

5 Insert the invisible zipper (see p.132) in the outside seam of the left leg.

6 Sew the inside seam of the left leg and press open.

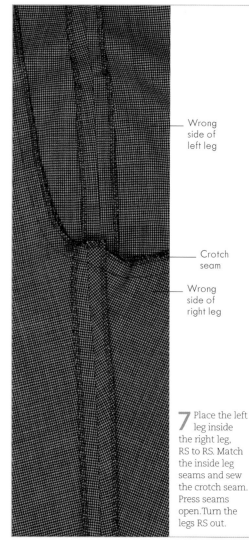

Wrong side of left leg

Crotch seam

Wrong side of right leg

7 Place the left leg inside the right leg, RS to RS. Match the inside leg seams and sew the crotch seam. Press seams open. Turn the legs RS out.

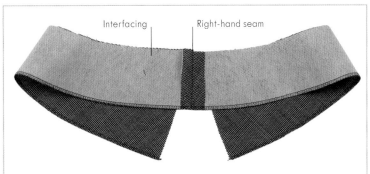

Interfacing   Right-hand seam

8 Attach medium-weight fusible interfacing (see p.102) to the WS (wrong side) of the waist facing pieces. Join the waist facings on the RH (right-hand) seam only. Press the seams open. Neaten lower edge of the facing using a 3-thread overlock stitch or a small zigzag stitch.

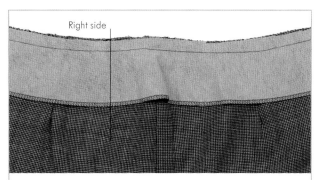

Right side

9 Attach the interfaced waist facing to the pants, matching RH seams.

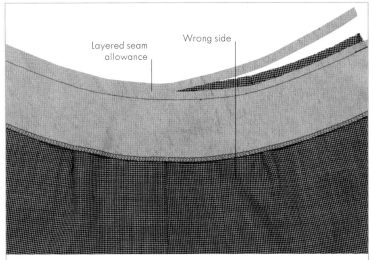

Layered seam allowance   Wrong side

10 Layer the seam allowance by trimming the facing to half its width (see p.97). Clip into the seam so it lays flat.

Wrong side

11 Press the seam toward the waist facing and understitch (see p.98). Turn the waist facing to the WS.

12 At the zipper, fold the edge of the waist facing under to meet the zipper tape. Pin and hand stitch to the zipper tape. Hand stitch a couple of small stitches to attach the facing at the side seams and CF (center front) so the waistband stays in place during wear.

13 Neaten the hem edge of the pant legs using a 3-thread overlock stitch or a small zigzag stitch. Turn up a 1½in (4cm) hem allowance, pin and press, and hand stitch in place.

PANTS PATTERN ONE VARIATION

CROPPED CIGARETTE PANTS

The pants pattern has been altered to make these chic cropped cigarette pants. They are ideal for summer and make an easy pack for your holiday suitcase. Go for a denim jean-style look or choose a bright and bold fabric with a summer print. They look good with a cropped top or under a loose fitting summer tunic. Choose a contrasting thread for the topstitching feature. To determine your leg length, measure down your inside leg to mid-calf.

YOU WILL NEED

- 51in (1.3m) x 59in (150cm) fabric
- 36in x 10in (90cm x 25cm) medium-weight fusible interfacing
- 1 x spool of matching all-purpose sewing thread
- 1 x spool of contrasting all-purpose sewing thread for the topstitching
- 1 x spool of contrasting all-purpose sewing thread for pattern marking
- 1 x 8in (20cm) invisible zipper

PREPARING THE PATTERN

The pants are made by altering Pants Pattern One. Follow the instructions to download the pattern in your size (see pp.10–11).

GARMENT CONSTRUCTION

The pants have an invisible side zipper, front and back darting at the waist, and a narrow leg with side leg slits that finish mid-calf. The pants fit close to the body, with a self-lined facing and topstitch detailing.

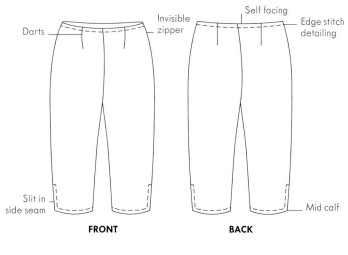

Darts — Invisible zipper — Self facing — Edge stitch detailing

Slit in side seam — Mid calf

FRONT   **BACK**

Bio-linen

Ramie

These cropped pants were made in 8oz light blue denim, but bio-linen or ramie would also work very well.

▶ HOW TO MAKE THE CROPPED CIGARETTE PANTS

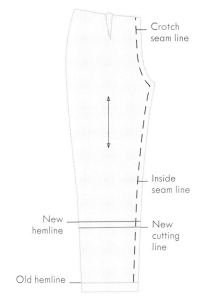

1 Prepare the front leg pattern and mark the seamlines and hemlines. Measuring upward from the hemline, draw a line for the new hemline. Measure ¾in (2cm) below this line and mark a new hem cutting line.

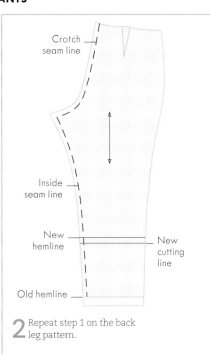

2 Repeat step 1 on the back leg pattern.

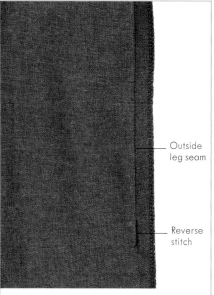

3 Make up as for the Classic Cigarette Pants steps 1–12 (see pp.220) but stitch the outside leg seam to 3¼in (8cm) above the cutting line to make the side split. Reverse stitch (see pp.222) at the end of the seam to provide extra seam strength.

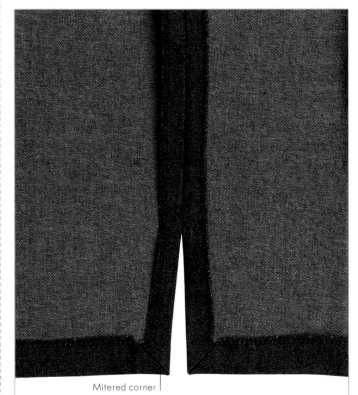

Mitered corner

4 Neaten the hem edge using a 3-thread overlock stitch or a small zigzag stitch. Press the hem allowance to the WS (wrong side). Miter the hem at the bottom of the split and pin in place.

5 With the contrasting thread, topstitch (see p.98) ³⁄₈in (1cm) up from the hem and around the split.

6 With the contrasting thread, topstitch (see p.98) around the waistfacing.

PANTS PATTERN TWO
CLASSIC PALAZZO PANTS

Wide-leg, or palazzo, pants are very flattering when worn with casual sandals or flats. These retain their smooth-leg look by having discreet in-seam pockets. Choose the pattern size by your full hip measurement (see p.61) and be sure to check your crotch measurements against the pattern. It is recommended to make the pattern in muslin first. These pants would look fabulous in fine wool crepe for evening wear or in linen or heavy cotton—even in medium-weight denim—for a more casual look.

YOU WILL NEED
- 107in (2.7m) x 59in (150cm) fabric
- 12in (30cm) x 59in (150cm) lining fabric
- 1 x spool matching all-purpose sewing thread
- 1 x spool contrasting all-purpose sewing thread for pattern marking
- 39in (1m) x fusible waistband interfacing
- 1 x pant hook and eye
- 1 x 7in (18cm) zipper

PREPARING THE PATTERN
These pants are made using Pants Pattern Two. Follow the instructions to download the pattern in your size (see pp.10–11).

Medium-weight denim

Crepe

We made our pants in linen, but you could try a crepe for evening or a medium-weight denim or printed linen for daytime. Medium-weight fabrics give maximum impact for this style.

GARMENT CONSTRUCTION
These wide-leg pants have a fly-front zipper opening and a fitted waistband. Belt loops on the waistband take a narrow belt. The pants feature in-seam pockets and front and back tucks at the waist.

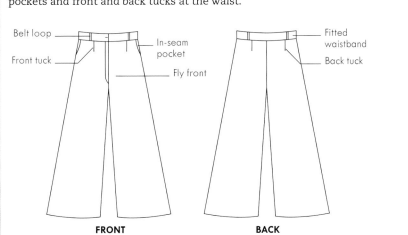

FRONT   BACK

These flowing palazzo pants epitomize 1940s movie-star glamour.

▶ **HOW TO MAKE THE CLASSIC PALAZZO PANTS**

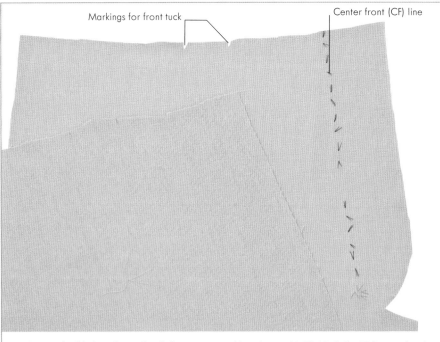

Markings for front tuck

Center front (CF) line

1 Cut out the fabric and transfer all the pattern markings (see pp.84–85). Mark the CF (center front) line, the front tuck, and the pocket opening with trace bastes (see p.84).

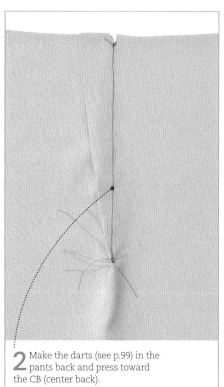

2 Make the darts (see p.99) in the pants back and press toward the CB (center back).

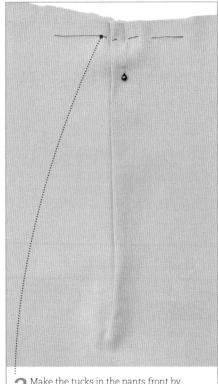

3 Make the tucks in the pants front by bringing the tuck lines at the waist edge together RS (right side) to RS. Pin and baste across the top.

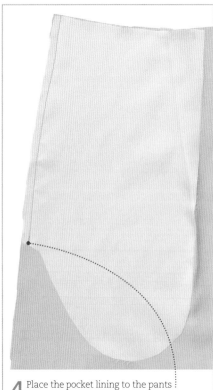

4 Place the pocket lining to the pants front, RS to RS. Pin and machine in place with a ⅜in (1cm) seam allowance.

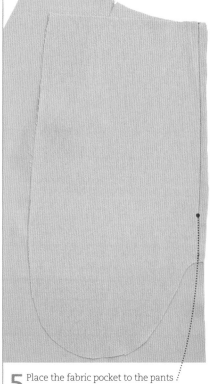

5 Place the fabric pocket to the pants back, RS to RS. Pin and machine in place with a ⅜in (1cm) seam allowance.

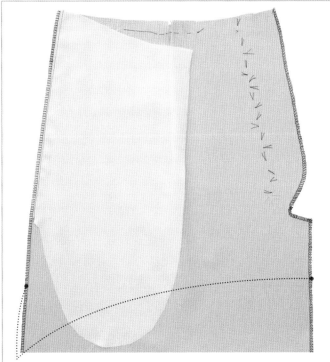

6 Neaten the side seams, the inside leg seam, and the CF and CB crotch seams using a 3-thread serger stitch or a small zigzag stitch (see pp.92–93).

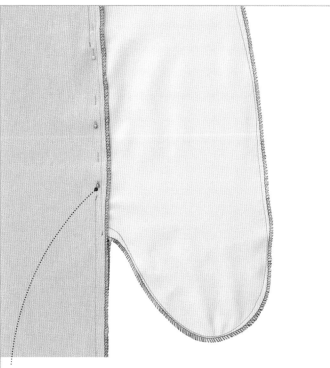

7 Join the pants front to the pants back at the side seams, leaving open above the point marked for the pocket opening. Stitch around the edges of the pocket bag and neaten.

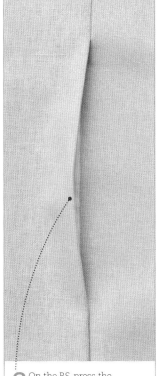

8 On the RS, press the side seam open and press the pocket toward the pants front.

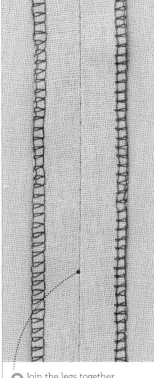

9 Join the legs together at the inside leg seam. Press the seam open.

Faced fly front zipper

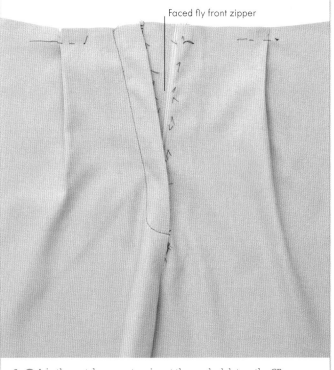

10 Join the crotch seam, stopping at the marked dot on the CF. Insert a faced fly-front zipper (see p.131).

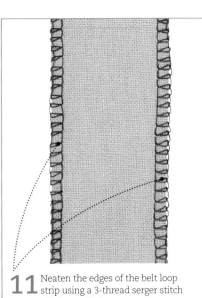

11 Neaten the edges of the belt loop strip using a 3-thread serger stitch or a small zigzag stitch.

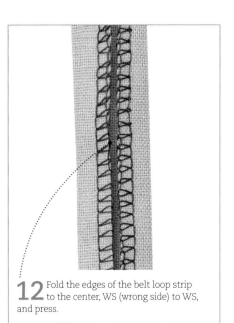

12 Fold the edges of the belt loop strip to the center, WS (wrong side) to WS, and press.

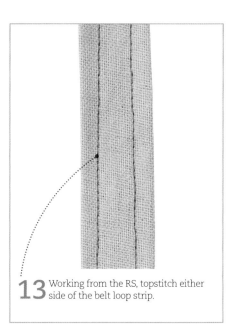

13 Working from the RS, topstitch either side of the belt loop strip.

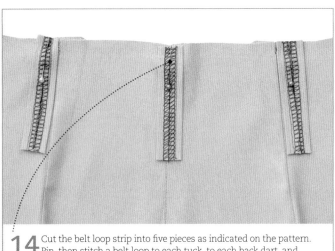

14 Cut the belt loop strip into five pieces as indicated on the pattern. Pin, then stitch a belt loop to each tuck, to each back dart, and to the CB seam.

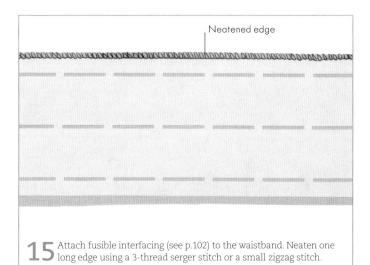

Neatened edge

15 Attach fusible interfacing (see p.102) to the waistband. Neaten one long edge using a 3-thread serger stitch or a small zigzag stitch.

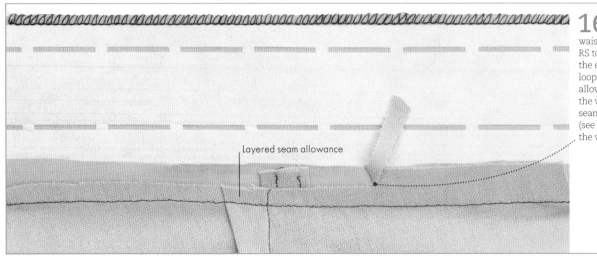

Layered seam allowance

16 Attach the other edge of the waistband to the pants, RS to RS, stitching over the ends of the belt loops. Layer the seam allowance by trimming the waistband side of the seam to half its width (see p.97). Press toward the waistband.

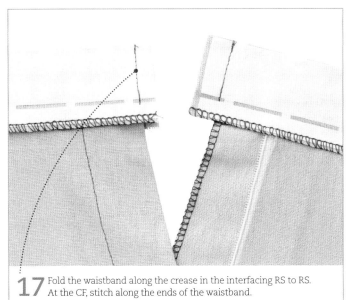

17 Fold the waistband along the crease in the interfacing RS to RS. At the CF, stitch along the ends of the waistband.

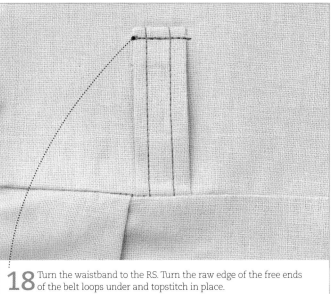

18 Turn the waistband to the RS. Turn the raw edge of the free ends of the belt loops under and topstitch in place.

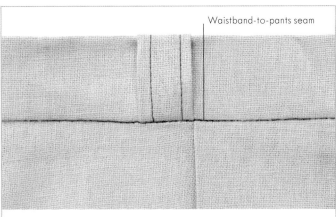

Waistband-to-pants seam

19 Fold the waistband WS to WS. Pin the free edge of the waistband to the waistband-to-pants seam. Working from the RS of the pants, stitch in the ditch—the line produced by the waistband-to-pants seam—through all layers to secure the waistband in place.

20 Neaten the hem edge by serging (see p.126). Turn up a 1½in (4cm) hem and hand stitch in place.

Hook   Eye

21 Attach a hook and eye to the waistband.

PANTS

PANTS PATTERN TWO VARIATION
PALAZZO SHORTS

Here the Classic Palazzo Pants have been shortened and given cuffs to create shorts that can be worn by any age. The cuffs are sewn in place to keep them in position. These shorts are comfortable to wear and, as with the pants, have belt loops. Wear the shorts with your favorite belt or make a sash belt (see pp.113) for a more casual vacation look. To make sure you have the correct finished length, measure your outside leg from your waist to just above the knee.

YOU WILL NEED
- 47¼in (1.20m) x 59in (150cm) fabric
- 1 x spool matching all-purpose sewing thread
- 1 x spool contrasting all-purpose sewing thread for pattern marking
- 39¼in (1m) x fusible waistband interfacing
- 1 x 7in (18cm) pant zipper
- 1 x pant hook and eye

PREPARING THE PATTERN
These shorts are made using Pants Pattern Two. Follow the instructions to download the pattern in your size (see pp.10–11).

These shorts were made in a lightweight slub-textured fabric but they would also work well in gingham or polyster.

Gingham   **Polyester**

GARMENT CONSTRUCTION
These shorts have a fly-front zipper opening and a fitted waistband with belt loops. There are front tucks, darts at the back, and the hem finishes just above the knee. The cuffs are made so that raw seams are hidden to give a professional finish.

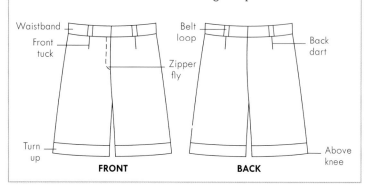

Waistband
Front tuck
Zipper fly
Turn up
FRONT

Belt loop
Back dart
Above knee
BACK

► **HOW TO MAKE THE PALAZZO SHORTS**

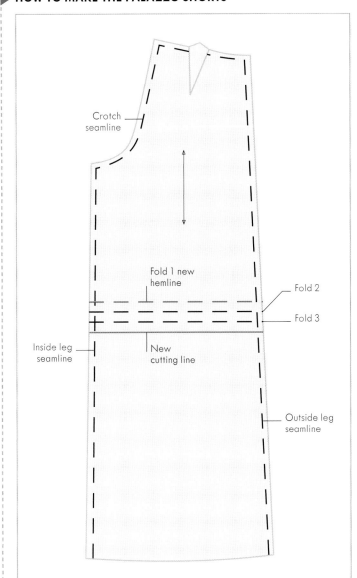

Crotch
seamline

Fold 1 new
hemline

Fold 2

Fold 3

Inside leg
seamline

New
cutting line

Outside leg
seamline

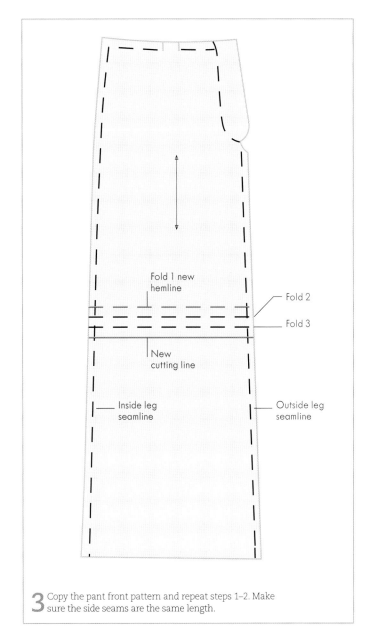

Fold 1 new
hemline

Fold 2

Fold 3

New
cutting line

Inside leg
seamline

Outside leg
seamline

1 Copy the pant back pattern and mark the seamlines. Mark a point equivalent to your measurement from the waist to above the knee. Draw a horizontal line across the leg from this point to make a new hemline. Mark this as Fold 1.

2 For the cuffs, measure 1in (2.5cm) down from Fold 1, draw a line and mark Fold 2. Measure 1in (2.5cm) down from Fold 2, draw a line and mark Fold 3. Measure 1in (2.5cm) down from Fold 3 and draw the new cutting line.

3 Copy the pant front pattern and repeat steps 1–2. Make sure the side seams are the same length.

4 Cut out the fabric using the new pattern pieces. Transfer all pattern markings (see pp.84–85). Pin the CF (center front) line and the front tucks and mark with trace tacks (see p.84).

Front tucks

CF (center
front) seamline

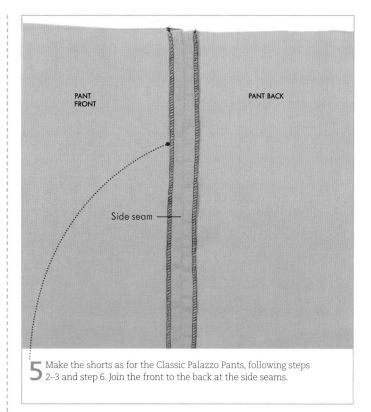

5 Make the shorts as for the Classic Palazzo Pants, following steps 2–3 and step 6. Join the front to the back at the side seams.

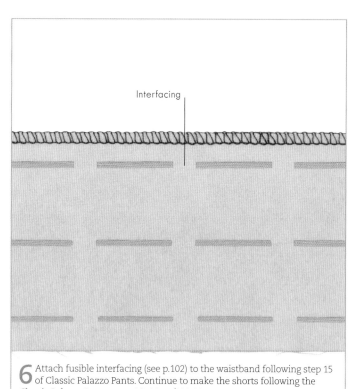

6 Attach fusible interfacing (see p.102) to the waistband following step 15 of Classic Palazzo Pants. Continue to make the shorts following the Classic Palazzo Pants steps 10–14 and 16–19.

7 Neaten the hem edge using a 3-thread overlock stitch or a small zigzag stitch (see pp.126–127).

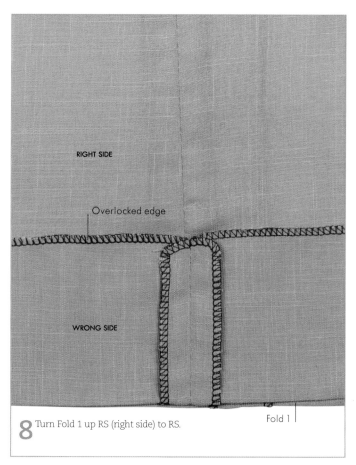

8 Turn Fold 1 up RS (right side) to RS.

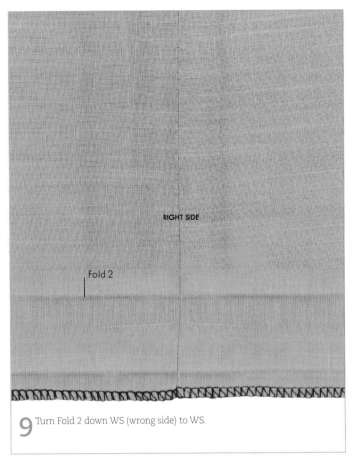

RIGHT SIDE

Fold 2

9 Turn Fold 2 down WS (wrong side) to WS.

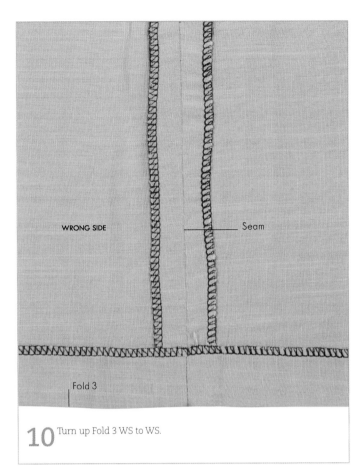

WRONG SIDE

Seam

Fold 3

10 Turn up Fold 3 WS to WS.

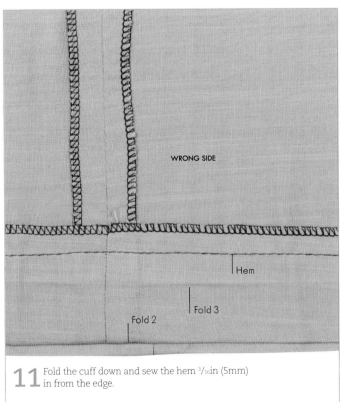

WRONG SIDE

Hem

Fold 3

Fold 2

11 Fold the cuff down and sew the hem ³⁄₁₆in (5mm) in from the edge.

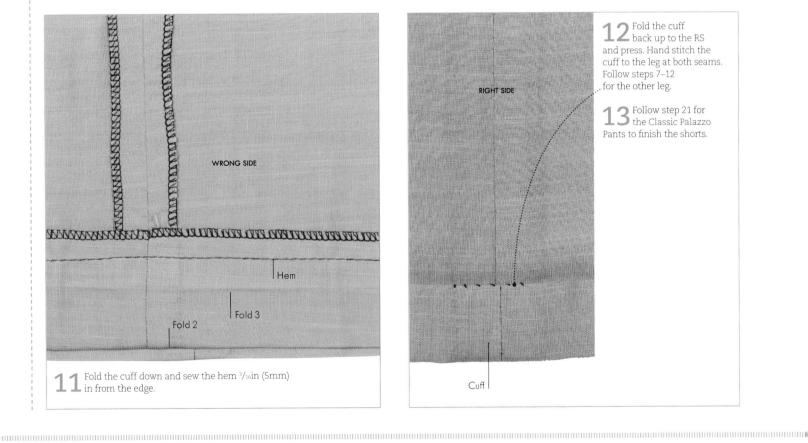

RIGHT SIDE

Cuff

12 Fold the cuff back up to the RS and press. Hand stitch the cuff to the leg at both seams. Follow steps 7–12 for the other leg.

13 Follow step 21 for the Classic Palazzo Pants to finish the shorts.

Page 238

TOP PATTERN ONE

CLASSIC SHELL TOP

VARIATIONS

Page 242

TIE-NECK TOP

Page 244

LONG-SLEEVED TUNIC

TOP PATTERN TWO

Page 246

CLASSIC PRINCESS-LINE BLOUSE

VARIATION

Page 251

SHORT-SLEEVED BLOUSE

THE TOPS

A quick change of shirt or top can transform a skirt or pair of pants from an outfit for the office into one to wear at a weekend in the country or at a cocktail party. The two basic styles here form the basis for five different looks.

TOP PATTERN ONE
CLASSIC SHELL TOP

The ultimate in simplicity, this style of top is known as a shell top, since it fits the upper body like a shell fits an oyster. The center-back zipper helps ensure a smooth line for a top that is easy office wear, whether under a jacket or on its own. It would comfortably tuck into a skirt or pants, or could be worn untucked. Choose the pattern by your bust measurement and, if necessary, widen at the hip.

YOU WILL NEED

- 69in (1.75m) x 59in (150cm) fabric
- 1 x spool matching all-purpose sewing thread
- 1 x spool contrasting all-purpose sewing thread for pattern marking
- 20in (50cm) x lightweight fusible interfacing
- 16in (41cm) zipper

PREPARING THE PATTERN

This top is made using Top Pattern One. Follow the instructions to copy or download the pattern in your size (see pp.10–11).

GARMENT CONSTRUCTION

The top is shaped with bust darts and has a round neckline finished with a facing. It has wrist-length, set-in sleeves that should sit comfortably at the end of the shoulder. There is a CB (center-back) zipper for ease of wear.

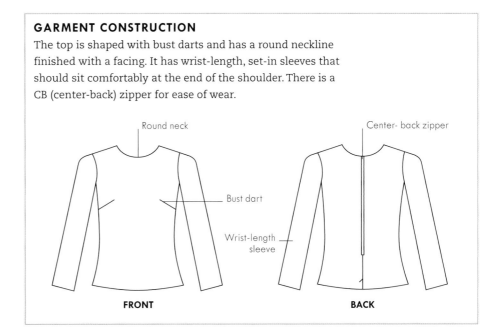

Round neck

Center-back zipper

Bust dart

Wrist-length sleeve

FRONT

BACK

Viscose

Silk satin

This top would work well in any lightweight fabric. Ours is in a polka-dot polyester, but it would also look great in plain silk satin, cotton, or viscose.

HOW TO MAKE THE CLASSIC SHELL TOP

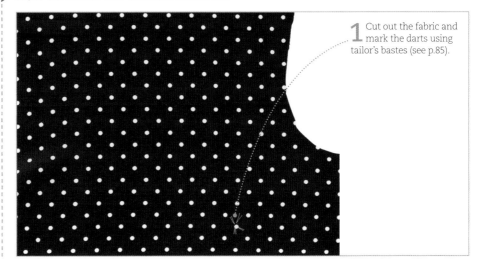

1 Cut out the fabric and mark the darts using tailor's bastes (see p.85).

The ultimate shell top, this versatile little number is great with a skirt or pants, tucked in or worn out

2 Make the darts in the front (see p.99) and press toward the waist.

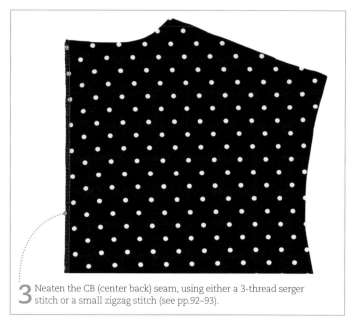

3 Neaten the CB (center back) seam, using either a 3-thread serger stitch or a small zigzag stitch (see pp.92–93).

4 Insert a 16in (40cm) zipper of your choice in the CB (see pp.129–132). Stitch the remainder of the CB seam.

5 Join the front to the back at the shoulder and side seams, RS (right side) to RS. Neaten the seam allowances together using either a 3-thread serger stitch or a small zigzag stitch.

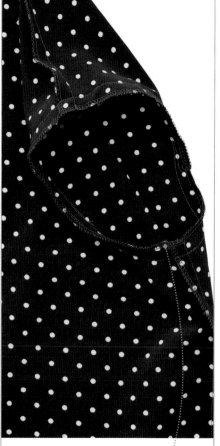

6 Neaten the lower edge of both sleeves using either a 3-thread serger stitch or a small zigzag stitch.

Ease stitches

7 Machine the sleeve seam. Neaten the seam allowances together using either a 3-thread serger stitch or a small zigzag stitch. Using the longest stitch available, machine two rows of ease stitches through the sleeve head (see p.114).

8 Fit the sleeve into the armhole, RS (right side) to RS, remembering to pin and stitch from the sleeve side (see p.114). Neaten the seam allowances together using either a 3-thread serger stitch or a small zigzag stitch.

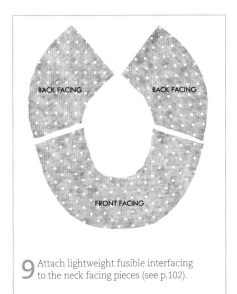

9 Attach lightweight fusible interfacing to the neck facing pieces (see p.102).

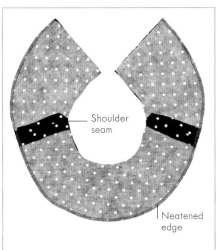

10 Join the facings at the shoulder seams and press the seams open. Neaten the lower edge (see pp.103–105).

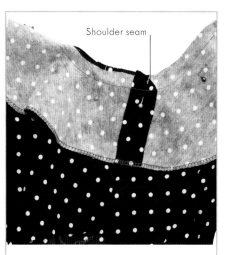

11 Place the facings to the neck edge of the top RS to RS, matching the shoulder seams. Pin and machine.

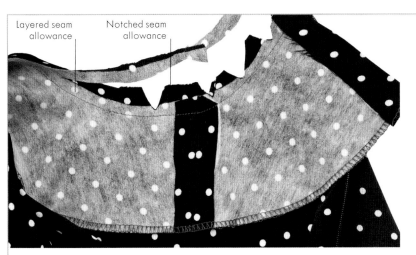

12 Layer the seam allowance by trimming the facing side of the seam to half its width. Notch the seam allowance to reduce bulk (see p.97).

13 Turn the facing to the WS (wrong side) and press.

14 At the CB, fold the edge of the facing in to meet the zipper tape. Pin and hand stitch in place.

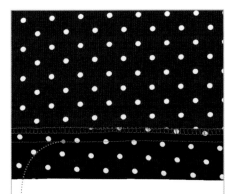

15 Neaten the lower edge of the top. Pin up 1½in (4cm) on the top and 1¼in (3cm) on the sleeves. Press and machine in place.

16 Topstitch around the neck, using stitch length 3.5.

TOPS

TOP PATTERN ONE VARIATION
TIE-NECK TOP

The shell top has now become a top with a slightly lower neckline, a tie neck, and a gathered sleeve. The back no longer features a zipper but is cut in one piece. This neckline flatters the face and is easy to wear with a skirt, pants, or jeans.

YOU WILL NEED

- 79in (2m) x 59in (150cm) fabric
- 1 x spool matching all-purpose sewing thread
- 1 x spool contrasting all-purpose sewing thread for pattern marking
- 20in (50cm) x ¾in (2cm) wide elastic

PREPARING THE PATTERN

This top is made using Top Pattern One. Follow the instructions to download the pattern in your size (see pp.10-11).

GARMENT CONSTRUCTION

This blouse has bust darts, a self-bound neck opening, a tie neck, and sleeves that are elasticated to fit the wrist.

Fine cotton

Satin

This top was made in polyester chiffon, but any soft fabric such as, fine cotton or satin, would work just as well.

▶ HOW TO MAKE THE TIE-NECK TOP

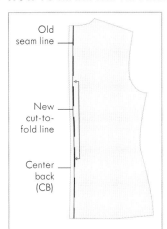

Old seam line
New cut-to-fold line
Center back (CB)

1 To cut the back as one piece, copy the pattern back and mark the CB (center back) seam line. Put a ruler along the seam line and rule a new straight line in its place. This line will be placed to a fold for cutting.

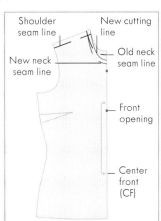

Shoulder seam line
New cutting line
Old neck seam line
New neck seam line
Front opening
Center front (CF)

2 Copy the pattern front and mark the seam lines. Mark a point on the CF (center front) 1⅜in (3.5cm) below the neck seam line. From here, draw a new neck seam line to the point where the neck and shoulder seam lines meet. Measure a ⅝in (1.5cm) seam allowance from the new neck seam line and mark a new cutting line. On the CF, mark a point 6⅜in (16cm) below the new neck seam line.

Old seam line
New seam line
New cutting line
Extended hemline

3 To widen the sleeve, copy the sleeve pattern and mark the seam lines. Extend the hemline by 2⅜in (6cm) on each side. Draw a slightly curving line from these two points to join them to the sleeve seam lines in the upper arm area. Draw new cutting lines ⅝in (1.5cm) below the new hemline and at either side of the new sleeve seam lines.

4 Cut out the fabric using the new pattern pieces. Mark the darts using tailor's bastes (see p.85). Make the darts (see p.99) and press toward the waist.

5 Make up as for the Classic Shell Top steps 5–8, using the seam for sheer fabrics method (see p.94).

6 Slash the CF of the blouse front to the point marked. Cut a piece of bias fabric 1½in (4cm) wide.

7 Use the bias fabric to bind the slashed opening (see p.118).

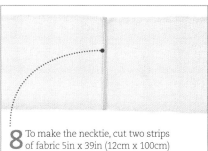

8 To make the necktie, cut two strips of fabric 5in x 39in (12cm x 100cm) on the straight grain. Join them together at the short end, RS (right side) to RS. Press the seam to one side.

9 Place the seam in the tie at the CB of the blouse, RS to RS. Machine around the neck edge. Clip the seam allowance and press toward the necktie.

10 Fold the tie, RS to RS. Starting at the slash in the neck, stitch the sides of the tie together, pivoting at the corners (see p.95). Clip the corners.

11 Turn the tie to the RS. Fold the raw edge of the tie under along the neck edge. Pin and hand stitch in place.

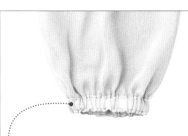

12 Machine a 1¼in (3cm) double-turn hem (see p.128) in the ends of the sleeve. Press. Insert elastic to fit the wrist (see p.117).

13 Complete as for the Classic Shell Top step 15.

TOPS

TOP PATTERN ONE VARIATION
LONG-SLEEVED TUNIC

This time our pattern has been altered to make an A-line tunic with a deep, topstitched V-neckline and a wide sleeve. It is quick and simple to make, and you will learn how to cut a neck facing. A tunic like this makes ideal casual or vacation wear.

YOU WILL NEED

- 87in (2.2m) x 59in (150cm) fabric
- 1 x spool matching all-purpose sewing thread
- 1 x spool contrasting all-purpose sewing thread for pattern marking
- 24in (60cm) lightweight fusible interfacing
- 1 x zipper

PREPARING THE PATTERN

This top is made using Top Pattern One. Follow the instructions to download the pattern in your size (see pp.10–11).

GARMENT CONSTRUCTION

This A-line, V-necked tunic has wrist-length, set-in sleeves. The faced neckline features topstitching and the tunic and sleeve hems are also machined in place. There is a CB (center-back) zipper.

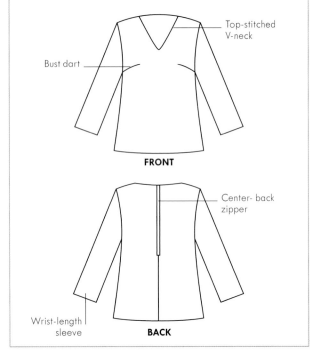

Top-stitched V-neck

Bust dart

FRONT

Center-back zipper

Wrist-length sleeve

BACK

Cotton

Acrylic knit

This top has been made in printed linen, perfect for wearing over jeans or leggings. Alternatively, try it in cotton for summer or in a knitted fabric for fall.

▶ **HOW TO MAKE THE LONG-SLEEVED TUNIC**

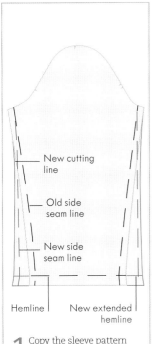

1 Copy the sleeve pattern and mark the side seam lines and the hemline. Measuring from the side seam lines, extend the hemline by 1¾in (4.5cm) on each side to widen the bottom of the sleeve. Join these points to the old side seam lines just under the arm. Measure a ⅝in (1.5cm) seam allowance from the new side seam lines and mark new cutting lines.

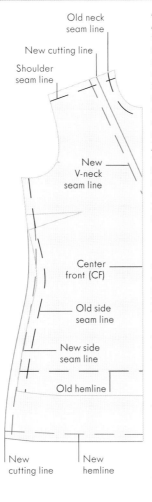

2 Copy the pattern front and mark the seam lines. Mark a point on the CF (center front) 6½in (17cm) below the neck seam line and another point 1½in (4cm) from the neck seam line along the shoulder seam line. Join the points for the new V-neck seam line. Measure a ⅝in (1.5cm) seam allowance from this new line and mark a new cutting line.

3 At the waist add ¾in (2cm) to the side seam line. At the hem edge, extend the side seam line 5in (12cm) to make the top longer. Join these two points to make a new side seam line and taper from here to the side seam line just below the bust dart. Measure a ⅝in (1.5cm) seam allowance from this new line and from the new hemline and mark new cutting lines.

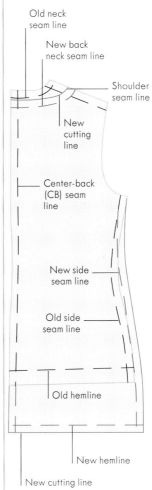

4 Copy the pattern back and mark the seam lines. Add to the side seam line and the hem to match the front. Mark a point on the CB (center back) 1in (2.5cm) below the neck seam line and another point 1½in (4cm) from the neck seam line along the shoulder seam line. Join the points for the new back neck seam line. Measure a ⅝in (1.5cm) seam allowance from this new seam line and mark a new cutting line.

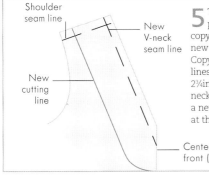

5 To make the new patterns for the facings, copy the neck area from the new pattern front and back. Copy the new neck seam lines. On the front, measure 2¾in (7cm) from the new neck seam line and mark a new cutting line, curving at the CF as shown.

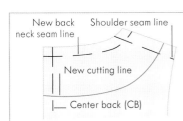

6 Make the back neck facing to match.

7 Cut out the fabric using the new pattern pieces and mark the darts using tailor's bastes (see p.85). Make up as for the Classic Shell Top steps 2–10.

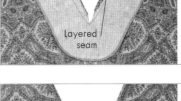

8 Place the facings to the neck edge of the tunic RS (right side) to RS, matching the seams. Pin and machine, pivoting at the CF (see p.95). Layer the seam. Turn the facing to the WS (wrong side) and press.

9 Top-stitch around the neck.

10 Continue as for the Classic Shell Top step 15, remembering that the hem allowance on the tunic is now ⅝in (1.5cm).

TOP PATTERN TWO
CLASSIC PRINCESS-LINE BLOUSE

This timeless blouse is very versatile. It will look efficient at the office in a plain fabric or a stripe, or try a cotton check for a more informal occasion. The princess lines at the front give the shirt a loosely fitted shape. Choose the pattern by your bust measurement; you should also check your neck measurement to make sure the blouse is comfortable.

YOU WILL NEED
- 94in (2.4m) x 59in (150cm) fabric
- 1 x spool matching all-purpose sewing thread
- 1 x spool contrasting all-purpose sewing thread for pattern marking
- 30in (75cm) lightweight fusible interfacing
- 9 x $1\frac{1}{40}$in (7mm) diameter buttons

PREPARING THE PATTERN
This blouse is made using Top Pattern Two. Follow the instructions to download the pattern in your size (see pp.10–11).

Cotton check **Chambray**

Made in striped cotton shirting, this blouse is very suitable for office wear, but in printed viscose, cotton check, or a chambray it will happily accompany you on a weekend in the country.

A crisp blouse is a must-have for every wardrobe. This princess-line version is an excellent choice.

GARMENT CONSTRUCTION
The long-sleeved, button-through blouse has princess-line seams at the front, deep darts at the back, and a one-piece collar. It also features a shoulder yoke that is topstitched to match the topstitched collar and buttoned cuffs.

Topstitched, one-piece collar   Shoulder yoke

Button closure

FRONT

Princess-line seam

Deep back dart   **BACK**   Buttoned cuff

▶ HOW TO MAKE THE CLASSIC PRINCESS-LINE BLOUSE

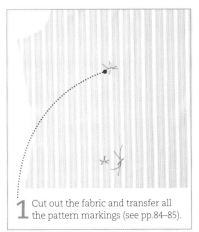

1 Cut out the fabric and transfer all the pattern markings (see pp.84–85).

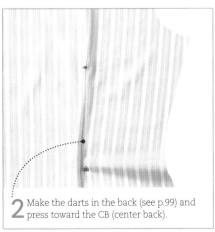

2 Make the darts in the back (see p.99) and press toward the CB (center back).

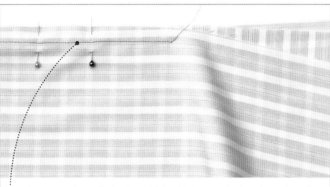

3 Place one yoke to the back, RS (right side) to RS. Pin the other yoke—the yoke lining—RS of the yoke to WS (wrong side) of the back. The back is now sandwiched between the yoke and the yoke lining. Pin and machine in place. If using a striped fabric, machine along a stripe.

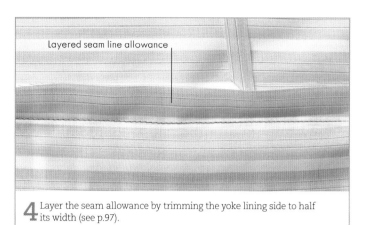

Layered seam line allowance

4 Layer the seam allowance by trimming the yoke lining side to half its width (see p.97).

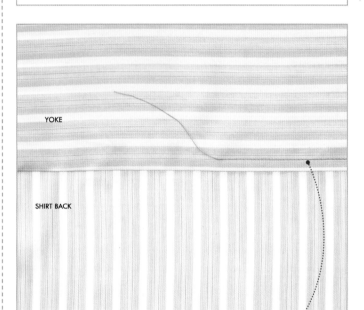

YOKE

SHIRT BACK

5 Press the seam allowances toward the yoke. Top-stitch using a slightly longer stitch length.

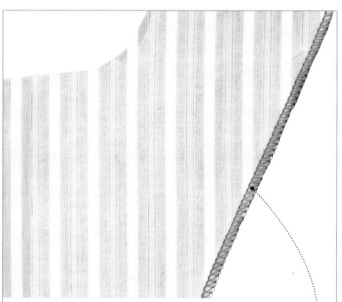

6 Attach lightweight fusible interfacing (see p.103) to the blouse fronts. Neaten the edges using either a 3-thread serger stitch or a small zigzag stitch (see pp.92–93).

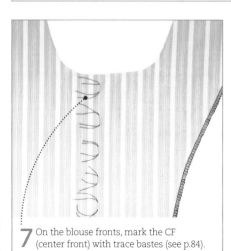

7 On the blouse fronts, mark the CF (center front) with trace bastes (see p.84).

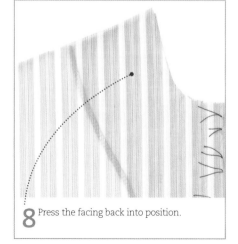

8 Press the facing back into position.

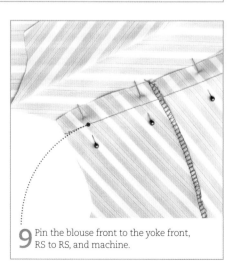

9 Pin the blouse front to the yoke front, RS to RS, and machine.

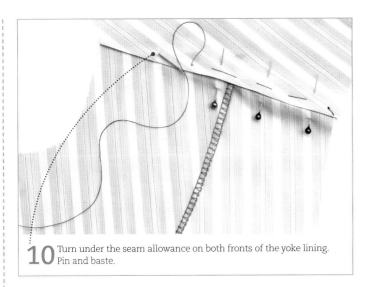

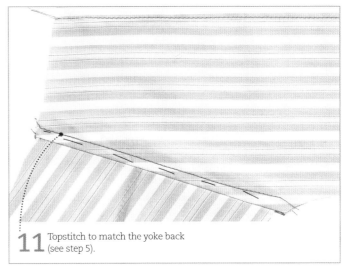

10 Turn under the seam allowance on both fronts of the yoke lining. Pin and baste.

11 Topstitch to match the yoke back (see step 5).

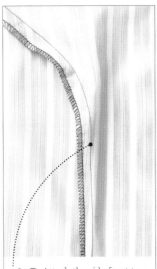

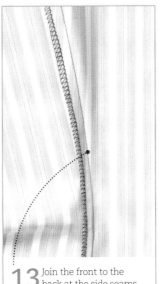

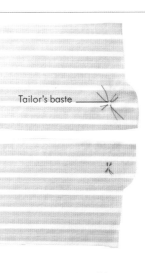

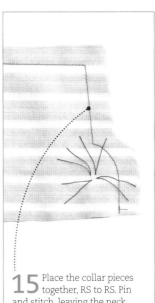

Tailor's baste

12 Attach the side front to the blouse front. Neaten the seam allowances together using either a 3-thread serger stitch or a small zigzag stitch. Press toward the side.

13 Join the front to the back at the side seams. Neaten the seam allowances together using either a 3-thread serger stitch or a small zigzag stitch. Press toward the back.

14 Attach lightweight fusible interfacing to both collar pieces and mark the location of the button and the buttonhole with tailor's bastes.

15 Place the collar pieces together, RS to RS. Pin and stitch, leaving the neck edge free.

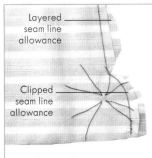

Layered seam line allowance

Clipped seam line allowance

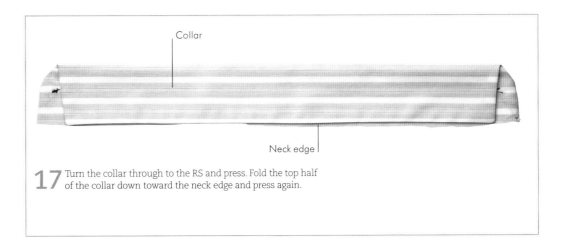

Collar

Neck edge

16 Layer the seam allowance by trimming one side to half its width. Clip the seam allowances around the curves.

17 Turn the collar through to the RS and press. Fold the top half of the collar down toward the neck edge and press again.

18 Attach the edge of the collar to the neck edge of the blouse, RS to RS, matching the pattern markings.

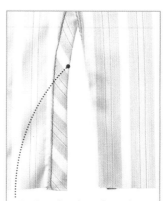

19 On the inside, turn under the raw edge of the collar, pin and hand stitch in place to the collar-to-neck seam.

20 Make a bound opening at the wrist of the sleeve as marked (see p.118).

21 Stitch the sleeve seam and neaten the seam allowances together using either a 3-thread serger stitch or a small zigzag stitch.

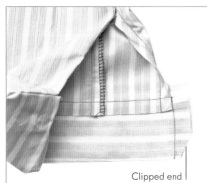

Clipped end

22 Attach lightweight interfacing to the whole cuff. Pin and machine one edge of the cuff to the sleeve end, RS to RS (see p.119). Turn the cuff RS to RS and stitch the short ends. Clip and turn.

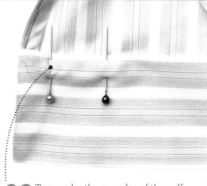

23 Turn under the raw edge of the cuff and pin. Hand stitch in place to the sleeve-to-cuff seam line.

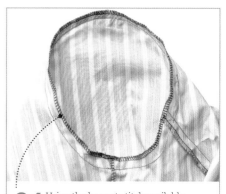

24 Using the longest stitch available, machine two rows of ease stitches through the sleeve head (see p.114). Insert the sleeve into the armhole, RS to RS (see p.114), pin and stitch. Neaten the seam allowances together.

25 Topstitch the collar to match the yoke back (see step 5).

26 Make six evenly spaced horizontal buttonholes on the CF of the right side as worn, as marked on the pattern, one on the collar, and one on each of the cuffs (see p.135). Attach buttons to correspond (see p.133).

27 Machine a ⅝in (1.5cm) double-turn hem along the bottom of the blouse (see p.128). Press.

TOP PATTERN TWO VARIATION
SHORT-SLEEVED BLOUSE

In this variation, the blouse pattern has been altered to eliminate the yoke, the sleeve has been shortened and widened to make a puffed sleeve, and the points of the collar have been rounded. This pretty little blouse would be good to wear in the summer with jeans or as summer office wear.

YOU WILL NEED
- 79in (2m) x 59in (150cm) fabric
- 1 x spool matching all-purpose sewing thread
- 1 x spool contrasting all-purpose sewing thread for pattern marking
- 30in (75cm) lightweight fusible interfacing
- Seven x ¼in (7mm) diameter buttons

PREPARING THE PATTERN
This blouse is made using Top Pattern Two. Follow the instructions to download the pattern in your size (see pp.10–11).

This blouse has been made in a brushed cotton print. A cotton with a floral pattern would also work well, or try a crisp eyelet or a soft rayon fabric.

Eyelet   **Rayon**

GARMENT CONSTRUCTION
The button-through blouse is fitted at the back with long back darts. It has a short puff sleeve finished with a band, and a collar with rounded ends.

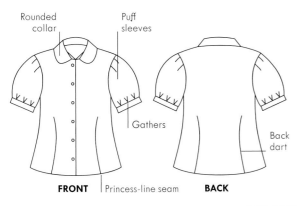

Rounded collar   Puff sleeves

Gathers

Back dart

FRONT   Princess-line seam   **BACK**

▶ **HOW TO MAKE THE SHORT-SLEEVED BLOUSE**

1 Copy the collar and mark the seam lines. Using a cup as a guide, round the corners of the collar to give new seam lines. Measure a ⅝in (1.5cm) seam allowance from the new seam line and mark a new cutting line.

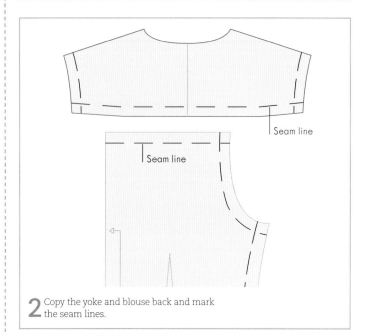

2 Copy the yoke and blouse back and mark the seam lines.

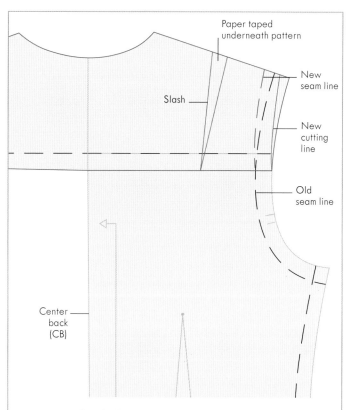

3 To remove the yoke from the pattern, overlap the yoke-to-back seam lines, matching at the CB (center back). Since the yoke is slightly shaped, slash the yoke through the shoulder so the seam lines lie on top of each other. Tape the pattern pieces together. The shoulder seam now needs to be shortened by the width of the slash. Measure this amount along the shoulder seam and draw in a new seam line. Measure a ⅝in (1.5cm) seam allowance from the new seam line and mark a new cutting line.

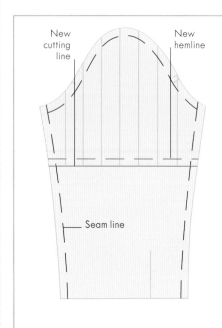

4 To shorten the sleeve, copy the sleeve and mark the seam lines. Mark a point on each side of the sleeve and 4in (10cm) below the armhole seam lines. Join these points together to make a new hemline. Draw a new cutting line ⅝in (1.5cm) below the new hemline.

5 To widen the sleeve, draw six vertical lines approximately 1½in (4cm) apart from the sleeve head to the new cutting line.

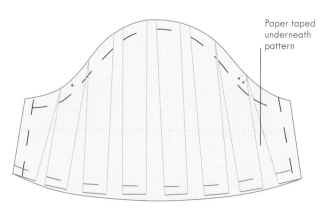

6 Cut through the vertical lines, place paper underneath, and spread the cut pattern pieces apart, leaving a gap of ¾in (2cm) between the three middle sections at the sleeve head and 1¼in (3cm) at the lower edge between all sections. Tape the pattern pieces to the paper. Mark dots between the notches to indicate where the gathers are to go.

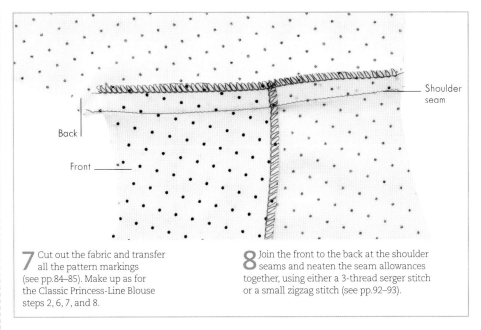

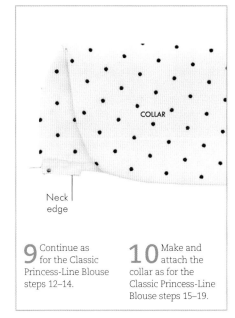

7 Cut out the fabric and transfer all the pattern markings (see pp.84–85). Make up as for the Classic Princess-Line Blouse steps 2, 6, 7, and 8.

8 Join the front to the back at the shoulder seams and neaten the seam allowances together, using either a 3-thread serger stitch or a small zigzag stitch (see pp.92–93).

9 Continue as for the Classic Princess-Line Blouse steps 12–14.

10 Make and attach the collar as for the Classic Princess-Line Blouse steps 15–19.

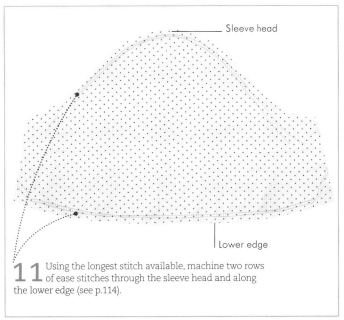

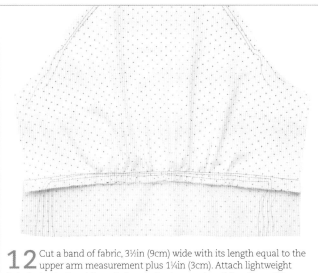

11 Using the longest stitch available, machine two rows of ease stitches through the sleeve head and along the lower edge (see p.114).

12 Cut a band of fabric, 3½in (9cm) wide with its length equal to the upper arm measurement plus 1¼in (3cm). Attach lightweight interfacing to the strip and place to the lower edge of the sleeve, RS (right side) to RS. Pull up the ease stitches to fit the edge of the sleeve to the band. Pin and stitch in place. Press the gathers toward the band.

13 Fold the sleeve, RS to RS, and machine the sleeve seam right through the band. Fold the band in half, WS (wrong side) to WS. Turn the edge of the band under by ⅝in (1.5cm), pin and hand stitch in place to the band-to-sleeve seam line.

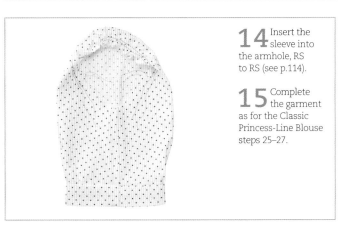

14 Insert the sleeve into the armhole, RS to RS (see p.114).

15 Complete the garment as for the Classic Princess-Line Blouse steps 25–27.

CLASSIC BOXY JACKET

Page 256

BOXY JACKET WITH COLLAR

Page 260

Page 264

CLASSIC BLAZER

Page 270

CROPPED BLAZER

THE JACKETS

The finishing touch for any outfit is the jacket. The four styles here prove that you do not have to be a tailor to create a head-turning look. Making these jackets will also add to the repertoire of sewing skills you have now acquired.

JACKET PATTERN ONE
CLASSIC BOXY JACKET

This simple boxy jacket looks good with pants or a skirt, or even over a dress. Choose your pattern by your bust measurement but note that if you have a fuller bust you may need to make a bust adjustment to make sure that the jacket meets at the front edges. This unlined jacket looks as good inside as out. The jacket and pocket flaps have been trimmed with grosgrain ribbon, while inside all the seams have been finished with bias binding.

YOU WILL NEED

- 69in (1.75m) x 59in (150cm) fabric
- 2 x spools matching all-purpose sewing thread
- 1 x spool contrasting all-purpose sewing thread for pattern marking
- 39in (1m) medium-weight fusible interfacing
- 5½yd (5m) x ³⁄₁₆in (5mm) grosgrain ribbon
- 16½yd (15m) x ¾in (2cm) bias binding

PREPARING THE PATTERN

This jacket is made using Jacket Pattern One. Follow the instructions to download the pattern in your size (see pp.10–11).

Linen   **Silk**

This jacket has been made in a medium-weight, firmly woven modern tweed. Other good choices include wool mixes, boiled wool, or linen. To wear as part of a wedding outfit, make it in silk.

A decorative ribbon trim gives the edge to a little boxy jacket—inside and out!

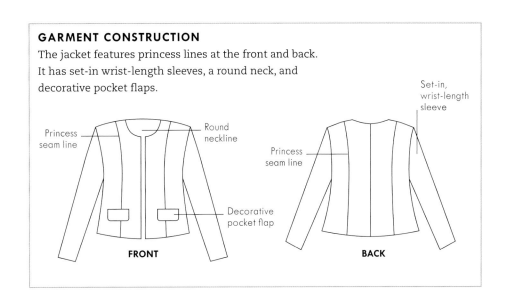

GARMENT CONSTRUCTION

The jacket features princess lines at the front and back. It has set-in wrist-length sleeves, a round neck, and decorative pocket flaps.

Princess seam line — Round neckline — Set-in, wrist-length sleeve — Princess seam line — Decorative pocket flap

FRONT   **BACK**

▶ HOW TO MAKE THE CLASSIC BOXY JACKET

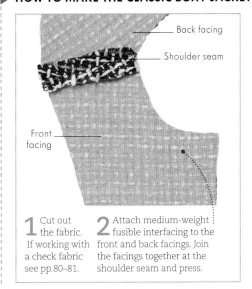

Back facing — Shoulder seam — Front facing

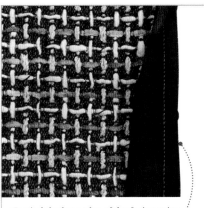

1 Cut out the fabric. If working with a check fabric see pp.80–81.

2 Attach medium-weight fusible interfacing to the front and back facings. Join the facings together at the shoulder seam and press.

3 Bind the long edge of the facing using a Hong Kong finish (see p.94) and ¾in (2cm) bias binding. Place the binding to the facing, RS (right side) to RS, and machine stitch in the crease line of the binding.

4 Wrap the binding around the raw edge of the fabric and secure by machining from the RS through the edge of the binding. Press.

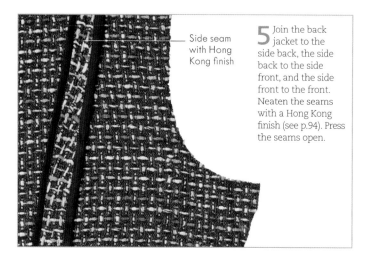

Side seam with Hong Kong finish

5 Join the back jacket to the side back, the side back to the side front, and the side front to the front. Neaten the seams with a Hong Kong finish (see p.94). Press the seams open.

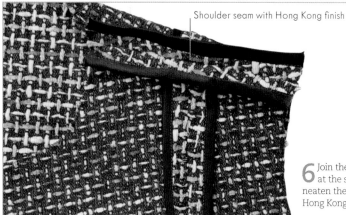

Shoulder seam with Hong Kong finish

6 Join the front to the back at the shoulders and neaten the seams with a Hong Kong finish (see p.94).

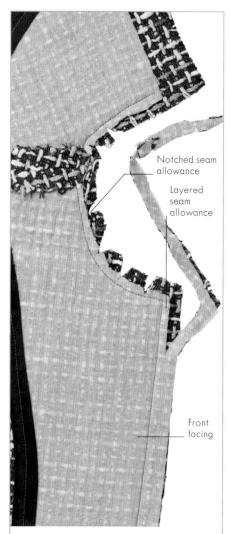

Notched seam allowance

Layered seam allowance

Front facing

Ease stitches

Sleeve seam

7 Machine the sleeve seams, neaten with a Hong Kong finish (see p.94), and press the seams open. Using stitch length 5, machine two rows of ease stitches through the sleeve head (see p.114)

8 Fit the sleeve into the armhole, RS to RS (see p.114). Join the armhole seam allowances together, wrapping them in bias binding and hand stitching the long free edge of the binding to secure (see p.107).

9 Attach the facing to the edge of the jacket, RS to RS. Pin and stitch. Layer the seam allowance by trimming the facing side of the seam to half its width. Notch the seam. Turn the facing to the WS (wrong side) and press.

10 Understitch the seam allowances to the facing (see p.98).

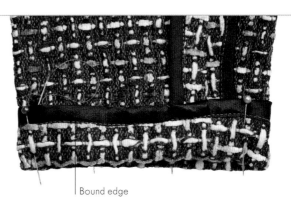

Bound edge

11 Bind the bottom edge of the sleeve using a Hong Kong finish. Pin up a ¾in (2cm) hem and hand stitch in place. Press.

12 Bind the bottom edge of the jacket but not of the facing, using a Hong Kong finish. Turn up a 1½in (4cm) hem on the jacket, pin, and hand stitch in place. At each CF (center front), turn under the lower edge of the facing, pin, and hand stitch in place. Press.

Clipped seam allowance

13 Attach medium-weight fusible interfacing (see p.102) to one half of a pocket flap and place one interfaced flap and one non-interfaced flap together, RS to RS (see p.122). Stitch together around lower edges using a ¼in (½cm) seam allowance. Clip, turn the flap to the right side, and press.

Folded corner

14 Pin decorative ribbon trim to the CF, around the neck, and around the pocket flap. Fold or miter the trim at the corners. Topstitch in place close to each edge of the trim. Press.

15 Trim flap to match. Press.

16 Pin the jacket flap to the jacket front, RS to RS, in a position of your choosing. Machine along the raw edge of the flap.

17 Press the flap into place and hand stitch at each side to secure.

JACKET PATTERN ONE VARIATION
BOXY JACKET WITH COLLAR

This version of the jacket is lined and has a heavy fringed trim. It would look great with a straight tailored skirt or maybe with the palazzo pants on pages 226–231. There are no alterations to the pattern pieces but this time the collar and lining pattern pieces are used.

JACKETS

YOU WILL NEED
- 87in (2.2m) x 59in (150cm) fabric
- 59in (1.5m) x 59in (150cm) lining fabric
- 2 x spools matching all-purpose sewing thread
- 1 x spool contrasting all-purpose sewing thread for pattern marking
- 39in (1m) x medium-weight fusible interfacing

PREPARING THE PATTERN
This jacket is made using Jacket Pattern One. Follow the instructions to copy or download the pattern in your size (see pp.10–11).

GARMENT CONSTRUCTION
This edge-to-edge lined jacket with wrist-length, set-in sleeves has princess-line styling. The pocket flaps have been omitted and a collar and fringing added instead. The jacket would also work without the fringing.

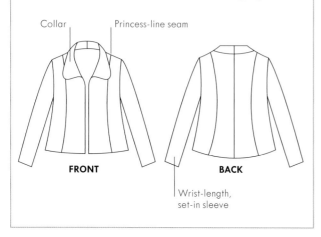

Collar — Princess-line seam

FRONT   **BACK**

Wrist-length, set-in sleeve

Traditional tweed

Gabardine

To get this exact look, use a tweed-type fabric. This jacket has been made in a check tweed. Other tweeds as well as gabardine would also work well.

▶ HOW TO MAKE THE BOXY JACKET WITH COLLAR

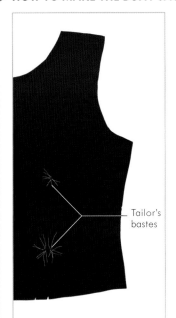

1 Cut out the pattern pieces from both the fabric and the lining. If using a check fabric (see pp.80–81). Transfer all the pattern markings to the lining (see pp.84–85).

Tailor's bastes

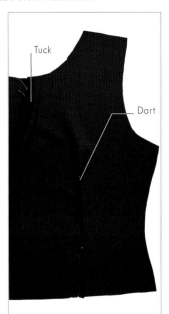

Tuck

Dart

2 Make the darts (see p.99) and stitch along the tuck lines.

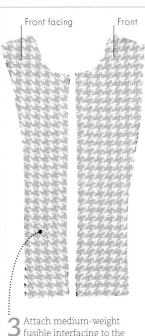

Front facing   Front

3 Attach medium-weight fusible interfacing to the front, front and back facings, and collar (see p.102).

Front   Side front

4 Join the jacket sections as for the Classic Boxy Jacket steps 5 and 6, omitting the seam neatening. Match the checks by pinning as shown. Press the seams open.

5 Make up the sleeve as for steps 7 and 8, omitting the seam neatening. The jacket should now be joined together.

6 Attach a 1¼in (3cm) wide strip of medium-weight fusible interfacing to the lower edge of jacket on the WS (wrong side). Clip to fit as required.

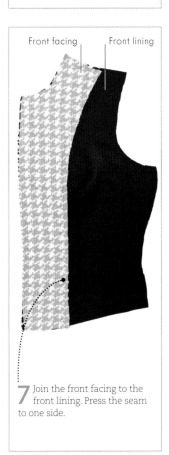

Front facing   Front lining

7 Join the front facing to the front lining. Press the seam to one side.

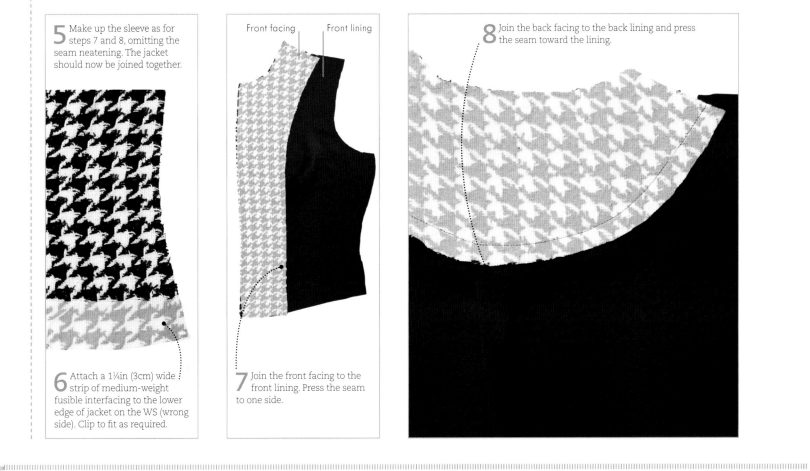

8 Join the back facing to the back lining and press the seam toward the lining.

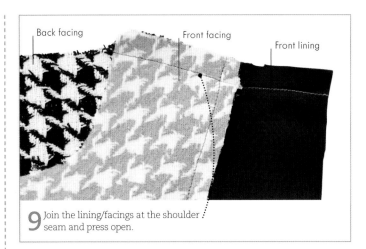

Back facing   Front facing   Front lining

9 Join the lining/facings at the shoulder seam and press open.

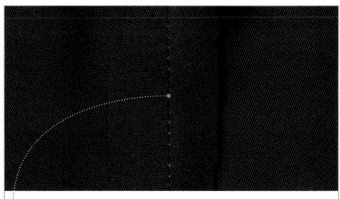

10 Join the front lining to the back at the sides and press open.

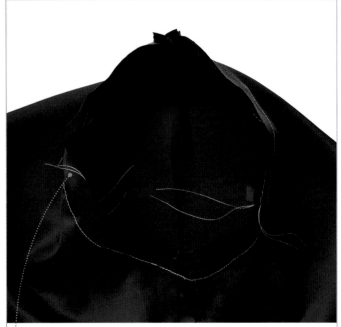

11 Make up the lining sleeve as for the Classic Boxy Jacket step 7, omitting the seam neatening. Fit the lining sleeve into the lining armhole, RS (right side) to RS.

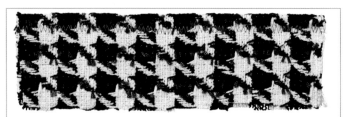

12 To make the fringing, cut strips of fabric approximately 4in (10cm) wide from selvage to selvage or along the straight grain—it depends on the weave of the fabric as to which produces the best-looking fringe. Fold the strips in half, WS to WS, and zigzag with stitch width 5 and length 2 close to the fold.

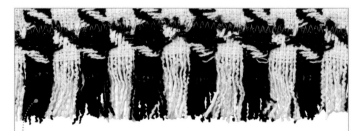

13 Fray the fabric along the raw edge, making enough fringing to go around the collar, around the hem of the sleeves, and around the lower edge and up the front of the jacket.

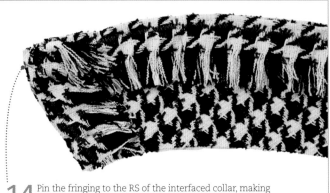

14 Pin the fringing to the RS of the interfaced collar, making a tight curve at the corners. Pin and baste in place.

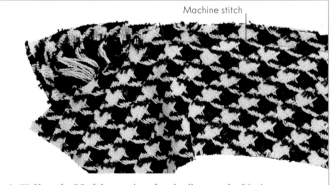

Machine stitch

15 Place the RS of the non-interfaced collar over the fringing and machine using a ⅝in (1.5cm) seam allowance.

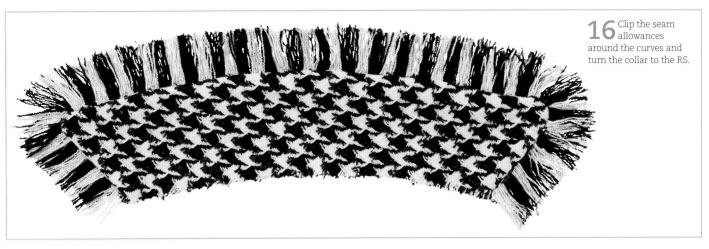

16 Clip the seam allowances around the curves and turn the collar to the RS.

17 Attach the collar to the neck edge of the jacket, WS of collar to RS of jacket. Pin and baste in place.

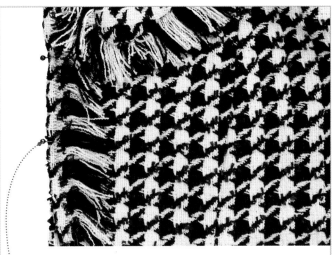

18 Pin more fringing around the hem of the sleeves and around the lower edge and up the front of the jacket. Baste in place.

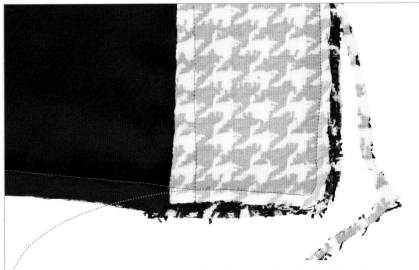

19 Place the lining/facings to the jacket, RS to RS, on top of the fringing. Stitch all around the edge leaving a 7in (18cm) gap at the CB (center back). Layer the seam allowances (see p.97) and clip the seam. Turn the jacket to the RS through the gap in the CB and press.

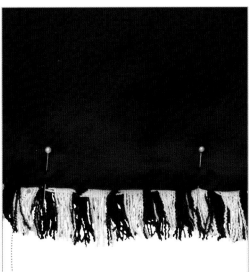

20 At the CB opening, fold under the raw edge of the lining to meet the top of the fringing. Pin and hand stitch in place.

JACKET PATTERN TWO
CLASSIC BLAZER

This classic, unlined blazer is a must-have for any wardrobe. The bust and waist darts give it a simple but flattering shape and it has a back center seam for a smooth fit. It sits just on the lower hip and would team well with the Classic Tailored Skirt (see pp.150-154) for more formal occasions or the Classic Flared Skirt (see pp.158-162) for something more casual. Its two buttons and patch pockets with a top cuff add interest and style.

YOU WILL NEED

- 79in (2m) x 59in (150cm) fabric
- 12in (30cm) x 12in (30cm) lining fabric
- 1 x spool of matching all-purpose sewing thread
- 1 x spool of contrasting all-purpose sewing thread for pattern marking
- 2 x 1⅛in (29mm) self-cover buttons
- 39¼in (1m) x 20in (50cm) lightweight fusible interfacing

PREPARING THE PATTERN

This blazer is made using Jacket Pattern Two. Follow the instructions to download the pattern in your size (see pp.10–11).

Bio-linen   **Ponte Roma**

This blazer was made from lightweight tweed but would also look great if made from bio-linen or ponte Roma.

This stylish yet relaxed blazer with matching buttons and deep front pockets is perfect for any occasion.

GARMENT CONSTRUCTION

This unlined blazer has waist darts at the front and back, bust darts, and a CB (center back) seam to give it shape. It has a narrow collar, two self-covered buttons, and two lined patch pockets with a top cuff. The pockets are topstitched with a triangle in each top corner for strength.

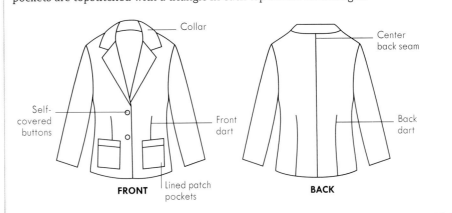

Collar
Self-covered buttons
FRONT
Lined patch pockets
Front dart

Center back seam
BACK
Back dart

▶ HOW TO MAKE THE CLASSIC BLAZER

1 Cut out the fabric and transfer the pattern markings using tailor's tacks (see p.99) at the point of the darts. Clip the raw edges for dart positions.

2 Sew the darts (see pp.99–100) in the front and back bodice. Press the front darts toward the CF (center front), bust darts downward, and back darts toward the CB (center back).

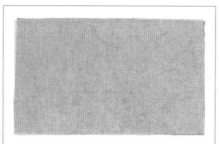

3 On the WS (wrong side) attach lightweight fusible interfacing to the pocket cuff.

4 On the RS (right side) sew the long edge of the cuff to the top of the pocket. Press the seam open.

5 With RS to RS, sew the pocket lining to the other side of the cuff. Press the seam open.

6 Fold RS to RS along the fold line of the cuff. Sew down both sides and snip at 45 degrees across the corners of the cuff.

Seam

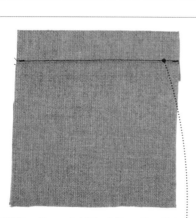

7 Turn the pocket RS out. Press. Topstitch along the bottom edge of the cuff.

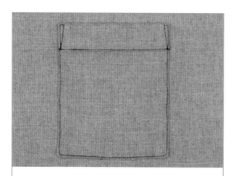

8 Turn ⅝in (1.5cm) of the lower edge of the pocket inside and press. Pin the pocket to the blazer front following the markings on the pattern. Sew ⅛in (3mm) in from the outer edges. Sew a triangle in both top corners for strength. Repeat steps 3–8 for the other pocket.

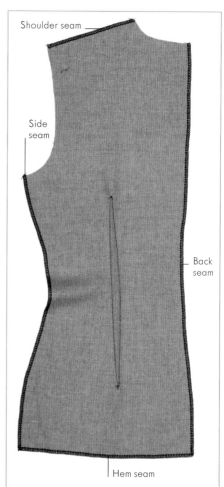

Shoulder seam

Side seam

Back seam

Hem seam

9 Neaten the seam allowances on the front and back shoulder seams, front and back side seams, front and back hems, and CB (center back) seams using a 3-thread overlock stitch or a small zigzag stitch.

10 Join the back blazer sections and press the seam open.

Center back seam

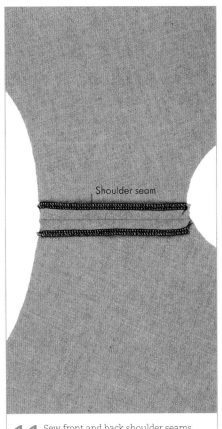

Shoulder seam

11 Sew front and back shoulder seams and press open.

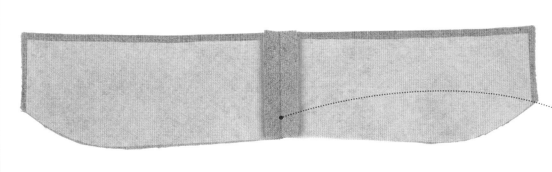

12 Cut out the lightweight fusible interfacing for the under collar pieces. Remove the seam allowance along the upper curve, CB seam, and short ends.

13 Attach the lightweight fusible interfacing to the under collar matching the bottom edges. Join at the CB and press the seam open.

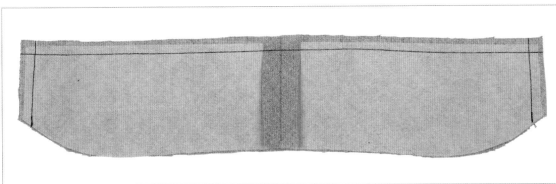

14 Join the collar pieces RS to RS, matching the curved edge, using the overstitched method (see p.110) and press the seam open.

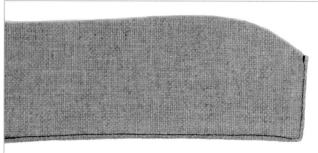

15 Turn the collar through to the RS (right side) and edge stitch around all the sewn hems.

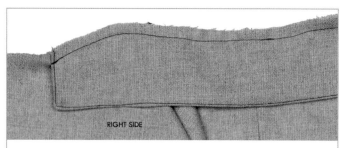

RIGHT SIDE

16 Pin and tack the collar to the blazer, RS to RS, matching the raw edges.

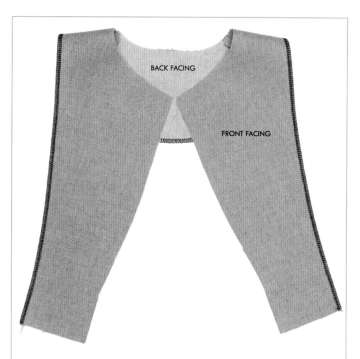

BACK FACING

FRONT FACING

17 Attach lightweight fusible interfacing to the WS of the front and back facings. Join the facings along the shoulder seam. Neaten the seams and press open.

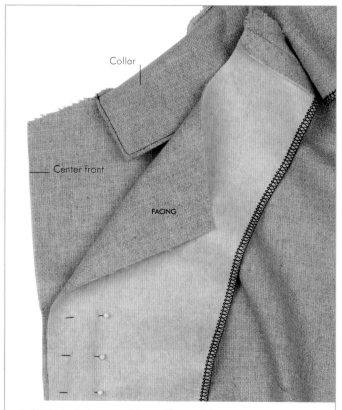

Collar

Center front

FACING

18 Pin the facing around the neckline and along the CF (center front), RS to RS, sandwiching the collar between both layers.

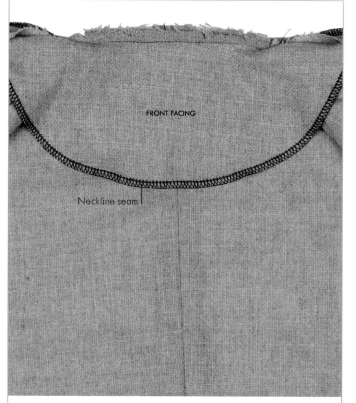

FRONT FACING

Neckline seam

19 Overstitch along both front facings. Layer the neckline seam (see p.97). Turn the facings using the same method as for the collar. Press.

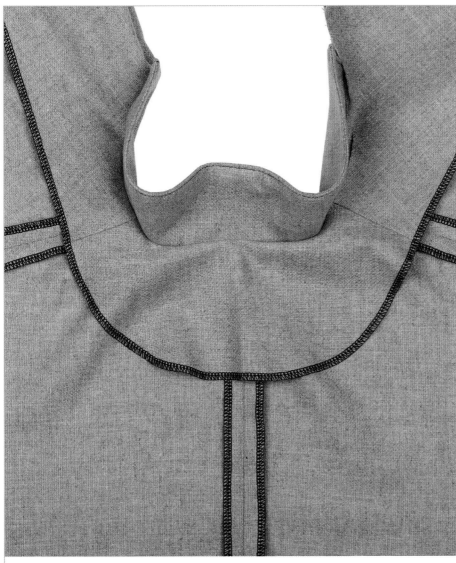

20 Handstitch the facing to the CB (center back) seam and the shoulder seams.

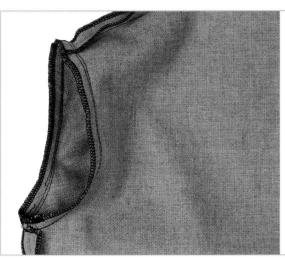

21 Neaten the sleeve seam allowances and sleeve hem using a 3-thread overlock stitch or a small zigzag stitch. Stitch the sleeve seam and press open. Turn up the sleeve hem and stitch in place (see p.117). Press.

22 Neaten the armhole seam allowance using a 3-thread overlock stitch or a small zigzag stitch. Fit the sleeve into the armhole RS to RS (see p.114).

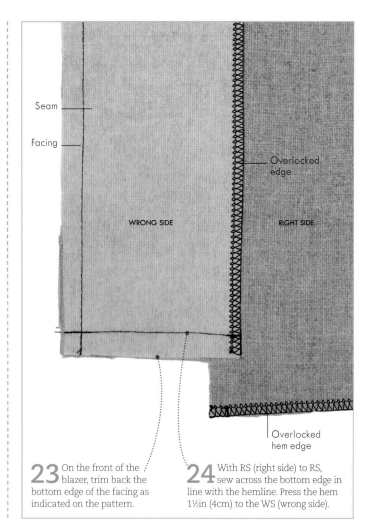

Seam

Facing

Overlocked edge

WRONG SIDE

RIGHT SIDE

Overlocked hem edge

23 On the front of the blazer, trim back the bottom edge of the facing as indicated on the pattern.

24 With RS (right side) to RS, sew across the bottom edge in line with the hemline. Press the hem 1½in (4cm) to the WS (wrong side).

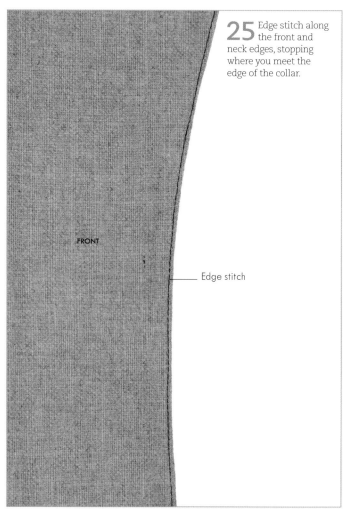

25 Edge stitch along the front and neck edges, stopping where you meet the edge of the collar.

FRONT

Edge stitch

26 Turn the facing to the WS and hand sew the hem in place (see p.89).

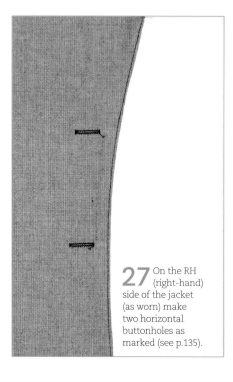

27 On the RH (right-hand) side of the jacket (as worn) make two horizontal buttonholes as marked (see p.135).

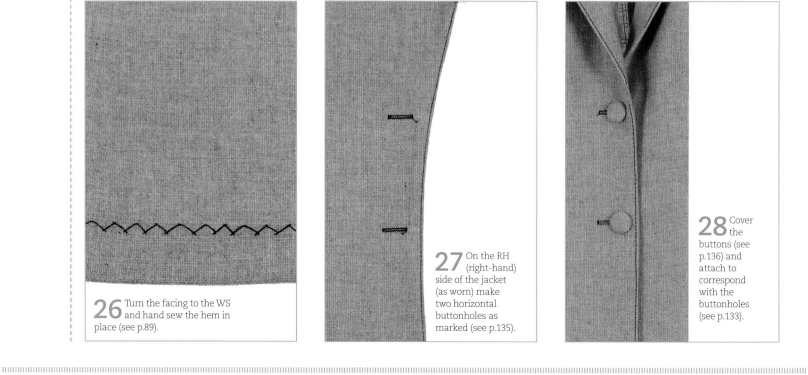

28 Cover the buttons (see p.136) and attach to correspond with the buttonholes (see p.133).

JACKET PATTERN TWO VARIATION
CROPPED BLAZER

This unlined blazer has simple shaping that gives it a flattering fit. It sits just on the upper hip, so it would look great teamed with the Sleeveless Shift Dress (see pp.177–178) for an informal evening or with the Classic Tailored Pants (see pp.220-225) for work. The blazer has a single button and two decorative pocket flaps. For a different look you could remove the bottom flaps and add a slightly shorter one as a breast pocket flap. Choose your pattern according to your full bust measurement (see p.60).

YOU WILL NEED
- 75in (1.9m) x 59in (150cm) fabric
- 10in (25cm) x 10in (25cm) lining fabric
- 1 x spool of matching all-purpose sewing thread
- 1 x spool of contrasting all-purpose sewing thread for pattern marking
- 1 x ⅞in (22mm) button
- 39¼in (1m) x 20in (50cm) fusible interfacing

PREPARING THE PATTERN
This blazer is made using Jacket Pattern Two. Follow the instructions to download the pattern in your size (see pp.10–11).

GARMENT CONSTRUCTION
This blazer has waist darts at the front and back, bust darts, and a shaped seam on the center back. It has a narrow roll collar, one large button, and two lined decorative pocket flaps.

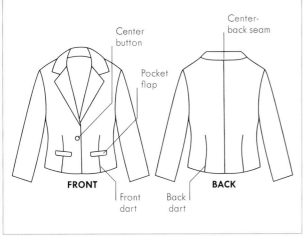

Center button

Pocket flap

Center-back seam

FRONT

Front dart

Back dart

BACK

Wool crepe

Corduroy

This blazer was made from a wool herringbone fabric but would also look great if made from wool crepe or corduroy.

▶ **HOW TO MAKE THE BLAZER**

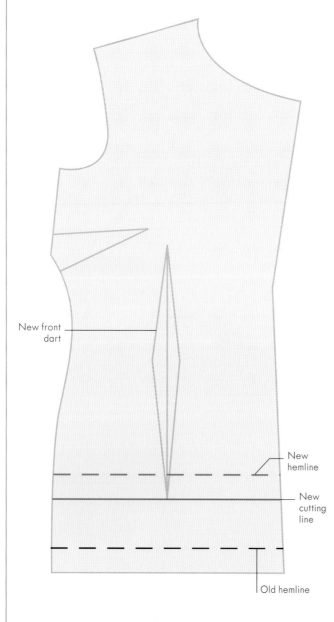

New front
dart

New
hemline

New
cutting
line

Old hemline

New
hemline

New
cutting
line

Old hemline

1 Copy the pattern front and mark the new cutting line 4in (10cm) up from the old hemline.

2 Draw in the new hemline 1½in (4cm) up from the new cutting line.

3 To lengthen the dart, draw a line through the middle of the waist dart to the new cutting line. On either side, draw a line from the widest point of the dart down to where it meets the new cutting line.

4 To make the new pattern pieces for the back and facings, follow steps 1–2.

5 Cut out the fabric using the new pattern pieces. Mark the darts using tailor's tacks (see p.99) and clip the raw edges. Make the darts in the front and back bodice (see p.99). Press front darts toward CF (center front), bust darts downward, and back darts toward CB (center back).

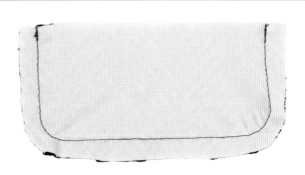

6 Cut two pocket flaps from the blazer fabric and two from the lining. Place a pocket flap main fabric and lining RS to RS for each flap. Sew around three sides, leaving the top open.

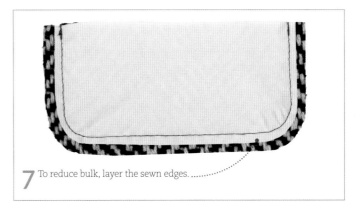

7 To reduce bulk, layer the sewn edges. ....

8 Turn the flaps to the RS and press. Topstitch all the sewn edges. Neaten the top raw edge using a 3-thread overlock stitch or a small zigzag stitch (see pp.92–93).

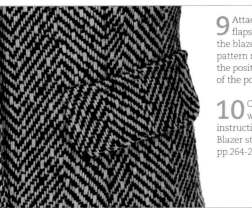

9 Attach the pocket flaps to the front of the blazer following the pattern markings for the position for the top of the pockets (see p.122).

10 Continue to work following instructions for Classic Blazer steps 9–26 (see pp.264-269).

11 On the RH (right-hand) side of the jacket (as worn) make one horizontal buttonhole as marked (see p.135). Attach the button to correspond with the buttonhole (see p.133).

MENDING
& REPAIRS

MENDING

Repairing a tear in fabric, patching a worn area, or fixing a zipper or a buttonhole can add extra life to a garment. Repairs like these may seem tedious, but they are very easy to do and worth the effort. For some of the mending techniques shown here, a contrasting color thread has been used so that the stitching can be seen clearly. However, when making a repair, be sure to use a matching thread.

UNPICKING STITCHES

Level of difficulty

All repairs involve unpicking stitches. This must be done carefully to keep from damaging the fabric because the fabric will have to be restitched. There are three ways you can unpick stitches.

▶ **SMALL SCISSORS**

Pull the fabric apart and, using very small, sharply pointed scissors, snip through the stitches that have been exposed.

▶ **SEAM RIPPER**

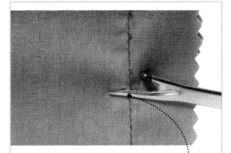

Slide a seam ripper carefully under a stitch and cut it. Cut through every fourth or fifth stitch and the seam will unravel easily.

▶ **PIN AND SCISSORS**

On difficult fabrics or on very small, tight stitches, slide a pin under the stitch to lift it away from the fabric, then snip through with a pair of sharply pointed scissors.

DARNING A HOLE

Level of difficulty ✶✶✶

If you accidentally snag a sweater or other knitted garment, it may make a small hole. A moth could make a hole, too. It is worth darning the hole, especially if the sweater was expensive or is a favorite. Holes can also occur in the heels of socks; these can be darned in the same way.

1 Even if the hole is small, the sweater will be unwearable.

2 Work several rows of running stitches vertically around the hole.

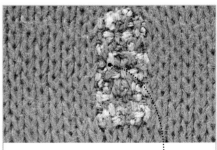

3 Complete the repair by working horizontal rows of running stitches through the vertical stitches.

REPAIRING FABRIC UNDER A BUTTON

A button under strain sometimes can be pulled off a garment. If this happens, a hole will be made in the fabric, which needs to be fixed before a new button can be stitched on.

1 On the right side of the fabric, the hole where the button has pulled off is clearly visible.

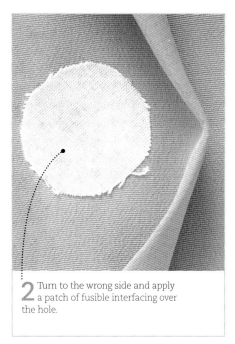

2 Turn to the wrong side and apply a patch of fusible interfacing over the hole.

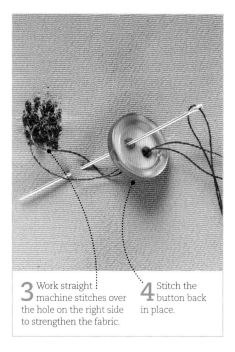

3 Work straight machine stitches over the hole on the right side to strengthen the fabric.

4 Stitch the button back in place.

REPAIRING A DAMAGED BUTTONHOLE

A buttonhole can sometimes rip at the end, or the stitching on the buttonhole can come unraveled. When repairing, use a thread that matches the fabric so the repair will be invisible.

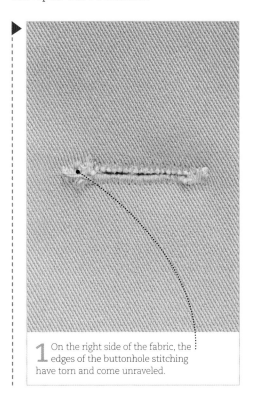

1 On the right side of the fabric, the edges of the buttonhole stitching have torn and come unraveled.

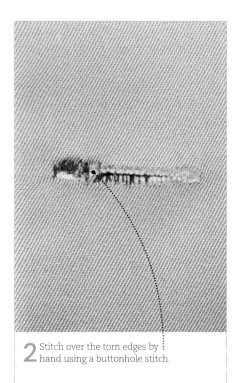

2 Stitch over the torn edges by hand using a buttonhole stitch.

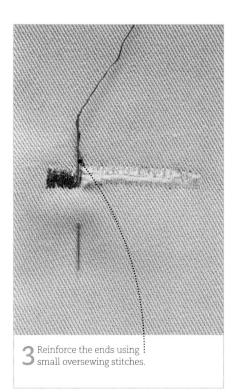

3 Reinforce the ends using small oversewing stitches.

MENDING A SPLIT IN A SEAM

Level of difficulty

A split seam can be very quickly remedied with the help of some fusible mending tape and new stitching.

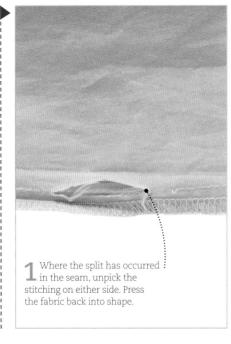

1 Where the split has occurred in the seam, unpick the stitching on either side. Press the fabric back into shape.

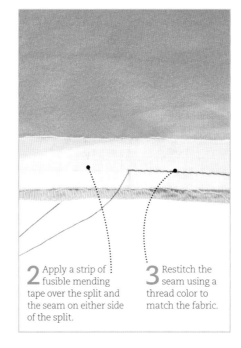

2 Apply a strip of fusible mending tape over the split and the seam on either side of the split.

3 Restitch the seam using a thread color to match the fabric.

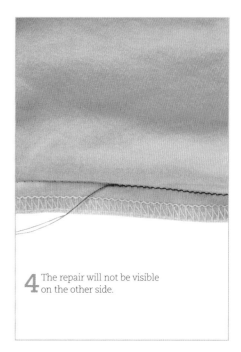

4 The repair will not be visible on the other side.

MENDING A TEAR WITH A FUSIBLE PATCH

Level of difficulty

Tears easily happen to clothing, especially children's wear. There are several methods for mending a tear. Most use a fusible patch of some kind, which may or may not be seen on the front.

▶ **FUSIBLE APPLIQUÉ PATCH**

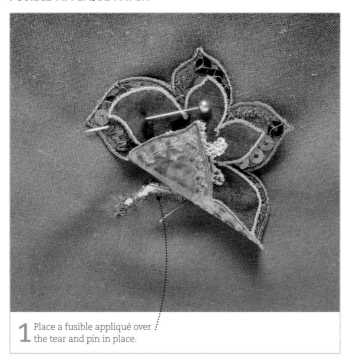

1 Place a fusible appliqué over the tear and pin in place.

2 Apply heat to fuse the decorative patch in place.

▶ FUSED PATCH ON THE RIGHT SIDE

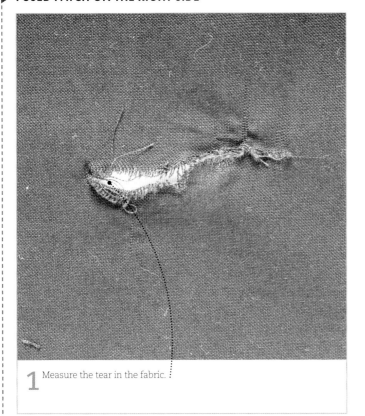

1 Measure the tear in the fabric.

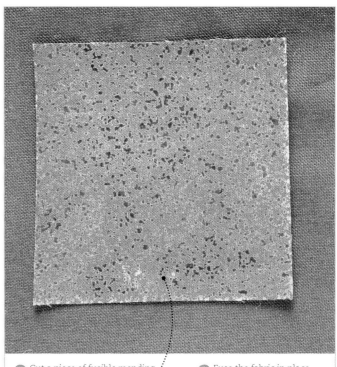

2 Cut a piece of fusible mending fabric that is slightly longer and wider than the tear.

3 Fuse the fabric in place on the right side.

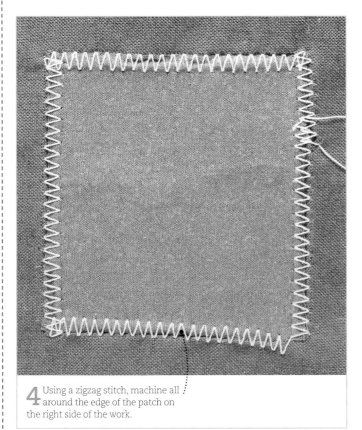

4 Using a zigzag stitch, machine all around the edge of the patch on the right side of the work.

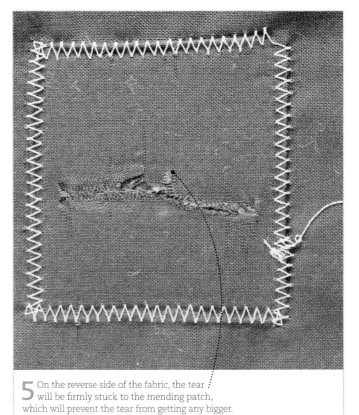

5 On the reverse side of the fabric, the tear will be firmly stuck to the mending patch, which will prevent the tear from getting any bigger.

▶ FUSED PATCH ON THE WRONG SIDE

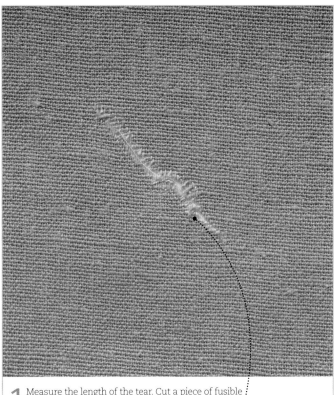

1 Measure the length of the tear. Cut a piece of fusible mending tape to fit.

2 On the wrong side of the fabric, fuse the mending tape over the tear.

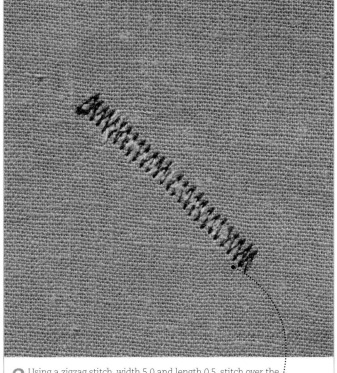

3 Using a zigzag stitch, width 5.0 and length 0.5, stitch over the tear on the right side of the fabric.

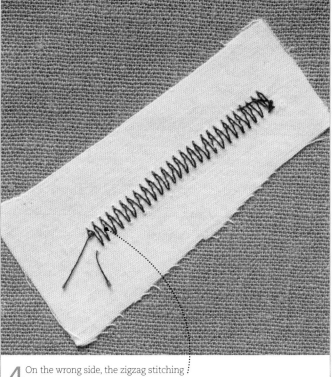

4 On the wrong side, the zigzag stitching will have gone through the fusible tape.

REPAIRING OR REPLACING ELASTIC

Level of difficulty ✱✱✱

Elastic can frequently come unstitched inside the waistband, or it may lose its stretch and need to be replaced. Here is the simple way to reinsert elastic or insert new elastic.

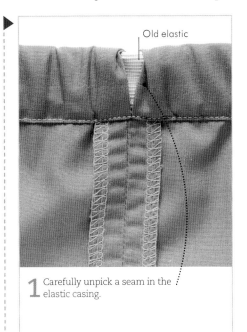

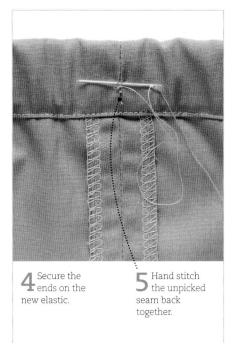

Old elastic

1 Carefully unpick a seam in the elastic casing.

2 Pull the old elastic through the gap in the seam and cut through it.

3 Attach new elastic to the old with a safety pin. Pull the old elastic through the casing. It will pull the new elastic with it.

4 Secure the ends on the new elastic.

5 Hand stitch the unpicked seam back together.

REPAIRING A BROKEN ZIPPER

Level of difficulty ✱✱✱

Zippers can break if they come under too much strain. Sometimes the zipper has to be removed completely and a new zipper inserted. However, if only a few teeth have been broken low down on the zipper and it can still be opened sufficiently, you can make this repair.

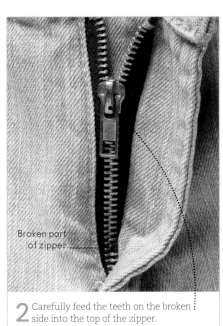
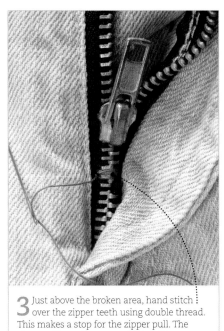

Broken teeth

Broken part of zipper

1 Where there are broken teeth on the zipper, the zipper pull will be attached to one side only. Move the pull up so it is alongside the gap in the teeth on the other side.

2 Carefully feed the teeth on the broken side into the top of the zipper.

3 Just above the broken area, hand stitch over the zipper teeth using double thread. This makes a stop for the zipper pull. The zipper will now have an extended life.

CUSTOMIZING

LENGTHENING A SKIRT WITH A CONTRAST BAND

Is last season's skirt just too short this year? Do you want to coordinate a skirt with a new jacket or with a top you have made? This simple technique shows you how to add a deep contrast band to the hem of a simple A-line or straight skirt.

YOU WILL NEED

- Skirt
- 20in (50cm) contrasting fabric of similar weight to the skirt
- 1 x spool matching all-purpose sewing thread

SIMPLE A-LINE SKIRT

Add a splash of color with a contrast band at the bottom of a simple skirt and perhaps complete your ensemble with a jacket or cardigan to match

▶ **HOW TO LENGTHEN A SKIRT WITH A CONTRAST BAND**

1 To make this project really easy, you will work on the front and back of the skirt separately, then join them at the side seams. Start by unpicking the skirt hem and 2–3¼in (5–8cm) of the side seams.

2 For the skirt front, cut a piece of contrasting fabric 9in (22cm) wide and at least 1¼in (3cm) longer than the front of the skirt is wide. Do the same for the back of the skirt. Fold the two pieces in half and press.

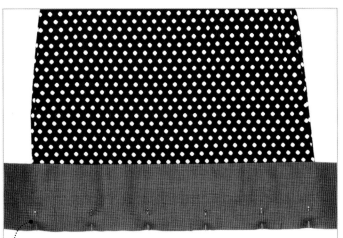

3 Pin the raw edges of the doubled contrast bands to the front and back hems of the skirt, RS (right side) to RS. Don't worry if the bands overhang at the sides of the skirt.

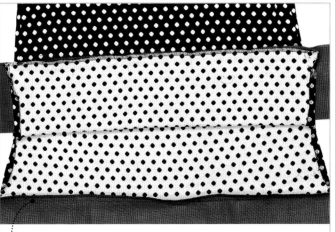

4 Machine the strips to the front and back hems. Neaten the seams using a 3-thread serger stitch or a small zigzag stitch (see pp.92–93).

5 Machine the skirt together at the sides, RS (right side) to RS, following the line of the original side seams.

6 At the hem edge, pin under the ends of the seam allowances. Hand stitch in place.

TURNING JEANS INTO A SKIRT

Turning old jeans that are too short or have ripped legs into a skirt is so easy. You don't even have to make a hem; a row of stitches at the bottom edge is enough to stop it from fraying. Wear it with a T-shirt for a casual yet fashionable vacation outfit.

YOU WILL NEED

- Pair of jeans
- 1 x spool topstitching sewing thread to match topstitching on jeans

OLD PAIR OF JEANS

Don't throw out those old jeans. Just a few cuts and topstitched seams will give you a sporty, casual skirt in no time at all

▶ **HOW TO TURN JEANS INTO A SKIRT**

1 Decide the length you want for your skirt and measure down from the waist of the pants by that amount. Add 1¼in (3cm) allowance for the hem, and cut through each leg at that point.

2 Carefully unpick the inside leg seams and the curved section of the crotch seam.

3 Cut off the curved part of the crotch seam on the front and back.

4 Cut through the side seams on one of the leg sections that you removed in order to make a single layer of fabric.

5 Place a piece of this leg fabric under each of the unpicked sections, front and back, to fill in the gap created by cutting away the crotch seam. Pin in place.

6 Starting at the crotch and matching the stitching lines, topstitch together using a longer machine stitch. Turn under a double-turn hem (see p.128), pin, and topstitch.

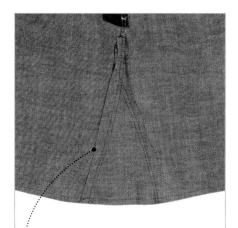

7 Remove any surplus fabric on the inside.

ADDING A COLLAR AND POCKETS TO A DRESS

It's easier than you think to add a contrasting collar to a simple round-necked dress. You can really create a whole new look if you add a pair of fake pockets, too. Try this on a simple cotton print dress for a retro look.

YOU WILL NEED

- Dress
- 20in (50cm) contrasting fabric for collar and pockets
- 1 x spool matching all-purpose sewing thread
- See-through nonwoven fabric
- 20in (50cm) lightweight fusible interfacing
- 20in (50cm) x ¾in (2cm) bias binding

SIMPLE DRESS

Give a plain shift dress a new lease on life by adding a neat little Peter Pan collar and oh-so-simple fake pockets

▶ **HOW TO ADD A COLLAR AND POCKETS TO A DRESS**

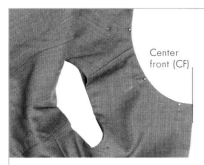

1 Fold the dress in half, pin around the neck and mark the CF (center front) with a thread marking.

Center front (CF)

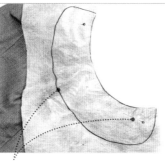

2 Pin some see-through nonwoven fabric to the neck edge and draw on the shape of your collar. We made our collar 2⅜in (6cm) deep.

3 Remove the drawing and add seam allowances of ⅝in (1.5cm). Do not add a seam allowance at the neck edge. Draw in the grain line at the CF.

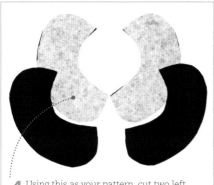

4 Using this as your pattern, cut two left and two right collars. Attach lightweight fusible interfacing to one pair.

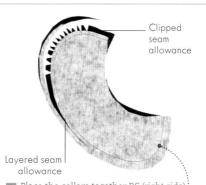

Clipped seam allowance

Layered seam allowance

5 Place the collars together RS (right side) to RS and stitch around the outside edges. Layer the interfaced side of the seam and clip.

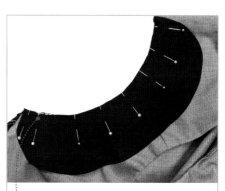

6 Turn the collar to the RS and press. Pin the collar to the neck, raw edge to finished dress neck edge.

7 Pin bias binding to the raw edge of the collar, RS to RS, and machine in place. Wrap the binding to the WS (wrong side) and hand stitch.

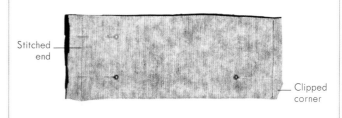

Stitched end

Clipped corner

8 make the false pockets, cut two pieces of fabric 8in (20cm) wide by 5¾in (14cm) deep and interface with lightweight fusible interfacing. Fold in half, RS to RS, along the length and machine the short ends. Clip the corners. Turn to the RS and press.

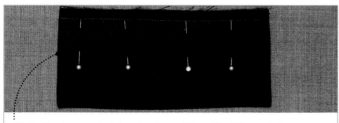

9 Try the dress on to determine the position of the false pockets, then pin and stitch them in place working from the RS.

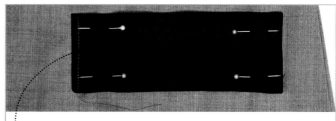

10 Turn the pocket upward over the stitching. Pin in place then stitch down the ends. The effect will be one of a pocket that is open at the top.

EMBELLISHING A DRESS WITH SEQUINS AND BEADS

This is a fabulously simple and inexpensive way to add sparkle to a day dress and turn it into a glamorous outfit in just an hour or so. All the sewing is done by hand, so settle down in a comfy chair and get creative!

YOU WILL NEED
- Plain dress
- Assorted sequins, pearls, and beads
- 1 x spool matching all-purpose sewing thread

PLAIN DRESS

Make a grand entrance in this sparkly little number created from a simple day dress

▶ **HOW TO EMBELLISH A DRESS WITH SEQUINS AND BEADS**

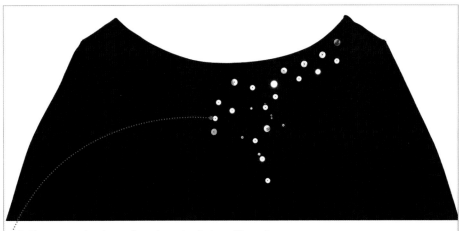

1 Choose some beads, pearls, and sequins that you like and scatter them on the dress to see which show up best.

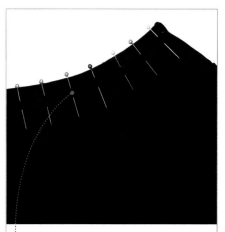

2 Mark the placement of the row of embellishment at the neck edge with pins. Make sure the pins are evenly spaced.

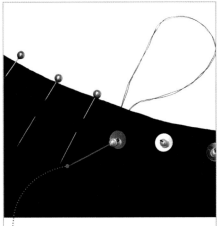

3 Hand stitch a sequin at each pin and add a small bead on top of each sequin.

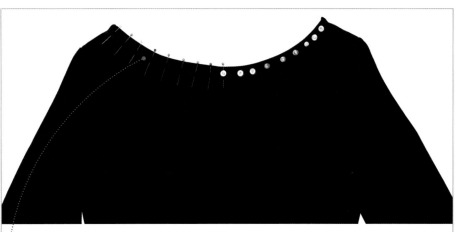

4 Continue adding sequins and beads all the way around the neck edge of the dress at the marked positions.

5 Add a scattering of beads and sequins to form a panel below the neck edge. Stitch from bead to bead without finishing the thread after each one, but don't attach more than 10 beads with one thread in case the thread breaks.

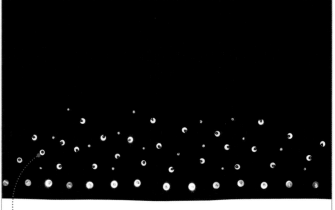

6 Add beads and sequins in the same way to create a border at the bottom of the dress.

ADDING A BOW AND GATHERS TO A T-SHIRT

Use this idea to breathe new life into an old T-shirt. Ribbon has been used to make a bow-and-gather feature at the hemline. If you are working with a quarter-length sleeve T-shirt, you could add this feature to each sleeve or adapt it to suit other garments, too.

YOU WILL NEED

- T-shirt
- 3¹⁄₈in (8cm) x 6in (15cm) piece of light cotton fabric
- 18in (46cm) x ⁵⁄₈in (1.5cm) wide grosgrain ribbon for the gathers
- 24in (60cm) x 1in (2.5cm) wide grosgrain ribbon for the bow
- 1 x spool of matching all-purpose sewing thread

PLAIN T-SHIRT

For the bow, you can either use ribbon in a complementary color, as shown here, or create a statement look with contrasting ribbon.

▶ **HOW TO ADD BOWS AND GATHERS TO A T-SHIRT**

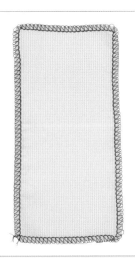

1 Neaten the edges of the light cotton fabric patch using a 3-thread overlock stitch or a small zigzag stitch.

2 On the WS (wrong side) of the T-shirt front, find the quarter point of the hem and draw a vertical line 6in (15cm) long. Fold the short ends of the gather ribbon over by ³/₈in (1cm). With the folded ends down, pin one end of the ribbon at the 6in (15cm) mark, ³/₁₆in (5mm) to the left of the line. Repeat with the other end of the ribbon, placing it ³/₁₆in (5mm) to the right of the line.

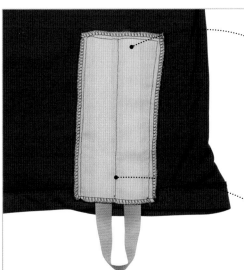

3 Lay the fabric patch ³/₁₆in (5mm) up from the hem over the vertical line to sandwich the ribbon between the T-shirt and the patch.

4 Using a ³/₁₆in (4mm) seam, sew up the right-hand side, across the top (making sure you sew over the ends of the ribbon to keep them in place), and down the left-hand side of the patch.

5 Sew a line of stitches between the two pieces of ribbon. Make sure you do not sew on the ribbon.

6 Pull on the ribbon loop gently to create the gathers.

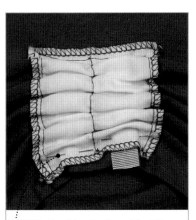

7 Pin the ribbon to the patch at the base to hold it in place and cut it ³/₈in (1cm) below the hemline. Tuck the ribbon ends into the patch.

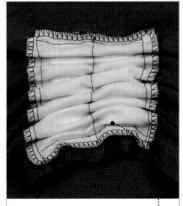

8 Sew across the bottom of the patch to close the channels and hold the ribbon in place.

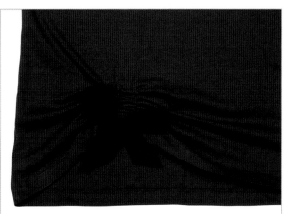

9 Make a bow from the 1in (2.5cm) ribbon and neaten the bow tails by trimming them at a 45 degree angle. On the RS (right side) hand stitch the bow in place at the base of the gathers. Use a couple of stitches at the base of each bow loop so they do not droop.

ADDING A RIBBON TRIM TO A CARDIGAN

Is your cardigan looking tired and dull? If so, why not add a pretty ribbon trim to the front edges and some decorative buttons? This technique could be applied to any style of cardigan. You could even embellish the neck and cuffs of a sweater in the same way, in which case you won't need the snap fasteners.

YOU WILL NEED

- A cardigan
- 80in (2m) firm ribbon, the width of the button band
- 15–20 assorted buttons
- Snap fasteners
- 1 x spool matching all-purpose sewing thread

PLAIN CARDIGAN

An assortment of buttons and a glam ribbon trim together give a tired old cardigan a quirky, handmade look.

▶ **HOW TO ADD A RIBBON TRIM TO A CARDIGAN**

1 Carefully remove the buttons using sharp scissors. Take care not to cut the fabric.

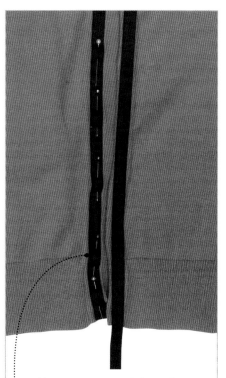

2 Taking care not to stretch the cardigan, pin a single length of ribbon, wide enough to cover the button band, from the hem of one front up, around the neck, and down to the other hem.

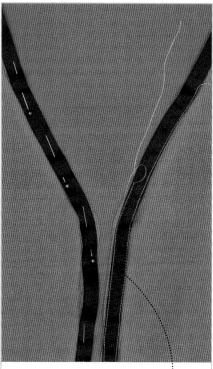

3 Machine carefully along both sides of the ribbon to hold it in place.

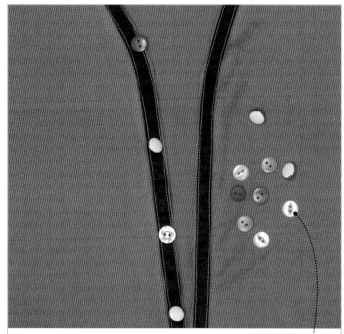

4 Evenly space assorted buttons, with a diameter no wider than the ribbon, the length of the ribbon, leaving it free of buttons where the two fronts will join. Stitch in place.

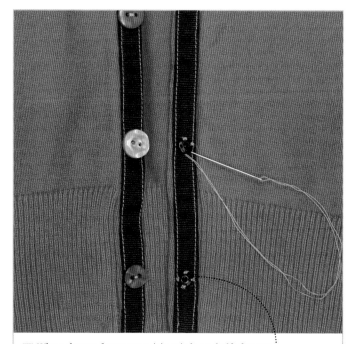

5 Where the two fronts are to join, stitch one half of a snap fastener beneath each button and the other half in the corresponding position on the other side of the ribbon trim.

GLOSSARY

Acetate Man-made fabric widely used for linings.

Acrylic Man-made fabric resembling wool.

Armhole Opening in a garment for the sleeve and arm.

Back stitch A strong hand stitch with a double stitch on the wrong side, used for outlining and seaming.

Basting stitch A temporary running stitch used to hold pieces of fabric together or for transferring pattern markings to fabric.

Belt loop Loop made from a strip of fabric that is used to support a belt at the waist edge of a garment.

Bias 45-degree line on fabric that falls between the lengthwise and the crosswise grain. Fabric cut on the bias drapes well. *See also* Grain.

Bias binding Narrow strips of fabric cut on the bias. Used to give a neat finish to hems and seam allowances.

Binding Method of finishing a raw edge by wrapping it in a strip of bias-cut fabric.

Blind hem stitch Tiny hand stitch used to attach one piece of fabric to another, mainly to secure hems. Also a machine stitch consisting of two or three straight stitches and one wide zigzag stitch.

Bobbin Round holder beneath the needle plate of a sewing machine on which the thread is wound.

Bodice Upper body section of a garment.

Boning Narrow nylon, plastic, or metal strip, available in various widths, that is used for stiffening and shaping close-fitting garments, such as bodices.

Box pleat Pleat formed on the wrong side of the fabric, and fuller than a knife pleat. *See also* Pleat.

Buttonhole Opening through which a button is inserted to form a fastening. Buttonholes are usually machine stitched but may also be worked by hand or piped for reinforcement or decorative effect.

Buttonhole chisel Very sharp, small chisel that cuts cleanly through a machine-stitched buttonhole.

Buttonhole stitch Hand stitch that wraps over the raw edges of buttonholes to neaten and strengthen them. Machine-stitched buttonholes are worked with a close zigzag stitch.

Button shank Stem of a button that allows room for the buttonhole to fit under the button when joined.

Cashmere The most luxurious of all wools.

Casing Tunnel of fabric created by parallel rows of stitching through which elastic or a drawstring cord is threaded. Often used at a waist edge. Sometimes extra fabric is required to make a casing; this can be applied to the inside or outside of the garment.

Catch stitch *See* Slip hem stitch.

Center back The vertical line of symmetry of a garment back piece. Often marked as CB.

Center front The vertical line of symmetry of a garment front piece. Often marked as CF.

Challis Fine woolen fabric with uneven surface texture.

Chambray A light cotton with a colored warp thread.

Cheesecloth Fine, plain, open-weave cotton.

Chiffon Strong, fine, transparent silk.

Clapper Wooden aid that is used to pound creases into heavy fabric after steaming.

Contour dart Also known as double-pointed dart, this is used to give shape at the waist of a garment. It is like two darts joined together. *See also* Dart.

Corduroy A soft pile fabric with distinctive ribs.

Cotton Soft, durable, and inexpensive fabric widely used in dressmaking. Made from the fibrous hairs covering the seed pods of the cotton plant.

Crease Line formed in fabric by pressing a fold.

Crepe Soft fabric made from twisted yarn.

Cross stitch A temporary hand stitch used to hold pleats in place and to secure linings. It can also be used for decoration.

Cutting line Solid line on a pattern piece used as a guide for cutting out fabric.

Darning Mending holes or worn areas in a knitted garment by weaving threads in rows along the grain of the fabric.

Dart Tapered stitched fold of fabric used on a garment to give it shape so that it can fit around the contours of the body. There are different types of dart, but all are used mainly on women's clothing.

Darted tuck A tuck that can be used to give fullness of fabric at the bust or hip. *See also* Tuck.

Denim Hard-wearing twill weave fabric with colored warp and white weft.

Double-pointed dart *See* Contour dart

Drape The way a fabric falls into graceful folds; drape varies with each fabric.

Dressmaker's carbon paper Used together with a tracing wheel to transfer pattern markings to fabric. Available in a variety of colors.

Duchesse satin Heavy, expensive satin fabric.

Dupioni Fabric with a distinctive weft yarn that is textured; made from 100 percent silk.

Ease Distributing fullness in fabric when joining two seams together of slightly different lengths, for example, a sleeve to an armhole.

Ease stitch Long machine stitch, used to ease in fullness where the distance between notches is greater on one seam edge than on the other.

Edge to edge A garment, such as a jacket, in which the edges meet at the center front without overlapping.

Enclosed edge Raw fabric edge that is concealed within a seam or binding.

Eyelet A fine plain-weave cotton embroidered to make small decorative holes.

Facing Layer of fabric placed on the inside of a garment and used to finish off raw edges of an armhole or neck of a garment. Usually a separate piece of fabric, the facing can sometimes be an extension of the garment itself.

Flannel Wool or cotton with a lightly brushed surface.

Flat fell seam *See* Run and fell seam.

Flat fell stitch A strong, secure stitch used to hold two layers together permanently. Often used to secure linings and bias bindings.

French dart Curved dart used on the front of a garment. *See also* Dart.

French seam A seam traditionally used on sheer and silk fabrics. It is stitched twice, first on the right side of the work and then on the wrong side, enclosing the first seam.

Fusible tape Straight grain tape used to stabilize edges and also replace stay stitching. The heat of the iron fuses it into position.

Gabardine Hard-wearing fabric with a distinctive weave.

Gathers Bunches of fabric created by sewing two parallel rows of loose stitching, then pulling the threads up so that the fabric gathers and reduces in size to fit the required space.

Gingham Two-color, checked cotton fabric.

Grain Lengthwise and crosswise direction of threads in a fabric. Fabric grain affects how a fabric hangs and drapes.

Grosgrain Synthetic, ribbed fabric often used to make ribbons.

Habutai Smooth, fine silk originally from Japan.

Hem The edge of a piece of fabric neatened and stitched to prevent unraveling. There are several methods of doing this, both by hand and by machine.

Hem allowance Amount of fabric allowed for turning under to make the hem.

Hemline Crease or foldline along which a hem is marked.

Herringbone stitch Hand stitch used to secure hems and interlinings. This stitch is worked from left to right.

Herringbone weave A zigzag weave where the weft yarn goes under and over warp yarns in a staggered pattern.

Hong Kong finish A method of neatening raw edges particularly on wool and linen. Bias-cut strips are wrapped around the raw edge.

Hook and eye fastening Two-part metal fastening used to fasten overlapping edges of fabric where a neat join is required. Available in a wide variety of styles.

Interfacing A fabric placed between garment and facing to give structure and support. Available in different thicknesses, interfacing can be fusible (bonds to the fabric by applying heat) or non-fusible (needs to be sewn to the fabric).

Interlining Layer of fabric attached to the main fabric prior to construction, to cover the inside of an entire garment to provide extra warmth or bulk. The two layers are then treated as one. Often used in jackets and coats.

Jersey Cotton or wool yarn that has been knitted to give stretch.

Keyhole buttonhole stitch A machine buttonhole stitch characterized by having one square end while the other end is shaped like a loop to accommodate the button's shank without distorting the fabric. Often used on jackets.

Layering Trimming one side of the seam allowance to half its width to reduce bulk at the seam.

Linen Natural fiber derived from the stem of the flax plant, linen is available in a variety of qualities and weights.

Lining Underlying fabric layer used to give a neat finish to an item, as well as concealing the stitching and seams of a garment.

Locking stitch A machine stitch where the upper and lower threads in the machine "lock" together at the start or end of a row of stitching.

Madras Brightly colored, unevenly checked cotton fabric from India.

Matka A silk suiting fabric with uneven yarn.

Miter The diagonal line made where two edges of a piece of fabric meet at a corner, produced by folding. *See also* Mitered corner.

Mitered corner Diagonal seam formed when fabric is joined at a corner. Excess fabric is cut away before or after stitching.

Mohair Fluffy wool yarn cloth used for sweaters, jackets, and soft furnishings.

Multisize pattern Paper pattern printed with cutting lines for a range of sizes on each pattern piece.

Muslin A plain weave, usually unbleached fabric.

Nap The raised pile on a fabric made during the weaving process, or a print pointing one way. When cutting out pattern pieces, ensure the nap runs in the same direction.

Needle threader Gadget that pulls thread through the eye of a needle. Useful for needles with small eyes.

Notch V-shaped marking on a pattern piece used for aligning one piece with another. Also V-shaped cut taken to reduce seam bulk.

Notion An item other than fabric needed to complete a project, such as a button, zipper, or elastic. Notions are normally listed on the pattern envelope.

Organza Thin, sheer fabric made from silk or polyester.

Overedge stitch Machine stitch worked over the edge of a seam allowance and used for neatening the edges of fabric.

Pattern markings Symbols printed on a paper pattern to indicate the fabric grain, foldline, and construction details, such as darts, notches, and tucks. These should be transferred to the fabric using tailor's chalk or tailor's bastes.

Pile Raised loops on the surface of a fabric, for example, velvet.

Pinking A method of neatening raw edges of fray-resistant fabric using pinking shears. This will leave a zigzag edge.

Pinking shears Cutting tool with serrated blades, used to trim raw edges of fray-resistant fabrics to neaten seam edges.

Pivoting Technique used to machine stitch a corner. The machine is stopped at the corner with the needle in the fabric, then the foot is raised, the fabric turned following the direction of the corner, and the foot lowered for stitching to continue.

Placket An opening in a garment that provides support for fasteners, such as buttons, snaps, or zippers.

Plain weave The simplest of all the weaves; the weft yarn passes under one warp yarn, then over another one.

Pleat An even fold or series of folds in fabric, often partially stitched down. Commonly found in skirts to shape the waistline, but also in soft furnishings for decoration.

Pocket flap A piece of fabric that folds down to cover the opening of a pocket.

Polyester Man-made fiber that does not crease.

Presser foot The part of a sewing machine that is lowered on to the fabric to hold it in place over the needle plate while stitching. There are different feet available.

Pressing cloth Muslin or organza cloth placed over fabric to prevent marking or scorching when pressing.

Prick stitch Small spaced hand stitch with large spaces between each stitch. Often used to highlight the edge of a completed garment.

Raw edge Cut edge of fabric that requires finishing, for example, using zigzag stitch, to prevent fraying.

Rayon Also known as viscose, rayon is often blended with other fibers.

Reverse stitch Machine stitch that simply stitches back over a row of stitches to secure the threads.

Right side The outer side of a fabric, or the visible part of a garment.

Rouleau loop Button loop made from a strip of bias binding. It is used with a round ball-type button.

Round-end buttonhole stitch Machine stitch characterized by one end of the buttonhole being square and the other being round, to allow for the button shank.

Run and fell seam Also known as a flat fell seam, this seam is made on the right side of a garment and is very strong. It uses two lines of stitching and conceals all the raw edges, reducing fraying.

Running stitch A simple, evenly spaced straight stitch separated by equal-sized spaces, used for seaming and gathering.

Satin A fabric with a satin weave.

Satin weave A weave with a sheen, where the weft goes under four warp yarns, then over one.

Seam Stitched line where two edges of fabric are joined together.

Seam allowance The amount of fabric allowed for on a pattern where sections are to be joined together by a seam; usually this is ⅝in (1.5cm).

Seam edge The cut edge of a seam allowance.

Seamline Line on paper pattern designated for stitching a seam; usually this is ⅝in (1.5cm) from the seam edge.

Seam ripper A small, hooked tool used for undoing seams and unpicking stitches.

Seam roll Tubular pressing aid for pressing seams open on fabrics that mark.

Selvage Finished edge on a woven fabric. This runs parallel to the warp (lengthwise) threads.

Set-in sleeve A sleeve that fits into a garment smoothly at the shoulder seam.

Serger Machine used for quick stitching, trimming, and edging of fabric in a single action; it gives a professional finish to a garment. There are a variety of accessories that can be attached to an serger that enable it to perform a greater range of functions.

Serger stitch A machine stitch that neatens edges and prevents fraying. It can be used on all types of fabric.

Sewing gauge Measuring tool with adjustable slider for checking small measurements, such as hem depths and seam allowances.

Sharps All-purpose needle used for hand sewing.

Shirting Closely woven, fine cotton with colored warp and weft yarns.

Silk Threads spun by the silkworm and used to create cool, luxurious fabrics.

Slip hem stitch Similar to herringbone stitch but is worked from right to left. It is used mainly for securing hems.

Snaps Also known as press studs, these fasteners are used as a lightweight hidden fastener.

Snips Spring-loaded cutting tool used for cutting off thread ends.

Staple fibers These include both natural and manufactured fibers such as cotton, wool, flax, and polyester. They are short in length, and relatively narrow in thickness.

Stay stitch Straight machine stitch worked just inside a seam allowance to strengthen it and prevent it from stretching or breaking.

Stitch in the ditch A line of straight stitches sewn on the right side of the work, in the ditch created by a seam. Used to secure waistbands and facings.

Stitch ripper *See* Seam ripper.

Straight stitch Plain machine stitch, used for most applications. The length of the stitch can be altered to suit the fabric.

Stretch stitch Machine stitch used for stretch knits and to help control difficult fabrics. It is worked with two stitches forward and one backward so that each stitch is worked three times.

Taffeta Smooth plain-weave fabric with a crisp appearance.

Tailor's bastes Loose thread markings used to transfer symbols from a pattern to fabric.

Tailor's buttonhole A buttonhole with one square end and one keyhole-shaped end, used on jackets and coats.

Tailor's chalk Square- or triangular-shaped piece of chalk used to mark fabric. Available in a variety of colors, tailor's chalk can be removed easily by brushing.

Tailor's ham A ham-shaped pressing cushion that is used to press shaped areas of garments.

Tape maker Tool for evenly folding the edges of a fabric strip, which can then be pressed to make binding.

Tape measure Flexible form of ruler made from plastic or fabric.

Tartan Fabric made using a twill weave from worsted yarns. Traditionally used for kilts.

Thimble Metal or plastic cap that fits over the top of a finger to protect it when hand sewing.

Toile A test or dry run of a paper pattern using muslin. The toile helps you analyze the fit of the garment.

Topstitch Machine straight stitching worked on the right side of an item, close to the finished edge, for decorative effect. Sometimes stitched in a contrasting color.

Topstitched seam A seam finished with a row of topstitching for decorative effect. This seam is often used on crafts and soft furnishings as well as garments.

Trace basting A method of marking fold and placement lines on fabric. Loose stitches are sewn along the lines on the pattern to the fabric beneath, then the thread loops are cut and the pattern removed.

Tracing wheel Tool used together with dressmaker's carbon paper to transfer pattern markings on to fabric.

Tuck Fold or pleat in fabric that is sewn in place, normally on the straight grain of the fabric. Often used to provide a decorative addition to a garment.

Tweed Traditional tweed is a rough fabric with a distinctive warp and weft. Modern tweed is a mix of chunky and bobbled wool yarns, often in bright colors.

Twill weave Diagonal patterned weave.

Understitch Machine straight stitching through facing and seam allowances that is invisible from the right side; this helps the facing to lie flat.

Velvet Luxurious pile-weave fabric.

Waistband Band of fabric attached to the waist edge of a garment to provide a neat finish.

Warp Lengthwise threads or yarns of a woven fabric.

Warp knit Made on a knitting machine, this knit is formed in a vertical and diagonal direction.

Weft Threads or yarns that cross the warp of a woven fabric.

Weft knit Made in the same way as hand knitting, this uses one yarn that runs horizontally.

Wool A natural animal fiber, available in a range of weights, weaves, and textures. It is comfortable to wear, crease-resistant, and ideal for tailoring.

Wool worsted A light, strong cloth made from good quality fibers.

Wrong side Reverse side of a fabric; the inside of a garment or other item.

Yoke The top section of a dress or skirt from which the rest of the garment hangs.

Zigzag stitch Machine stitch used to neaten and secure seam edges and for decorative purposes. The width and length of the zigzag can be altered.

Zipper Fastening widely used on garments consisting of two strips of fabric tape, carrying specially shaped metal or plastic teeth that lock together by way of a pull or slider. Zippers are available in different colors and weights.

Zipper foot Narrow machine foot with a single toe that can be positioned on either side of the needle.

INDEX

ACKNOWLEDGMENTS

PUBLISHER ACNOWLEDGMENTS

Second edition
DK would like to thank Lynne Garner for supplying new projects, Peter Stephens for new photography, Zebel Bespoke Exeter & London for tailoring assistance, Jennifer Wendell Kosek for her consultation on the US edition, and Millie Andrew for editorial assistance.

First edition
DK would like to thank Laura Palosuo, Hilary Mandleberg, Jane Ewart, Glenda Fisher, Hannah Moore, Charlotte Johnson, Jennifer Murray, Seyhan Esen, Sonia Charbonnier, Ruth Jenkinson, Nicola Powling, Penny Smith, Marianne Markham, Mary Ling, Jane Bull, Alicia Ingty, Neha Ruth Samuel, Mansi Nagdev, Ira Sharma, Zaurin Thoidingjam, Glenda Fernandes, Navidita Thapa, Pankaj Sharma, Sunil Sharma, Tarun Sharma, Nand Kishor Archarya, Manish Chandra Upreti, Alison Shackleton, Paula Keogh, Jane Ewart, Ruth Jenkinson, Rebecca Fallowfield, Claire Cross, Angela Baynham, and Marie Lorimer.

All images © Dorling Kindersley Limited.
For further information see www.dkimages.com

AUTHOR ACKNOWLEDMENTS

No book could ever be written without a little help. I would like to thank the following people for their help in making all the garments: Jackie Boddy, Averil Wing, Jenny Holdam, Christine Scott, Angela Paine, and Joan Culver. My darling husband, Nigel, and our children, Kathryn and Oliver, for all their support and endless cups of tea! Thanks must also go to the companies that have continued to support me: Janome UK, Coats Crafts, Fruedenberg-nw, Fabulous Fabric, Simplicity patterns, and MIG. Thank you to my editors Laura Palosuo—and Hilary Mandleberg, who I think I have inspired to take up sewing again!

ABOUT THE AUTHOR

Alison Smith A trained fashion and textiles teacher, Alison taught for many years at one of the largest schools in Birmingham, where she was Head of Department. In 1992 she set up the School of Sewing—the first of its kind in the UK—to teach all aspects of sewing, including dressmaking, tailoring, and corsetry. Alison has also taught at the Liberty Sewing School in London and at Janome's sewing school in Stockport. In 2004, she opened a fabric shop in Ashby de la Zouch to complement the School of Sewing. In 2013, Alison was awarded an MBE for her services to sewing and corsetry. She also teaches online for Craftsy.com and writes regularly for sewing magazines, including *Love Sewing*. Alison lives in Leicestershire with her husband and has two adult children.
www.schoolofsewing.co.uk
www.sewwardrobe.co.uk
www.etsy.com/uk/shop/SewWardrobe

Alison's projects in the book are the Classic A-line skirt (see pp.144–147), Button front A-line skirt (see pp.148–149), Classic tailored skirt (see pp.150–154), Tailored evening skirt (see pp.155–157), Classic shift dress (see pp.168–172), Short-sleeved shift dress (see pp.173–176), Sleeveless shift dress (see pp.177–179), Classic waisted dress (see pp.180–184), Short-sleeved waisted dress (see pp.185–186), Sleeveless waisted dress (see pp.187–190), Waisted cocktail dress (see pp.191–195), Classic empire line dress (see pp.196–200), Sleeveless empire line dress (see pp.201–203), Long empire line dress (see pp.204–07), Classic palazzo pants (see pp.226–231), Classic shell top (see pp.238–41), Tie-neck top (see pp.242–243), Long-sleeved tunic (see pp.244–245), Classic princess-line blouse (see pp.246–250), Short-sleeved blouse (see pp.251–253), Classic boxy jacket (see pp.256–259), and Boxy jacket with collar (see pp.260–263).

ABOUT THE CONSULTANT

Lynne Garner started her dressmaking career while she was at college, working in the wardrobe department of her local theater. Since then she has taught sewing at Hertford Regional College, Harlow College, and for the WEA. Lynne has written for *Popular Crafts* and *Sewing Magazine*, as well as writing her own books on dressmaking.

Lynne's projects in the book are the Classic flared skirt (see pp.158–162), Flared skirt with yoke (see pp.163–65), Classic shirtdress (see pp.208–13), Shirtdress with roll-tab sleeves (see pp.214–17), Classic cigarette pants (see pp.220–23), Cropped cigarette pants (see pp.224–25), Palazzo shorts (see pp.232–235), Classic blazer (see pp.264–70), and Cropped blazer (see pp.271–273).

DK | Penguin Random House

SECOND EDITION
Designed, edited and project managed for DK
by Dynamo Limited

DK UK
Project Editor Amy Slack
Senior Designer Glenda Fisher
Senior Jacket Designer Nicola Powling
Jackets Co-ordinator Lucy Philpott
Pre-production Producer David Almond
Senior Producer Kariss Ainsworth
US Editor Karyn Gerhard
Managing Editors Ruth O'Rourke
Managing Art Editor Christine Keilty
Art Director Maxine Pedliham
Publishing Directors Mary-Clare Jerram, Katie Cowan

DK INDIA
Senior Editor Janashree Singha
Assistant Editor Ankita Gupta
Managing Editor Soma B. Chowdhury
DTP Designers Manish Upreti, Satish Gaur,
Rajdeep Singh, Anurag Trivedi
Pre-production Manager Sunil Sharma

This American Edition, 2021
First American Edition, 2012
Published in the United States by DK Publishing
1450 Broadway, Suite 801, New York, NY 10018

A catalog record for this book
is available from the Library of Congress.
ISBN 978-0-7440-2689-4

DK books are available at special discounts when purchased in bulk
for sales promotions, premiums, fund-raising, or educational use.
For details, contact: DK Publishing Special Markets,
1450 Broadway, Suite 801, New York, NY 10018
SpecialSales@dk.com

Printed and bound in China

For the curious

www.dk.com

This book was made with Forest Stewardship
Council ™ certified paper—one small step in
DK's commitment to a sustainable future.

For more information go to www.dk.com/our-green-pledge